A FIDDLER TELLS ALL

by

Ralph Nicholson *A.R.C.M. (b. 1907)*

Ralph Nicholson (b. 1907)

Published by the Author - Ralph Nicholson
9 Barton Green, Trull, Taunton, Somerset.

Copyright - Ralph Nicholson 2000.

ISBN 0-9539286-0-8

Printed by The Taunton Printing Company
11 & 12 Belvedere Trading Estate
Taunton, Somerset TA1 1BH

Acknowledgements

I am most grateful to all those people - friends, former colleagues, and family members - who encouraged and persuaded me to put pen to paper. Particular thanks go to Barbara Scott and Tessa my niece in Harrogate who first made a start on deciphering mounds of script on their word-processors. But I am especially indebted to Chris Markwick who completed the task and arranged both the text and illustrations so effectively for publication. R.N.

The extract from pp376 - pp378 of <u>The Baton and the Jackboot :</u> <u>Recollections of a Musical Life</u> by Berta Geissmar (Hamish Hamilton, 1944) is reproduced by kind permission of Penguin Books Ltd.

Illustrations

*To the memory
of Gill my late wife*

A Fiddler Tells All

CONTENTS

Preface

The late Gerald Finzi, who composed delightful music, both memorable and unashamedly tuneful, once told me that he had thought of a splendid ten-word opening to a book - if ever he got round to writing one - I don't think he ever did - and these were the words: "He raised the lid of the dustbin, and" - after a suitable pause - "peered out". What an inspired opening!

I have no intention of "pinching" it, nor have I the permission of his two sons even to mention it. At least I have admitted the source of the quote; mine would be mundane in comparison. In fact what I have written in the following pages will, I hope, be of "public interest". Many friends and colleagues have said it needs to be written. I have the advantage of having been a professional musician for a good many years during which I have met a great many people and had a considerable number of varied experiences with notable events and inspiring occasions to savour - and a lot of humour. And I have been lucky in possessing a surprisingly good memory - especially for quite detailed happenings.

If there is one thing I can claim without hesitation it is that everything I have mentioned is the truth - as far as I can remember it - and in no way am I fantasising, and all personalities were real and not a figment of my imagination.

There is a remarkable television programme, presented by Michael Buerk, of unbelievable events in which he often concludes: "What happened next?". This is a question that I rather too often have to ask myself, which I suppose is inevitable with advancing years. The events themselves are often clear and memorable, but then one is bound to ask what happened just before or what occurred next? It is almost impossible to make a narrative continuous without some details getting lost in the mists of time.

Probably, as much as anything, it has been the humour and fun that I have enjoyed most in the course of making music of a high quality. Without a sense of humour life is hardly worth living. A person who lacks this commodity - and who takes the most absurd remarks literally - has no place in my list of friends of whom I have, and have had, many. Perhaps also I may have acquired a useful sense of observation of events and people, which possibly goes right back to a report I had at the end of a term at my kindergarten before the first world war which said: "Inclined to look out of the window!"

R.N. 1999

1. EARLY LIFE

The fact that I was a "musical child" does not mean I was by any means a prodigy, but I was born into a small family in which music was going to be an important factor in my life. My brother, Clive, was over three years older than me and was showing an aptitude for the violin at an early age. We were both born in London - the Finsbury Park area - Clive in 1904 and myself in 1907, but after only two more years we moved to Sutton, and I lived in Surrey for the greater part of my life, until quite recently when I moved to Somerset - a couple of miles from Taunton.

My (our) father was the leading light. He lived for music. He was a more-than-useful pianist and a sympathetic accompanist. (As a cellist it would be kindest just to say his playing was unmemorable - or perhaps even just the opposite!) His music probably emanated from his cousin, Dr. Frank Nicholson Abernethy, who lived in Dulwich, and - among other things - taught impecunious elderly ladies the piano for practically nothing.

"Uncle Frank", as we called him, was a brilliant musician who had no "push", and therefore never really achieved his desserts. As a composer of Church music he must have become quite well known, especially among the non-conformist fraternity. His many chants, hymns etc. were published in Church literature and, for all I know, are still in use.

Life was not always fair to him, but if he had possessed more gumption and "go", and perhaps had sought the help and influence of someone of distinction in religious circles, he would have achieved his rightful place in the musical world. My father said he never heard him play a wrong note, and he used to tell the story - not quite accurate perhaps - of some occasion when, at a concert, a clarinettist had brought the wrong instrument, a "B flat" instead of an "A", and Uncle Frank transposed the music at sight. (Father always claimed it was Mendelssohn's *Elijah*, but this would have been impossible as the whole orchestra would have had to transpose! However, there could have been some truth in the story.)

But the point of all this is that there was an advertisement for an organist in the City of London - actually it was for Southwark Cathedral, on the South side of London Bridge. Uncle Frank applied for the post and, among about 80 other applicants, in fair competition, he came out on top and apparently had the job. But unfortunately, it was a bad time for father's cousin as it coincided with a change of Bishop. The new Bishop was informed of the appointment of a new organist, but he declared he was not interested - he had brought his own organist with him from his previous living. So that was the end of my Uncle Frank's chance of starting what might have been - what should have been - a new and interesting change in his career, and no-one knew what opportunities might lie ahead. For a man of such distinction - he had gained one of the highest honours, for he was a Mendelssohn Scholar - it was a sad and undeserving full stop. In fact it was a disgraceful rebuff. He retired to his piano- and organ-teaching in Dulwich. When he died, he left about £95, and it was a long time before anyone could find his will. It eventually turned up in a hymn book on his shelves!

Uncle Frank never married. He had a sister, known as Aunt Sarah, who was a spinster. I only knew her when she was "full of years" - and she lived to well into her 90s. We were told she had a beautiful soprano voice when she was young. I only remember her with rather a croaky voice, and becoming increasingly deaf. But one thing she retained right through her long life was her sense of humour. She could be very funny, and this trait in her nature could not have been enhanced by her living alone!

An example of her wit can be illustrated when, during the last war when she lived in Camberwell, she wrote to my father when the intensity of the blitz had become more serious, saying that she had decided to "evacuate". She told him she was moving from the 4th floor to the 2nd! A delightful event took place at the old Queen's Hall when we, in conjunction with my cousin, felt we ought to do something to celebrate an impending special birthday of our redoubtable aunt. We decided that Aunt Sarah would enjoy a concert on her 90th birthday, for even if she couldn't hear very well, she would enjoy the "antics" of the great conductor, Sir Thomas Beecham. No-one would have guessed that the croaky voice would hold up the start of the concert by a minute or so - but more of that in a later chapter.

Going back to my extreme youth before the Great War, I suppose it must have been about 1913 or -14 when I began to show some signs of musical tendencies. I was dispatched to "play-in" the children of our kindergarten in Sutton, as they marched to their places in the school garden. It was a summer term, the instrument I was allotted being a side-drum. I merely had to give an even beat so that they could march in time as they lined up at the annual prize-giving, producing nothing more complicated than a regular beat. (I never could - even to this day - do a proper side-drum "roll".)

Clive and I were lucky in having a first-rate violin teacher named Miss Winifred Amos, who used to come over once a week by train from Croydon. She was very pleasant but very strict. She was an excellent teacher who insisted on our devoting a lot of time mastering technique - i.e. scales and exercises - and not just learning what were mostly well-known tunes for violin and piano. Quite early on we were made familiar with the music of the great masters of the standing of Bach, Handel, Purcell and Corelli. And, inevitably, as soon as my technique approached the standard of Clive's, we were playing the well-known *Double Concerto* of Bach together, he having, of course, a three year start over me.

Among other things, we had to keep time books, 3 to 4 hours practice a day being about the "norm". Father kept a "weather eye" over us both, and practising had priority over most other activities while we were at home.

Clive did a number of things better than me. For instance, he had - and always had - a much freer left hand vibrato, and it was not long before he developed "absolute" pitch. He was able to name any note played on the piano without hesitation. I couldn't (at first), but my father used to play a chord and I would say, for example, "4 white, 3 black", referring to the notes of the keyboard.

How I found I was able to say the names of the actual notes came through a rather unusual ruse. I would take up my fiddle and immediately play the note I heard, and I would at once name it, or them, if it was a chord. I was then able to simplify the process when I realised it was not necessary to use a fiddle - I just imagined I had a fiddle under my arm and quickly thought what finger I would use to reproduce the note. And I still adopt this method if I have any doubts in my mind - which happens sometimes. Some years ago I was encouraged when Clive admitted that there is a tendency, as one grows older, for one's sense of pitch becomes somewhat less reliable, and I have found that that is so.

In the 1920s, as regards music making, it was very much a case of "do it yourselves". There were, of course, concerts in London, and our parents were regular subscribers to monthly Monday concerts given at the Queen's Hall by the London Symphony Orchestra. The L.S.O. was formed in 1904, chiefly as a result of a row with Sir Henry J. Wood who formed his own orchestra. Some of the trouble was caused by the so-called "Deputy System", where a player would send another man to rehearsals and do the concert himself - admittedly a somewhat bizarre arrangement. "Henry J" was naturally averse to such goings-on. He had actually formed his own orchestra in about 1895 for his own series of "Henry Wood Concerts".

2. SCHOOL-DAYS

I suppose it was not long after the end of the first World War, in 1919, that I became aware that music could become a "passport", so to speak, to certain privileges and advantages over other mortals, and would add other, so far unknown, joys to life. Our rather misguided but quite jolly Dr. Sutton, whom my grandfather couldn't tolerate because of his rather blustery attitude, diagnosed my having curvature of the spine (later to be found as straight as a die), and said that I must be dispatched to school by the sea for my health. So I was sent to a very nice "prep" school in Margate - a town not to be recommended in the height of the winter months when a strong NE wind is blowing off the North Sea!

The school was called Laleham, and was where my favourite cousin, Alan Heath, had been a boy some years before. I put "prep" school in inverted commas deliberately, as it was not a prep school as such, since it was the last term when boys of public school age were there, going on till they were up to 17 or 18 years of age. And they had, that term, the best soccer team of any school around, with an unbeaten record, and were anticipating a successful end to the term before the school reverted to one of prep school age. But I, in my innocence, somewhat "blotted my copybook". Early on in the term I developed chicken pox. Immediately I was isolated, and I remember counting my spots which I seem to remember amounted to approximately 18! I know the disease can be very unpleasant but I was never ill in the real sense.

You would think this would cause me to lose any possible friends in the school. I felt dreadful at having - quite unwittingly of course - been the cause of such mayhem. I know I was quite ashamed and embarrassed at what I had done - a really nasty little boy of 12! But not a bit of it. I had, eventually, a lovely term. The saving grace? Music! It was soon discovered I played the fiddle reasonably well and I almost immediately began to realise the significance of the word "privilege". One of the senior boys was an excellent pianist, so instead of repairing to bed with the juniors at an early hour, I was allowed to stay up late and play Handel and Bach sonatas etc. And it gave me quite a standing in the eyes of the school, and to me much enjoyment. I don't know if my violin playing improved during my two years at Laleham for I was "taught" by a piano teacher. So little did he know about violins that at one "lesson" he actually brought a violin along - which he was getting for another pupil - for me to try and see what I thought of it!

Whether or not living near the sea straightened my spine, I think it toughened me up, especially in the winter months. In the dormitories, there were hand basins, filled with cold water before we went to bed. I well remember, especially in the coldest days of February, that quite often - since the windows had been wide open all night - we would have to break the ice before we could wash in the mornings!

I was really happy at Laleham - the first time I had lived away from home - and I put it down to the splendid broad-minded headmaster, S.C. (Sam) Hester. He had a delightful personality, and incidentally had a love of music. I got on with him famously. Not long ago I came across a personal letter from him to me - an extremely nice one - written some years after I had left the school, and I think he had heard a broadcast on the radio in which he thought (wrongly) that I had taken part. But, I well remember the time he said to me something which I have found true right through life. His wise words were, "If the headmaster is right, then the whole school will be right". And I have found that applies not just with a school head, but also the conductor of an orchestra or the C.O. of a company of an Army unit or a platoon in the R.A.F., or whenever any group of men relies on the character and leadership of the man at the top.

Looking back it is odd how often in my life I have been picked out to do odd jobs for people - usually an orchestra conductor - which I shall be referring to later in this narrative. While I was still at Laleham there was an assistant master named "Adamthwaite" whom I, even at quite a young prep school age, decided was a slightly disreputable character (I don't know anyone else who felt the same). I do know that he used to "employ" me to run little errands for him in the morning when I should have been at school. I am not sure whether it was every day, but it was certainly quite often. I believe they were betting slips, and he was obviously having a bet on horses at various race meetings. How I, at my "tender" age, was allowed to do this, or where I took these slips I can't remember as there were no betting shops as there are today, but it was a small episode in my career. I did form an opinion of this man - who was of course very pleasant to me - that I wouldn't trust him as far - to quote my late father-in-law - "as I could throw a grand piano"!

From Laleham I moved on - still by the sea - to the Sussex town of Eastbourne. It was while I was at Eastbourne College that my life and early signs of my future began to form, develop and "take off". And it was a happy five years that I had at the College.

Eastbourne

We had a science master at Eastbourne who appeared rather repellent - anyway, anything but pleasant. He always looked disagreeable, and this was his general demeanour - later to be revealed as something of a facade. He had a gruff manner and was far from popular, and quite frightening to some of the smaller boys. His name was Temperley, and this seemed somewhat appropriate at the time. His nickname was "Crippen"! He sometimes sat at his desk - he even used to put his feet on the desk itself - and, at times when parents were being shown round, he wouldn't always rise to his feet. In the chemistry laboratory there were numerous experiments and many smells permeated the air, not least the very unpleasant gas H_2S. Temperley himself would fiercely call out: "Some boy has made a smell in the laboratory", - accenting the first syllable! He would also occasionally become rather vague, as though he was thinking of something else, and once, while setting the "prep" for the next lesson, he announced rather slowly: "Now, for preparation, you will prepare pages 157-8-9", and then after quite a pause "10"! But I found, after I had become more senior, that "Crippen" had a much warmer side to him and he became quite "human". He showed quite an intelligent interest in music, with more than a little knowledge of good music, and he seemed to enjoy discussing it. I think it was another case of a bark being worse than a bite.

There is usually one master who is considerably less popular than the rest, often someone who is unable to keep discipline, and schoolboys are very quick to take advantage or "the mickey" as we now call it, and even "rag" a teacher who displays certain weaknesses - and who usually lacks a sense of humour - and woe betide such a master. And so it was at Eastbourne, and how often it is the French master who suffers. We had a French master - not himself French - by the name of Waterfield, who was generally known as "Bubbles". One day when he was writing on the blackboard, a boy took advantage of Bubbles having his back to us and climbed up on to the rafters. He immediately noticed the defaulter and called out: "What are you doing up there, boy?" "Looking for something, Sir", replied the boy. "What are you looking for?", asked Bubbles. "Trouble, Sir", came the reply. Many boys attending his classes would take the precaution of padding their trousers!

I don't think that I exactly distinguished myself academically, but in most other activities I think I can say, with all modesty, that I more than "filled the bill" and made many friends. Most of these are no more in this world, including one - John Underhill - who I sadly learned passed away not long ago. He was a year senior and older than I. Though he was in a different House, we were both in the Shooting VIII together, and captain in successive years. He and Eliza had been married for over 62 years. Gill and I were to miss our half century by a year and a half.

It is an indication of how things have developed over the years when one compares the changes from 1921 - my first term at Eastbourne College - with, say 10 years later. And, of course, nowadays the standard of performance is remarkably high in schools even before the more musically gifted have gone to music college. As a new boy, in December 1921, at the end of term concert, I was the only boy taking part, when I played a violin solo with piano. I can't remember what it was but it caused a minor sensation where previously instrumental music was practically nil. My "stock" shot up overnight and I achieved (temporary) popularity. But there must have been hope for the future as the facilities at the College were good - and I was to benefit from them. There was a modest little lady called Elsie Reed who taught the piano and played the organ in Chapel, and there was another piano teacher called Alcock, with a shock of black hair, whom I always considered something of a "rough diamond". He was also a minor composer who turned out to be a rather unlikely brother of Sir Walter Alcock, one-time organist of Salisbury Cathedral. But I, naturally, felt the best hope for instruments in the College was the teacher of violin, W.J.Read. He was a splendid player and teacher, and I learned a lot from him during my five years there and we became firm friends. He had a son, named Cyril, who possessed a first class technique and seemed destined for a musical career as a soloist.

I rather lost touch with him. His father was somewhat old-fashioned in dress; he was a stoutish man and used to wear a double-breasted waistcoat!

He had a number of quirks, one of them being his use of a pencil. He used to take whatever piece he had brought me and run his pencil along, rather at the speed of a typewriter, but very untidily. In violin playing - or any other string instrument - there are only two directions for the bow to travel, down-bow and up-bow. In many straightforward pieces for violin it is often unnecessary to mark in any bowing at all, except where a special effect is required. It is ideal to see string players in an orchestra bowing precisely together, just as it is lovely, for instance, to watch the precision and perfect movements of troops at the Trooping of the Colour. But for Read, this was not the point. He marked the bowing on every note of every bar with a sign for up- or down-bow. I still have some of the copies of music I learnt with him, and I would be ashamed to lend one of these to anyone - at least without some explanation. He once told me he had been amused by one girl he had taught at an Eastbourne school who had said to him: "I think I'm old enough now not to have every single bar marked with the bowing!" His argument was that should you stop for any reason, you would know exactly which way to bow when you restarted. I quite agreed (not verbally!) with the schoolgirl. All very odd! Another thing about Willie Read was that he was mad keen on the great violinist Kreisler, and would make sure he was present when the great man was giving a concert at the local Devonshire Park concert hall. And I had to learn all Fritz Kreisler's many arrangements of well-known tunes for violin and piano.

Again I was to find music to be a "passport to privilege". My housemaster, H.F.Morres, was very keen on music too. He had quite a passable baritone voice. He loved singing, and I will never forget his annual performance of an aria from "Chu, Chin, Chow" and his rendering of "I cobble, and cobble and cobble all day"! He often allowed me special privileges. One was when there was a special concert at Devonshire Park - at the bottom of our road - often when Kreisler was playing, and Morres used to let me slip out of prep to walk down to the theatre.

There is a nice story about Kreisler. He was due to play a concerto, many years ago - I believe it was the Beethoven concerto - at one of the three cathedrals - possibly Worcester - during a Three Choirs Festival. Years ago, we violinists could not rely on our gut strings not breaking unexpectedly, especially the very thin top E string - this was before the long lasting wire string was adopted - and, if one broke, it needed a lot of running in or it tended to become flat. Kreisler broke a string within 20 minutes of going on to play his concerto, so - it is alleged - he sat at the back of the 2nd violins during the previous work, giving his new string time to settle down as he played with the orchestra - unseen by the audience no doubt!

My musical career did not progress much except as a soloist, for at last I was being taught by a good teacher and performer for five happily spent years. If I did not show any outstanding talent in the main sports of the school I did achieve some satisfaction in gaining promotion to Sergeant in the O.T.C. I was a passable long distance runner and actually came in 2nd, as 2nd string in the mile, in an Old Boys match a year or two after I had left school - the 1st string had to give up as he drank too much over lunch! But my "forte" was shooting. I was in the VIII for the last three years of my school career, being captain in my final year (just as my brother had been three years previously while at Epsom College). It was that year that our House won nearly all the inter-House cups. Had we won them all it would have created a record, and we should have done this easily but for my crass carelessness.

The master in charge of shooting was a certain Major Stephen Foot, the author of a book called *Three Lives*, about his army career, his life as a schoolmaster, and his involvement in some religious cult - possibly the Oxford Group (but I hope not!). It happened that, during one occasion on the Crumbles, a boy's bullet did not fire after he had pressed the trigger. (Why does everyone these days talk about "pulling" the trigger? It is the one thing you are taught not to do. If you do you miss the target!) Anyway, the Major told the boy (possibly me!) to unload and remove the offending bullet from the magazine. Major Foot put it in his pocket, then changed his mind and flung it away in the shingle. Within a minute it exploded!

We used to shoot at the Crumbles, a large area of shingle between Eastbourne and Hastings, which was open to the wind which blew straight off the English Channel, usually from the direction of Beachy Head, with no protection whatsoever apart from a few Martello towers, built many years ago as protection against attacks from the French fleet in a war long forgotten.

By early July in the summer term, the Shooting VIII went to Bisley for the annual Ashburton Shield Rifle Competition between 70 and 80 public schools. We had three days there, and again I was to benefit by privilege. The great majority of the schools were accommodated in tents in the grounds not far from the actual ranges, but for some reason, never explained and a mystery to this day, Eastbourne together with three or four other schools (I think they were something like Harrow, Wellington, Sherborne and one other) had been singled out as guests of the Inns of Court. We slept separately from all the other schools and what was a new experience for most of us was that the meals were served by white-collared waiters. Not only that but we had cider with our meals! Before the Ashburton itself there was another competition sponsored by a photographic firm from Aldershot called "Gale and Polden", which was rather fun. And there was also another schools event called the "Cadet Pair" in which just two boys shot together, and the result depended on their combined total. In this event we usually did quite well and one year went quite near to winning it.

The night before the Ashburton we used to receive a pep talk from Major Foot. He used to tell us to walk round the camp before turning in for the night and select a "worm" from another school. A "worm" was the most miserable looking boy we could find and he was to be fixed firmly in our minds as the one we were up against while we were shooting - a bit quaint, but quite amusing, though I can't say it did much good.

9

We never really did ourselves justice when it came to the actual day and we usually finished up "well down the field". I used to put it down - probably fairly correctly - to the big difference in conditions between the usually windy weather of the south coast and the often very hot and sultry conditions, often with no wind at all, at Bisley in the early days of July. It is true that we tended, so to speak, to "lean up against" the prevailing sea breezes we were used to. We quite enjoyed the Crumbles, for we lay on our tummies on the loose shingle and could sort of dig ourselves into the most comfortable position to fit our bodies.

I must just mention the cause of my "gaff" which lost us the particular shooting prize. As I have mentioned, all shooting competitions we took part in consisted of a specified number of shots fired, first at a range of 200 yards followed by 500 yards. The nearer distance tended to be easier than the further one, where you had to be more accurate. For this particular event Major Foot decided to eliminate some of the less efficient shots - "duffers" if you like - by reversing the usual procedure and starting the event at the more difficult 500 yards range, but I never expected to be counted among them. Because of this change we naturally had to adjust the sights on our rifles accordingly. Yours truly, who should have known better as Captain, omitted through carelessness to do this and shot as from 200 yards, and I couldn't think why I was getting such poor results. I did continue from the 200 yards, just to "make up the numbers", but I never forgave myself and I doubt if anyone else did!

Among a number of lasting disappointments in my life was that while I was teaching at the Royal College I unexpectedly heard from Stephen Foot who had discovered my whereabouts. He had moved to a flat in a block off Victoria Street near Westminster Abbey. He said he'd love to see me again and asked me to call on him sometime. I regret I never did. These personal weaknesses seem to stay with you for the rest of your life!

But I did have the pleasure at my very first "Ashburton" in my first year (1924) in the Shooting VIII, of being "mentioned in dispatches". I was still only a lance-corporal. An early report of the event appeared in the *Evening Standard*. It is true I started rather well at 200 yards. The report began by mentioning three boys from other schools who scored 33 out of 35 points. I, in my "exalted" rank, was given a new sentence which began: "Others who also scored 33 were Sgt. Nicholson of Eastbourne . . .". I was glad that the reporter had no time to stay for the shooting at 500 yards for I did less well, scoring 27! But my total of 60/70 was quite reasonable. It is true that when you have responsibilities you tend not to do so well yourself while you are encouraging and helping others, and this occurred in my case in my last term, but I didn't let the side down. Before the end of the term I took part in an open tournament, anyone in the town being eligible to enter, and I managed to win it. As far as I can remember my reward was a silver cruet. What happened to it I know not, but I was not paid for winning so I retained my amateur status!

We used to enjoy our trips to the Crumbles, travelling on a double-decker

Eastbourne bus. Once the site of a rather unpleasant murder in the early 20s, the Crumbles are alas no more - the whole area has been converted into a marina.

My school education ended on a good note since I won the music prize. It was presented on Speech day by the then headmaster, E.C.Arnold - a relation of the well known head of Rugby School, Matthew Arnold - who was not the least bit interested in music. The prize was a beautifully leather-bound book on some obtuse subject, which I admit I have never got round to reading, but it looks very impressive among others in my bookcase. As my father had given the prize, hoping to encourage instrumental music at the College, he was slightly embarrassed when he heard I had won it and felt he ought to award a second one that year, which he did.

Arnold distinguished himself in many ways, but especially with his priceless collection of stuffed birds and a fine collection of carved woodwork done by many past boys of the College, which adorned the walls of Big School. He would have been devastated had he lived to see, not many years ago, the Big School Hall go up in flames one night, due to an electrical fault. Only the shell of the building remained. Arnold, who was mad keen on rugby was known universally as "Og". He used to pace up and down the touch line in his long green overcoat - very similar to a recent Foreign Secretary's - where the cry of "Take the runner!" was frequently heard from him.

The development of music soon became apparent. Having myself appeared as a new boy in 1921, playing a violin solo and being the only member of the school to take part in the Christmas concert, I found a remarkable change ten years or more later when I was invited back to lead the violas in a choral and orchestral concert in Big School. I was probably the only person outside the immediate circle of the College taking part. I believe the work performed was Coleridge Taylor's *Hiawatha's Wedding Feast.* Whether or not this was so, I, playing viola, was sitting square on to the audience, looking straight down the hall. Not being able to see what was going on behind me, I was suddenly aware of something unusual when I chanced to look round. It was certainly something puzzling. A boy was sitting behind the orchestra with his back to the audience, facing the choir. He seemed to have a pile of cards in his hands, and from time to time held one aloft for the choir to see, but from where I sat they appeared to have nothing on them. After holding them up for a couple of seconds, he would drop the card on the floor. It was, I suppose, about the same size as the metal discs used in the more old fashioned cricket scoreboards or "tally wags". When a suitable moment occurred I asked my partner in the orchestra if he knew what was going on behind our backs. He was able to give me the answer. Apparently it was a new experience for the choir to sing with an orchestra, so, to assist any member of the choir who may have got lost, or needed confirmation of where they had got to, he held up the numbers - or more probably letters - we had reached in the printed score. A good idea and an unusual one.

A good many years later, when my eldest son David was a boy at the College, I went down and joined in the choir, singing in a worthy performance of

Bach's *St John Passion*, in the large Congress Theatre quite near the College. It was most encouraging to find such a "musical revolution" had taken place since I left.

My father continued the Music Prize under the name of E.B.Nicholson until I took it over as the R.W.Nicholson music prize. It has been in abeyance for some years now. I felt I should perhaps - as two of the family are O.E's - reinstate the prize in some form, in spite of them having quite a number of awards for music these days, and this has now been done.

The decision that I would be devoting my life to music really came about when we lived in Sutton. Nearly opposite our house there lived a large family named Sharp, and naturally their numerous children and my brother and I went to school together. Mr Sharp's sister was Ethyl Hobday, a noted professional pianist who was married to Alfred Hobday, principal viola of the L.S.O., and it was suggested that I played my violin to them when they were visiting. As a result of this, the verdict was that I seemed to be on to a good thing - and that's really how it all started. While we were talking to them, Mrs Hobday told us that when she was about 5 years old, she actually played to Brahms! And she had never forgotten - nor have I - that he said to her: "Never play my fast movements too fast". What splendid advice to some up-and-coming conductors!

3. YEARS AS A MUSIC STUDENT IN LONDON

Royal College of Music

The transition from schoolboy to student was quite marked. For instance,. where one would call a master at school "Sir" all the time, there was a tendency, if one got to know one's professors really well, to call them by their first names, though I never called my violin professor "Maurice" - and I would never have thought of doing so - but always "Mr Sons" (pronounced like "songs" without the "g"). Any way, they talked to you more on equal terms and soon became personal friends.

When I arrived at the Royal College in September 1926, I really felt I had "come of age". I did not enter for any scholarship but started as an ordinary fee-paying student. My father did not have to "fork out" too much in fees. If your first study was for half- hour lessons (which seems very little as regards time), the fee was 14 guineas a term, and if for 20 minutes, 12 guineas. For my last two years at the College I was awarded the Gowland Harrison Scholarship, and the award was worth £200 a year, if I remember correctly. Naturally this was a considerable saving to my parents and they were pleased for me to continue at the R.C.M. for two more years.

During my time at the College, it was a period of great activity, and I became involved in absolutely everything. I was very contented with life generally. The world was mainly at peace and there was little urgency in life. If, as a result of taking part in so many varied activities I "fell between a number of stools", I didn't really care. Nor do I regret anything that I did, for life was very full and exciting and I enjoyed every minute of it. Studying the violin was not my only concern, but I did allow enough time for practice.

When I started at the Royal College, I was quite a shy boy, especially with the opposite sex, believe it or not! It was not really surprising for a young boy coming straight from - not exactly a monastic life - but five years in an entirely boys' public boarding school. (It was many years before girls were accepted in the VIth form at Eastbourne.)

At the R.C.M. one was immediately aware of the segregation of the sexes as far as possible, but this could not realistically be sustained. There was, for instance, nothing to prevent a male student coming away from his first study lesson to be followed immediately by a young lady. But the two notices which "welcomed" us when we arrived at the College must have been relics of the days when the building was first opened in the 1890's. There are two side staircases leading to the upper floors as well as down to the basement, one to the left and the other to the right, and at the bottom of each of these were small printed boards, one with the instruction "Male Staircase" and the other, equally unbelievable "Female Staircase"! Whether we took the slightest notice is doubtful, but the boards were still in place when I entered the College in 1926.

An example of my lack of self-assurance (repeated 10 years later when the Boyd Neel String Orchestra were playing in Salzburg - but that's another story), was illustrated when it came to lunch time. In my very early days at the College I could not brace myself to confront a mixed crowd of students in the dining rooms downstairs in the basement. For quite a long time I religiously walked down to the ABC by South Kensington Underground Station - about a ten minute walk - and ate the simplest of lunches which was invariably soup, a roll and butter and a cup of coffee, costing a total of one shilling and a penny half-penny (1/1½d). I soon got used to female company!

My violin professor, a little Dutchman called Maurice Sons, was a fine teacher and was the first person I'd known with whom I did not want to disagree or argue. Everything he said - based of course on vast experience - was sound good sense. He was the leader of Henry Wood's old Queen's Hall Orchestra. Although small in stature he had a big tone and it was once said that he could be heard above everyone else in the Orchestra! His playing of the music of J.S.Bach had a very special quality about it. In 1929 Sons got me a violin from the famous violin makers of New Bond Street, W.E.Hill & Sons. It was one of their red fiddles and was made in 1914, being modelled on the "Messie" Strad. It had a fine tone and I was, and still am, the only person to have played on it. Hills did not sell their violins until 15 years after their manufacture. In the meantime they would be hung up in a loft to give the special varnish time to really dry and to mature. I cannot imagine, in today's life of commercialism, anyone could afford to wait so long. The violins all "hung up to dry" reminds one of a butcher's shop where the turkeys are hung from the ceiling to mature for Christmas!

Hill's shop in New Bond Street was quite unique with its attractive little bow window at the front. Inside there was quite an air of mystery. The man at the shop's counter would greet you with great courtesy and then disappear into the bowels of the earth, going down the long flight of stairs, either with the fiddle you had brought in for repair, or whatever, or to collect a fiddle you had previously taken in. You rarely saw anyone else on any particular visit. One never knew what went on there, whether there was a big repair room, how many worked there, etc. If you wanted to try a fiddle you did so in the shop itself. This delightful small building is no longer Hill's.

My violin was said by Mr Sons to be the second best "Hill" he'd ever seen, second only to his own of 1895. It cost me £70 in 1929 and is now in safe custody and worth several thousand pounds!

Sons had a dry sense of humour and tended to end a remark with the expletive "Hein?", which one had to presume meant "If you see what I mean", or something similar. He was outspoken and did not mind showing when he did not think too much of other musicians. Of Fleisch, the well-known violinist, he would say: "Fleisch? He is just a flash in the pan, hein?", and he seemed to have no time either for the "pioneer" viola player, Lionel Tertis, who did so much to popularise the viola with his many arrangements of violin pieces, and who designed a very a large viola. Sons seemed to have scant respect for Tertis and said: "He is aggressive and common, hein?".

14

I did not care for the playing of Tertis either, but that is by the way. What used to make Sons laugh was the story of the schoolboy who, when asked how many symphonies Beethoven wrote, thought for a moment and then answered: "Beethoven wrote four symphonies - the 3rd, the 5th, the 7th and the 9th!" In a string quartet in his teaching room where he was coaching, a 2nd violinist was counting time by tapping the floor rather noisily with his foot, Sons angrily hit his foot with his bow and said to the student in his broken English: "Leave your foot at home". He admonished one student whose rather fast vibrato irritated him. "Zat ees not a vibrato", he said to the student, "It ees a nervous vobble!"

Maurice Sons lived in a house in St John's Wood Road, only about a cricket ball's throw from Lord's. During the war the house was bombed. When I heard the news I called on him and found the bomb had luckily only grazed the side of the house. "I am still here, Nicholson, the house is still here, so I shall continue to live here, hein?" - and he did.

During the late 20s and early 30s the tempo of life was slower and there was a lack of urgency and people were able to enjoy life - not that there was any relaxation of standards. There was more time to savour what was on offer without the relentless pressures of these days. There were a number of extra-musical activities at the College. On each side of the R.C.M. there was a certain amount of open space; the next building on one side was the School of Mines and on the other was Imperial College. On the latter site there was evidence of the generosity of a lady benefactor who presented a hard tennis court for the benefit of students. The only thing she failed to realise would be necessary was a supply of red top-dressing. But the court became popular and was in frequent use. As usual it always seemed to fall on me to organise things, and I did organise an annual tournament. I remember one year playing in the Men's Doubles with the violinist Ronald Onley and we managed to win the final. What happened to the Silver Cup I've no idea!

I was a 2nd study pianist. I never did play the piano well, though probably well enough to accompany violin students. For some reason my father never encouraged me to learn the piano in my youth - especially since he spent half his life playing the piano - whereas my brother Clive was not only a proficient pianist but good enough to play the organ for occasional services at Epsom College chapel. My 2nd study professor at the R.C.M. was a delightful man name Henry Wilson, with whom my elder daughter, many years later, also studied. He had recently married an excellent teacher of singing, Kathleen McQuitty. They happened to have adjacent teaching rooms which looked directly over the tennis court. With such "ringside seats" it was not unnatural for one or other to come to the window briefly and look out while their pupils were performing. It always reminded me - if I happened to be playing - of those little figures of long ago of a man and a woman in a small box with two doorless openings, on a sort of movable swivel, which were supposed to predict the weather. If the little man swung out it was going to be fine, if the woman, then we could expect poor weather. I believe they were completely inaccurate but quite decorative.

It is funny how small incidents often remain with you though quite unimportant in themselves. One such involved the very first student I met when we both arrived at the R.C.M. on the same September day in 1928. His name was Jimmy Whitehead. I was 19, he was a 14 year old schoolboy, still in shorts, who came from Bacup in Lancashire. He was to become a distinguished cellist, including being principal of the original Boyd Neel String Orchestra. I believe he originally wanted to be a County cricketer. I'm sure he could have been; he was a "natural" in any sport he took part in.

Jimmy was in the student's lunch room, which had a good view of the tennis court, when two men went on to play a singles match. At the moment when Jimmy was watching, both players were facing each other and served simultaneously at each other. jimmy nearly had hysterics, laughing at this very odd but unintentional event. I must say I've never seen it happen again since, and when you come to think of it it is rather funny.

As I have said, he was adept at all sports and I can remember, to my cost, when I played him at croquet while we were on holiday together at the Lizard in Cornwall. The small hotel we were all staying at had quite a nice lawn. I was in a good position and about to beat him easily when Jimmy played a devastating shot from the far end of the lawn and sent my ball flying. That was the sort of player he was, and I found out too that he was equally adept at tennis and golf.

After leading the cellos at Glyndebourne (before the R.P.O. became the resident orchestra), and at other venues, Jimmy decided to emigrate. He formed a piano trio with the pianist Lance Dossor and another ex-Collegian, dug up his roots and settled in Adelaide, Australia, where he remained for the rest of his life. He was to be joined by his wife, Nora, a violist - also at the R.C.M and in the "Boyd Neel" with me - and their four daughters. I once asked Jimmy, with five in the same family all having the initial J, who would cash a cheque made out to J.Whitehead. Without hesitation Jimmy, who never really lost his North Country accent, firmly replied, "I would!". My silly nick-name for Nora was "Bone". Oddly enough it seemed to have stuck. The last I heard of her was that she was well and cheerful but in a nursing home with failing sight. Jimmy died a few years ago, but he did not devote his whole life to music for he played golf regularly with the great cricketer Sir Donald Bradman in Adelaide. I once asked him what it was like and he said: "All right so long as you took the game seriously".

While I was at the College I became involved in many and varied activities, and some might say I fell between a number of different stools. I wouldn't agree for I gained a great deal not only musically but in lasting friendships, both with other students and with members of the teaching and office staff too. Among my "sidelines" was to contribute, from time to time, lighthearted - I suppose you could call them humorous - articles to the R.C.M. Magazine, as a sort of antidote to more serious and profound articles on some musical subject or other. For instance, I wrote a "spoof" dictionary of musical terms. I even "invented" a large instrument which I called a "viopiccolodillytuba" based on three different instruments. My very close friend the late Jimmy Phillips (cellist) and I wrote an article based on words common to music and wines and spirits. It was surprising how many we found, perhaps one rather more obvious one being "portamento". On another occasion I wrote a review of an imaginary concert where the music critic had been taken ill and the job had been allocated to the cricket correspondent. For example - "There was a sudden collapse of the stand between the conductor and orchestra", and "The conductor, with a big swoop of his baton towards the first violins, nearly bowled a maiden over!".

These articles no doubt caused a titter or two at the time, but of course those days are in the past - maybe we didn't take ourselves too seriously at the time but there is, of course, nothing like that now. Today the R.C.M. magazine is a much larger and dignified journal with "high-powered" articles and reports of musical events and the successes of up-and-coming young artists on the brink of brilliant careers as befits a representative of a great musical institution of world-wide fame, established in the late 19th century, and adorned from the very beginning with such great names as Sir Arthur Sullivan, Sir Charles Villiers Stanford, Ralph Vaughan Williams, and many others, either as professors or students. Any such frivolities as described above would, of course, be completely out of place these days where competition is greater and the standard of performance of the young is unbelievably high.

But I do not regret being around in those slightly "easier-going" days when there was less officialdom and a minimum of security. Even during my fourteen years of teaching at the College there were two incidents of theft - the first being completely "bare-faced" when two men in long white coats walked the whole length of the passage to the New Building, calmly removed a T.V. set and walked out of the building unchallenged, naturally presumed to be on official business. That was the last ever seen of the television set! It was quite unbelievable that anyone could carry out such a mean, comparatively small crime as the other theft. There was, and still is, a charming small statue of Mozart holding a violin and bow in the short passage of the gallery on the first floor, immediately above the main entrance to the College. The violin bow was stolen, and as far as I know it has never been found.

But I must return to the days of the late 20s and early 30s when so much took place, including memorable concerts and opera performances. The fairly frequent visits of Sir Thomas Beecham deserve special mention since they contain a great deal of fascinating details which I will deal with fully in a later chapter. I am only so lucky to have witnessed, and even taken part in, so much of it.

There is much more to what I might call the "domestic" scene where one had an opportunity to "let one's hair down". It was not long after I arrived at the R.C.M. that I realised that there was a wealth of humour, especially among the staff. I always maintain that one of our most precious assets is a sense of humour. I cannot get on with people who have no humour and take all remarks literally.

One of the delightful institutions of the College was an association of friends known as the R.C.M. Union (completely different from the Musicians Union), rather a club consisting of past and present students who paid an annual subscription. It is all, again, different now and renamed the R.C.M. Society. It was this Association that was the precursor of the annual Union "At Home" that took place in the summer term. It was a most enjoyable event which consisted of a serious concert of moderate duration, performed by distinguished past students of the College. After excellent refreshments with wine, provided and served in the concert hall by a firm of caterers, there followed - sometimes in the same hall but more recently in the opera theatre, a floor below - the entertainment, known by the then Hon. Sec. of the Union and one of the Times music critics, a little lady called Marion Scott, as "The Funniment". This gave scope for the display of much talent at the College, often extremely funny and provoking much laughter, though I must be careful to display a degree of modesty since I eventually became responsible for quite a number of these entertainments. But it takes more than one to create laughter and there was certainly no lack of talent at the College, especially with students whose principal subject was opera, where a number of them were to spend their working days performing on the stage.

It was soon apparent to me in my very early days that these annual events were not the sole preserve of the students for a lot of humour also emanated from the professors and staff. We had, at that time, a delightful Registrar called Claude Aveling. He was one of the great characters of our profession. He was rather short-sighted, but behind a somewhat lugubrious expression hid a man of well-known scholarship, possessing a very subtle sense of humour, and he was also a man of kindliness who often displayed in my presence a trait of generosity. I had reason to collect money for various "local" causes from time to time, whether it be merely selling sweepstakes tickets for the Derby or, for instance, asking for contributions towards the expenses in connection with dances which I organised fairly often at Imperial College, opposite the rear of the Albert Hall. Claude Aveling would always be willing to contribute, often more generously than anybody. And I was able to witness his great gift of humour at one of the first "At Homes" I attended. Unfortunately I have temporarily forgotten the details, but if I could find the report of the occasion in the relevant issue of the R.C.M. magazine which I have (somewhere) I am sure many of the details will come flooding back to my receptive memory. But I do know it was extremely funny and clever.

Aveling had a daughter, Elizabeth - a singer. She remained as a student at the College for some fifteen years, which must be some sort of record. I shall be mentioning Elizabeth again, a little later on, in connection with another "At Home" in which she took a most prominent and important part, the event being a quite brilliant revue devised by "Dr" Malcolm Sargent after he had caused me almost to have kittens by his elusiveness due to pressure of work. Almost at the last moment he came up with a quite incredible "sketch" if you like, but worthy of a more appropriate epithet, as a result of less than a quarter of an hour's thought during a 1st orchestra tea-break. The result, unfortunately put on in his absence, was a fantastic success. I've never ceased to marvel at Sargent's quickness of brain, but more of that anon. I had good reason to worry on that occasion as I was responsible for the evening's entertainment!

Another "At Home" during my early days - when I was unconsciously learning the "tricks of the trade", so to speak - was also something devised by a then professor of the College, this time the ubiquitous character, "Willie" Reed, the well-known (Dr) W.H.Reed, leader of the L.S.O., friend of Elgar and of everyone else who came in contact with him. He advised Elgar on various points in the Cadenza of his Violin Concerto among other things. He also showed a practical side of his sense of humour when he devised a priceless sketch which he called "Passmarks". The main gist of it was that he had discovered that the opening of the Mendelssohn *Violin Concerto* and the main theme of the *Die Freischutz* overture by Weber could be played with exactly the same accompaniment. There was a shortage of rooms so that the examining of violin and voice had to take place at the same time! I had been selected as the violinist. There was a dramatic end to this to this short episode for the sequel was that for some reason I had to be shot, and I believe it was quite effective as a "blank" was fired. As I fell to the ground the violin was smashed to smithereens (it had to be of no value, of course) and I was carried off. The rest of the story is - as they say - confined to history. But it was a small example of some of the things we got up to in those days, which was all the greatest fun and never anything but well organised chaos.

I was involved in a number of other "At Homes", which I enjoyed. The memories tend to be spasmodic with some details forgotten and I tend to say to myself, since the events are now a long time ago - what happened next? or - what happened just before? But I can remember enough of the general events to make them interesting and often funny. For one of my first "At Homes" I thought of a ridiculously elaborate title like: "A grand special rehearsal/concert performance for the Patron's fun". Unfortunately I had to submit it for some reason to the Registrar, Claude Aveling, for approval and he did not approve. He explained to me why he dissuaded me from using it at the time. We had a benefactor at the College in the person of Sir Ernest Palmer, founder of the famous Reading biscuit firm of Huntley and Palmer, and one of the activities he financed was a termly visit of one of the London orchestras, often the L.S.O., for advanced students to conduct one work on a certain Friday morning in term time. The session was from 10 a.m. until 1 p.m. The chosen student was given a stipulated time to rehearse the work chosen and then, after a 15 minute break, would conduct, or possibly play part of a concerto, as if part of a concert. I was one of those chosen in my final term and my choice Brahms' *Tragic Overture* with the L.S.O.

Aveling explained to me the reason for his decision not to allow my title. These one-off concerts were sponsored by a fund instituted by our benefactor Ernest (later Lord) Palmer, and known as the "Patron's Fund". "Between you and me, Nicholson," he said, "your title is amusing but we cannot afford to offend our benefactor. We might perhaps use it on another occasion when our Patron is not around!" This small display of censorship was just because ëfuní sounded a bit too much like ëfundí for comfort, so I had to abandon my title and think up something else.

With an orchestra available for College "At Homes" one had endless opportunities for frivolity. On one occasion we had a large girl soprano, Margaret McArthur, who had a lovely sense of humour. With her massive frame she could claim a wide range of voice, from a top G in the treble clef down to a low note in the bass clef. Her contribution to the programme was to sing a very popular and very much in vogue aria from *Samson and Delilah*, by Saint Saens.

At that time the College organ was situated centrally and just behind the orchestra at a higher level. I had as the organist an old friend of mine - a fellow student whom I met when he came to the R.C.M. for the first time in 1928 - and we've been friends ever since. He's a year older than I am and lives now in Cheltenham, his name being Laurence Hudson. We had arranged the organ to develop a cipher - that's to say a note that sticks down, usually in the wrong key, which brings any performance to a halt. Lawrence had arranged for this note to be prolonged by wedging a coin between two keys and turning off the air. This left enough in the pipes for the note to continue for about half a minute or so, at which point it died with a wail as it finally gave up and silence descended. Whilst all this was happening Laurence had slipped off the organ seat and disappeared into the area of the pipes through a small door to the left of the organ, it being assumed that something had blocked one of the pipes. In a short while, with all eyes - including those of the soprano soloist, Margaret McArthur - trained on the organ, he reappeared holding aloft by its tail what appeared to be a dead rat. Margaret shrieked in terror and feigned a realistic swoon and was, with difficulty, carried out by three or four strong men! The "rat" was a very realistic creation made out of brown cloth by a very dear lady, a Mrs Gotch, whose main responsibility was to dress all the ladies - soloists and chorus - for R.C.M. performances of operas in the old Opera Theatre. I still have that "rat" somewhere!

The "revues" continued in the same vein each year, and another occasion must be recalled. Some time earlier there had been in London, and elsewhere, a solo pianist who was rather more than somewhat eccentric. There must have been embarrassing moments, but basically he was a fine pianist. Stories, of course, abounded about his antics. One day, when the audience were all in their seats - perhaps at the Wigmore Hall in London - he was practising away at the piano, quite oblivious of anyone else, when he suddenly realised the audience were already in their seats. He was alleged to have exclaimed: "Oh, there you are!" His name, by the way, was Pachmann. There was another occasion which must have caused a certain amount of concern, especially for people who had paid quite a high price for their seats, when he started off by making a most unpleasant noise, playing a lot of wrong notes and discordant harmony. After a few moments of this he stopped, and addressing the audience said: "Zat is how some people play. Now listen to how Pachmann plays!", and order was restored, with the audience sitting back and enjoying the remainder of the recital.

At one particular College "revue" we had one item based on some of the eccentricities of Pachmann, the soloist representing this rather odd individual being one of the most distinguished and respected professors of cello at the College - Ivor James. He was particularly noted as a teacher and player of chamber music. He had his own well-known string quartet, and was frequently joined by Helen Just who was also a professor at the College. She had once been a pupil of Ivor's and later became his wife. For this particular "take-off" we had available a full orchestra and, of course, a grand piano. It might have been thought, at the time, a rather strange choice, to have Ivor James impersonate Pachmann, but he made a brilliant success of it. He did not pretend to be a first class pianist but he possessed a reasonable enough technique to provide a surprisingly good fake. He did not have to play very much, but what he had to achieve was far from easy. The two passages which had to fit into our plan were the opening bars and the final (quite tricky) passage from César Franck's *Symphonic Variations* for piano and orchestra. But before we came to the actual "performance" - such as it was - we had some delightful antics from Ivor in the guise of Pachmann. For instance, after he had been "doodling away" at the keyboard for a little while, he looked up and saw me waiting on the conductor's rostrum, ready to begin. He immediately got off his stool and came and gave me a hug! Then, again causing much laughter, he returned to his stool and started a chromatic scale from the centre of the keyboard and went right round the piano, pretending to be playing, to the far end and back again down the left hand side of the instrument, arriving at the bass end and then finished in the middle, form where he had started! At last we got going on the Franck of which he gave quite a passable rendition.

I had a splendid suggestion for one "At Home" from the flautist John Francis which must be recorded for it illustrates a number of things. Apart from anything else, the suggested piece was unavailable in this country and the actual performance was to be in two days' time! The piece was called "Elephunt und Müke (The Elephant and the Flea). It seemed it was a German publication and was composed for Piccolo and Bass Trombone. It was then Tuesday and the "At Home" was on the Thursday. The only people that might be able to help were a well known music firm in the West End (I do not wish to name it as I might have something derogatory to say about them!). I rang them up and a very helpful assistant looked it up and found it was available in Germany. "When do you require it?" he asked. "Thursday - urgently. Any chance, do you think?" "I'll do my best", he replied. Miraculously it arrived, and in time for the rehearsal. This was, of course, in the 1930s. The performance went down like a bomb. John Francis played the piccolo and the trombonist came on with a bucket while John's piccolo was full of French chalk! Before any reasonable sound could be produced, the two soloists had some difficulty in producing anything at all from their instruments. When John blew into his piccolo, clouds of white dust caused a temporary mist, while the trombonist could only produce a gurgle from his instrument until he'd emptied out about a gallon of water into the bucket! The next day I wrote to the music firm saying how delighted I was with their service and suggested their music assistant should be commended. What did they do but put my letter to them re the music assistant, whose name was Sidney Horwood, on his desk as though I had written it to him and not to the firm. They obviously did not want him to gain any kudos from the occasion. How mean can you get? I got to know Sidney Horwood well after this. He was a nice little man with a quietly efficient demeanour. He also had a lovely sense of humour. It transpired he was an alto in Westminster Abbey Choir.

In my early days at the R.C.M. I lived in Sutton, in Surrey. I had been under (Dr) Gordon Jacob for the study of orchestration. He was universally claimed to be the master of the subject. I know of no-one else who had the same knowledge and expertise in this important subject. The surprising thing about him was that apart from the piano, he did not play any other instrument, and yet he wrote concertos and other works for practically every instrument one can think of - or a combination of them - and everything he composed "came off" with unquestionable brilliance. And his music was invariably effective, enjoyable and memorable. It is hard to believe that, for a time, he was ignored as a member of the R.C.M. teaching staff. They were soon to realise that here was a man who could be described as unique, the likes of whom "would not be likely to come this way again". Jacob's clear and concise Orchestral Technique has been my bible since its publication in about 1933. During the First World War he was taken prisoner, but this did not cause him to abandon his music for the duration and deprive the world of his skill and dedication to the subject. With his ingenuity he collected all the plain paper he could lay his hands on and converted it into musical manuscript by ruling out the necessary five lines of the stave, and it was even said that he was able to devise some kind of instruments for his fellow prisoners to play and they performed new music he had composed!

Gordon and I became firm friends and on one occasion we were both asked to produce a "funniment" for the next "At Home". At that time Gordon was living in Ewell, Surrey, and I was not much more than 10 minutes away. What I do remember well - if not all the details of the show which we cooked up together - was the hilarious time we had one sunny day, sitting in the Jacobs' garden planning our programme. There were some outrageous things we wanted to include, but we knew they would be likely to shock some of the more staid and serious-minded members of the Committee. But during that day we caused each other to laugh heartily as we applied our own unofficial "censorship" on ourselves at the same time regretting that we would not get away with putting in certain things.

Though Jacob was a serious-minded composer, he was not averse to including some delightful humorous touches in his works, and there is one published work that is unashamedly written in a light-hearted vein. It is the Overture *The Barber of Seville Goes to the Devil*, which is guaranteed to bring the house down. So he was the ideal person to compose the music for our "show", and I've never forgotten the opening music, the details of which I can roughly remember, and I believe I still possess the music somewhere. Gordon had assembled a brass band, complete with bass drum and other percussion instruments, with all the players dressed in ridiculous clothes and straw hats. They were to march down the length of the Concert Hall and on to the stage, The memorable opening music was entitled *The March of the Burbleton-on-Trout Brass Band*. The tune at the start contained an octave leap that wasn't quite an octave, about a semitone short, which made it all the funnier. It is a shame that these little gems of humour get lost for all time after only one performance. But perhaps this one may not be lost after all!

My biggest undertaking for these annual events, and probably my most successful "solo" effort - though I did have some valuable assistance with some of the music from John Wilson - was a pantomime called *Cinderella*. It was basically the traditional story but with a difference. For instance, the essential 'fairy coach' was my own Austin 7, and the 'glass slipper' - to be produced by midnight - turned out in this case to be a double bass! A college of music is an ideal place for putting on such a venture. I had everything "on tap" from an opera theatre, with every facility, to many budding actors and actresses and, of course, as many singers as may be required, for special songs had to be written, and there was scope for involving the names of a number of professors and staff members in a special version of "Widdecombe Fair".

With so much talent abounding and such a perfect setting I had a chance to produce a worthwhile evening. It was up to me, among others, to meet this challenge. I must say that with so many other happenings at the R.C.M. - especially in the summer term - I did once start to panic a bit as I felt things were beginning to get on top of me, especially as the event got too close for comfort. But, after a number of late nights, and with the invaluable skill and imagination of John Wilson who wrote and arranged the music for one of the songs - one of the successes of the performance - I was able to relax a bit and regain my optimism and confidence.

A brief pen picture is required of John Wilson who was a splendid person. With his subtle sense of humour and his scholarship he was the ideal person to have around. He was actually a nephew of Sir Walford Davies. John and I were contemporaries at the Royal College and got to know each other well. For three years in the 30s I taught the fiddle at Tonbridge School where he was the Assistant Director of Music. He later moved on to Charterhouse where he remained Director of Music for many years. His dear wife, Mary, died sadly at an early age. John kept on until his retirement but this was not the end of his connection with Charterhouse for he continued to teach there till he was well into his 80s and he only died a few years ago. A large congregation of his many friends gathered in the School Chapel for the service of thanksgiving for his long life. The very moving tribute by his successor,

Bill Llewellyn, to a man of so many talents, not least his work for the Church of England's Hymnal, showed with what high esteem he was universally held.

I remember one sunny day, many years ago, when John was carrying out research for Arthur Mee and his famous books for children, and I joined him. We drove around Hampshire and Surrey visiting old churches, some of them quite small, hoping to glean interesting information on their history from gravestones and other sources, including - who were long-standing vicars? etc. I don't think I was much help to him but it was an enjoyable day out.

To return to the pantomime, I had driven round to the back of the College, where you could still drive behind the tennis court and up to the theatre stage exit. Luckily it was wide enough to accommodate my little Austin 7, and I left it outside. I had washed it and cleaned it so that it looked at its best. Later in the day it poured with rain and I was devastated. I saw one of the stage hands, called Leslie Hughes, who was a typical "servant of the College", and who was completely unflappable and could be relied on to deal successfully with any minor crisis, be it a lighting fault or mechanical failure. He could see my despair over the rain (I wasn't used to owning a car), and he just said: "Leave it to us". By the evening there was my vehicle, all dry and gleaming, but as yet out of sight in the wings. The climax of the pantomime was seeing if a very small violin (about 6 inches or so in length), would fit exactly into a large double-bass box lying on its back in the centre of the stage. Enter the fairy coach "up-stage left", bearing Cinderella herself, a rather attractive student soprano, Freda Jackson. She stepped out of the coach carrying the tiny fiddle, with a look of disbelief on her face as, at one minute to midnight she is invited to place the miniature fiddle in the double-bass case. Still in considerable doubt she does so, leaning into the case with the small fiddle and stands back as a foot pump is taken out of my car. This is attached to the inside of the wooden case and a succession of men take turns at pumping away until eventually a full-size double-bass is removed from the case, amid scenes of triumph. End of story - blackout!

This was not in fact quite the end of the story. I felt strongly that it was a shame that all this - if not "tears and sweat" - hard work, thought and organising should, after a mere two hours at one R.C.M. Union "At Home", be lost for ever and relegated to the memory after a single performance. So strongly did I feel about it that, soon after the occasion, I asked for a private interview with the Director, Sir Hugh Allen. This was granted and I was ushered into his office. I had great respect for Sir Hugh and always got on well with him. On this occasion I felt I had a good case to put to him and he listened sympathetically. My case, which I presented quite forcibly, was that I had put a great deal into writing this pantomime. It had entailed getting the "book of words" written out and duplicated, as well as the music, and it had resulted in "popular appeal", and after just one solitary performance it was going to be lost for all time. Would he consider allowing a second performance? He said he didn't think it would be possible to include it in the normal College curriculum, about which he was quite adamant, though he would like to say 'yes' to my proposal.

I did not think my request unreasonable and I had already decided that I would not leave that room until Sir Hugh had agreed! As a result of my persistence he did eventually agree to a second performance. How it fitted into a fixed programme I shall never know, but fit in it did. Even this took quite a bit of organising - getting the cast together again, advertising the event, etc. etc. The performance took place not long after the first, and although there is always a danger in repeating what has been deemed to be a success, or causing an anti-climax, I am glad to say this did not happen, and I found the extra effort had been worth it. And so it appeared did other people. I must say the success of my persistence even surprised myself. It reminded me of my own mother who could be as stubborn as anybody. She was the author of a "quote" in our family.

We lived in Sutton in those days and used to employ a builder who went by the name of Bye. One day mother had asked him to call round as she had a job at our house which needed attention. He examined the job and then, scratching his head, said he felt he wouldn't be able to tackle it. To which my mother immediately responded by saying: "I think you will find you can Mr Bye!", and, of course, he did! Hence the much-used family "quote".

One other Union "At Home" must be mentioned before, later, I describe the memorable triumph which must be attributed to one man - "Dr" Malcolm Sargent. Once again an orchestra had been assembled. Any irregularity in our profession, or newsworthy scandal or event would be a godsend to anyone prone to wanting to take off or ridicule such a happening. At this particular time there had been a lot of controversy and bad publicity on a subject that had dogged the profession since the early days of the century when Sir Henry Wood himself decided to stamp out the practice by forming his own orchestra. The trouble was called the "Deputy System", the general idea that a player would attend a rehearsal but send someone else - a "deputy" - to play at the concert. And that was what we were about to take off. But that was not the only bone of contention.

At this time there was a lot of controversy about demands that musicians should receive pensions at the end of their careers. One particular person was strongly against it, and he did not do his popularity much good for he publicly said so. Of all people, this was Malcolm Sargent himself. Quite apart from anything else, it was a tactless thing for him to do. I thought it was at the time, and still do. His argument against the proposal was feeble and silly. He stated that if a man knew he had a pension to look forward to at the end of his playing days, he would not give one hundred per cent to his playing now. Just sit back and wait for the great day, I suppose. Not surprisingly I don't think this idea got very far. It was a strange side of Sargent's nature which was difficult to understand, especially as there was quite a lot of unemployment in the profession at the time.

There was one light-hearted moment concerning Sir Thomas Beecham, who had suffered as much as anyone from "deputies" at rehearsals and concerts. There were very many stories about "Tommy", some of which must be called "alleged" (I shall be quoting many later on, which I know to be absolutely true). One "alleged" one reflects the kind of things that even Beecham had to encounter. The story goes that he had called for say four rehearsals for a particular concert. This was most unusual since most concerts required one rehearsal of three hours only. But the exception was when a little-known or unknown work came along, presenting extra difficult passages both of playing and ensemble. At the last rehearsal, Beecham was said to have addressed the orchestra, saying: "Gentlemen, I would like to bring to your notice one of your colleagues, Mr So-and-so (possibly the 2nd oboist), who is the only member of the orchestra who has personally attended every rehearsal for this concert. I should like to commend his sense of duty and assiduous example to you", to which the player replied: "I am sorry Sir Thomas, but I cannot do the concert!"

Our jollification at the R.C.M. started with two upright pianos placed on the floor below the stage and facing it so that the two players had their backs to the audience. On their backs were pinned large notices which read "NO PENSIONS". (As it happens, I heard afterwards that this didn't go down too well. I can't think why not!) The two pianists continued playing away while an orchestra assembled on the platform.

When the tuning was completed, I came on and stepped up to the conductor's rostrum followed by a violin soloist. Bach wrote two violin concertos; the one in A minor starts with the soloist coming in immediately at the first bar with the orchestra, whereas the other one is in E major and has about 8 bars of *tutti* (all the orchestra alone) before the violin joins in at the 9th bar. Off we went, but in no time at all the sound was awful. I stopped the performance and made a brief apology to the audience - "There has been a little misunderstanding" - and we started again. Of course, the same thing happened. This time I had to speak to the Orchestra. I had to admit I hadn't been at the rehearsal. "Which concerto are you playing?" I asked. "The E major", came the reply. "What did you rehearse?" I asked. No-one knew as they had all sent deputies to the rehearsal! I then had to enquire of the soloist what he had prepared to perform. "The A minor", he replied. "Well, what did you rehearse with the orchestra?" I asked him. "I didn't attend the rehearsal, so I don't know. I had to send a deputy!" So the concerto collapsed. I think we made our point, but whether we affected anything I know not. At least the audience enjoyed our opening number of the "funniment". I wonder how many people still remember any of our frolics?

There was one "At Home" which was entirely serious but nonetheless thoroughly enjoyable and sometimes quite exciting. It was, I believe, a concert to celebrate the 25th anniversary of the founding of the R.C.M. Union. The orchestra which had been invited to perform was nothing if not a "star-studded" group of players consisting of distinguished past students of the College. Such an assemblage had probably never been brought together as a unit before, nor has been since. A large number of players came from the B.B.C. Symphony Orchestra and some were present professors. I can remember quite a few of those playing, including Marie

Wilson (violin), Alfred Hobday and Bernard Shore (violas), Ambrose Gauntlett and Purcell Jones (cellos), and Alfred's brother, Claude Hobday (double-bass). In the wind section were Robert Murchie (flute), Léon Goossens (oboe), "Jack" Thurston (clarinet) and Aubrey Brain (horn). In the percussion department were Guy Warrack and Fred Wheelhouse, by whom, incidentally, I was taught timpani.

The printed programme for this special concert left one gap in the usual details - who was going to conduct the *Meistersingers* Overture, which was the final work in the programme? There had been no rehearsal of it and the gap naturally created a feeling of considerable anticipation, if not anxiety. The only clue we had in the audience was that the Overture was to be conducted by "a student who was at the R.C.M. from 1892 to 1895". We hadn't any idea who it was, and we had to wait with keen anticipation - with some guessing which was well off the mark - until all was revealed when a brisk figure came through the door opposite the stage at the end of the hall, with white flowing hair, almost bouncing on to the rostrum. It was none other than Leopold Stokowski! With very little in the way of preliminaries, the baton-less maestro set off to conduct an electrifying performance of the Overture. With everyone so keyed up such a performance was inevitable. Although it was an obvious place to look for a special thrill, it nevertheless happened. Towards the end of the work, there is a cymbal clash. This is usually played by one player. On this occasion there were two players to undertake this straightforward but very important task, producing the usual sound at this point. It might be assumed that at such a moment one would expect to be thrilled by it and that I am making rather a lot out of it, but it is proof that it was a very special moment that, after all these years, I can still remember and feel the thrill it gave me at the time. The two players were Guy Warrack, who taught me musical theory and later became a close friend, and Freddie Wheelhouse of the B.B.C. Orchestra, from whom I gleaned a lot through his experience as a percussionist and timpani player. I hope that very special concert is somewhere recorded in the annals of the College. Unfortunately it can only be a "written" recording as actual sound recording was not, sadly, yet available to the individual as it is today.

It might surprise a lot of people when I say that it is often harder to play a few notes or even just a single note in a piece than to play nearly all the time, like a string player. And I don't mean technically, but knowing exactly when to play (and where to shut up!). It sometimes requires a lot of counting of bars, and you also need a strong nerve and a positive approach. You can't get away with clashing the cymbals in the wrong place.

There was a silly story of an inexperienced North Country (choral) conductor who was conducting his choir and an orchestra when a cymbalist did an almighty "clash" in the wrong place, which caused the conductor, more used to dealing only with choirs, to turn to the 1st violins asking: "Who done that?" I happen to have had quite a number of solo percussion experiences over the years with various London orchestras, but again they must keep for the chapter on conductors since they are - oddly - all in connection with Malcolm Sargent.

Regarding the "one note" man, sometimes referred to in connection with some percussionists, numerous artists have had a field day in the past describing in pictures the details of the movements of a particular player who only had to play one note in a concert. One showed him waking up in the morning, getting out of bed, shaving, dressing, having breakfast, walking to the station, catching a train to London and eventually arriving at the hall for the rehearsal where he had to play his one note at the appropriate moment. Then the same palaver of returning home only to have to return again in the evening. Even funnier was the cartoon where the player - again with just one note to play - went through all the preparation for the event - and then missed it! Too easily done! The famous cartoonist of the day, who so often picked on some happening for his pictorial wit, was one H.M.Bateman.

That sort of thing can sometimes get you down. Endless counting of bars causes timpani players to worry, especially when there are no cues to check where you are, or there are misleading ones. I was caught out once for, though the unimaginative copyist or printer had put a cue in, it did not occur to him to put "2nd time" where a certain passage is repeated and I crashed in after the first appearance of the passage. It was about 8 bars too soon! I once described the endless counting of bars, and the accompanying anxiety of it all, as a malady and named it "percussion of the brain"!

During my time at the Royal College, I got to know a number of interesting people. One such was a lady who worked in the reference library which contained many old and rare prints. Ironically this library was situated in one of the highest spots in the College, in the top of one of the twin towers of the building. The only means of access - there being no lift - was by relying on "Shanks's mare". I say ironically since this elderly lady - a Mrs Doisly - was very crippled and found walking extremely difficult, though I never once heard her grumble about her disability. It was hard to believe that she had once been an international lacrosse player, representing England.

This dear lady became a very good and kind friend of mine and seemed to take to me. She was a personal friend of Sir Edward Elgar. She once showed me a postcard she had received from the great composer, signed by him, and she kindly presented this to me. After living most of my life in Surrey and having moved as a widower to the West Country not many years ago, it is not surprising that not everything has so far found its appropriate place, but I know that postcard is "somewhere"!

There were two "loyal servants of the College" - that's to say, members of the permanent office and domestic staff - whom I must also mention, although all of them contributed to a particularly happy atmosphere there. One of these two was a real character whom everyone entering the R.C.M. could not fail to notice. He was always known as "Mr Parker" and was usually in his little "box" by the College entrance. He was quite small and had a club foot - something you never see these days - and he invariably wore a shiny top hat! One of his duties was to pump air into the College Concert Hall organ. This was before the days when the air needed to make an organ function was provided electronically. I can remember during my schooldays being allocated this duty in chapel when you went through a little door at the side of the organ, out of sight of the congregation. There was a wooden lever - rather like part of an oar - which you raised and lowered to fill the organ with air. And there was a small lead weight hanging from the side of the organ to let you know the state of the bellows. As the weight was approaching the bottom you had to blow furiously to bring it to the top again. If one lost concentration, or had begun to doze off, there would be a general groan from the organ, like some dying creature, and you quickly started operating again. I believe there was a small warning sound to bring you to your senses. You could not retain air for future use, so as the sermon was coming to an end the organist would press this small buzzer and you started operations again.

Mr Parker also had to be available for other special duties. From time to time there would be examinations for the A.R.C.M diploma, and organ examinees were allowed half an hour to practice on and familiarise themselves with the organ. These were usually non-students of the College who might be visiting the R.C.M. for the first time. Parker had no formal musical training and was not particularly conversant with the subject, but somehow - rather like John Hare, the head of the General Office - he seemed to have acquired a special instinct regarding music. One day a prospective candidate was practising away when Parker came round from the side of the organ and said to the young man: "Where do you come from?", to which came the reply: "Birmingham". Parker then said to him: "Well, you'd better get back there, you don't stand a chance!"

I was once involved in a small ceremony which also included Mr Parker, and was again in the Concert Hall. The occasion was the College's farewell to that distinguished and delightful character who was the Registrar - Claude Aveling. The hall was crowded with professors and students, and five or six of us, representing various aspects of the life of the College, were seated on the platform to pay our various tributes, . I had the honour of representing the students, and there was also, of course, Mr Parker. I always remember his contribution which he read from a large sheet and included a memorable phrase: "We have seen our professors and students comin' and goin' - day and night - I mean - day after day." He was definitely one of the memorable characters of the College who probably knew more about the place than most people.

The other person I must refer to was the maintenance man named English. The particular occasion I recall was rather less charming than that involving Mr Parker. The Director of the R.C.M. at the time was Sir Hugh Allen. One day he decided to go round the College with English to check that everything was being attended to properly. They had gone to one of the Students' lavatories - with the old-fashioned wide "basins" - and the last student hadn't bothered to check it had cleared properly after the flush. "What's the meaning of that, English", he enquired. "I don't know, Sir. It's a stranger to me", he replied!

In my days at the College - i.e. the 1930s - I still possessed an Austin 7, better known as a "Baby Austin". Parking was no problem as there were no meters to deter your stay, as there are now, and I would just leave the car outside the College in Prince Consort Road. Sir Hugh Allen was not only Director of Music at the R.C.M. but also held a Chair of Music at Oxford University where he would spend his week-ends, leaving the College late on a Friday afternoon. Many a time I would receive a message from his secretary saying: "Would you drive Sir Hugh to Paddington to catch the 4.45 train to Oxford?", and I would duly drive him across the Park in good time to catch his train. There were few traffic problems in those days and the journey took no more than 10 minutes. There was one occasion when the message had a variation: "Would you drive Sir Hugh and Sir Walter Alcock to the Athenaeum in Pall Mall?" They were both members of the Club, Sir Walter being organist at Salisbury Cathedral at the time. When I told a fellow student rather proudly after I'd got back to the College, that I'd had two knights in my Austin 7, he said, with a naughty twinkle in his eye: "Who with?"

I must now refer back and describe the Union "At Home" already mentioned which I consider the most brilliant of all and illustrates the incredible brain and ingenuity of Malcolm Sargent. Although, as I have said, I had been asked to co-operate with Sargent to provide the entertainment on that occasion, I hadn't an idea in my head and was becoming rather desperate. It was up to him now. I decided to tackle him at the 15 minute break in the rehearsal of the First Orchestra one Friday afternoon. He said: "Come and talk to me while I have my tea". This took place in the Director's private room. I duly followed him in. For the first few minutes there was silence as he sorted things in his mind. Eventually he said: "Have you a pencil and paper? Take this down. You will have a full orchestra on the stage and eventually you will appear at the far end of the Concert Hall, made up as Sir Thomas Beecham, and walk slowly down and make your deliberate progress to the rostrum and take a bow. Having prepared to start the music, there will be a distraction - a disturbance in the audience - a late arrival, a short-sighted lady is trying to reach her seat in the 4th row, clambering over people as she does so, noisily dropping her umbrella on the floor and eventually finding that her seat is already occupied. She then has to turn back amid more clatter, when it is discovered that she is in the wrong row - her seat is in the 3rd row - and she has to make her way back, much to everybody's annoyance. While all this is going on you will have on the score on your conductor's stand, a flat cardboard box. In it will be a bald wig, some spirit gum and a mirror. You will then remove the "goatee" beard and small white moustache, pull the wig over your head and stick on a black moustache with small points at each end, all the time appearing to be studying the score. You will now be Sir Adrian Boult! You will look round to see if the disturbance is over and the audience will see a completely different conductor and wonder how he got there!"

Not only did no-one in the audience see what had been going on on the rostrum, neither had the orchestra. I had written on a piece of paper on every stand in large letters DON'T LAUGH! This proved to be unnecessary since they were apparently so intrigued by the antics of the "short-sighted old lady" - who incidentally was Elizabeth Aveling, and acted superbly - they had not noticed what I was up to. This was a fantastic success with which to start the entertainment, and I can only claim a comparatively small part in its triumph. I had naturally wondered whether the idea would come off and I showed some doubt, but Sargent, in his "quicksilver" way said emphatically: "I am quite sure it will work very well". And it was outstandingly successful. What a man! Sadly he was too busy to be there to witness his triumph.

4. CHAMBER MUSIC

Although I had all the chances of chamber music playing while I was at the College - I was in a quartet coached by my own Violin professor - I never followed this line as strongly as the orchestral side. There are many musicians who will tell you that the String Quartet is the highest form of music making. I am sure they have a lot to support their views. After all, the greatest quartets were written by Mozart, Haydn, Beethoven, Mendelssohn and countless others. The dedicated string chamber music lover - and particularly if he is a professional - must have a really fulfilling life. Four players, though of course they add to their number when necessary for quintets or sextets and other combinations, is an ideal number to work, play and travel together. I cannot imagine it would ever become really boring. I suppose playing in Orchestras was never the end all, be all, for me and I soon had an ambition to be a conductor and this desire was eventually fulfilled. This was based on the variety of invaluable experience I had gleaned over the years which cannot be learnt in a day. this was of course invaluable. But I was not averse to playing in a Quartet professionally.

My chance to do this came both suddenly and unexpectedly. I was enjoying a summer golfing holiday with relations in the Scottish Highlands, something I did frequently. It was actually Pitlochry in Perthshire - not very far from Balmoral - where I remember you could play golf all day for a mere two shillings and if you were extra keen and got up early enough, it would be possible in the summer to fit three rounds in the day! I was just about to set off to play a round when the 'phone rang from London. It was Alan Bartlett, a colleague of mine from the R.C.M. He led a String Quartet aptly named "The Portland" since the B.B.C. is in Portland Place!

He wanted me to return at once as his 2nd fiddle had been taken ill and they were booked for a broadcast, very soon, of Dvorak's *Piano Quintet*. He was not all that concerned whether I knew the work or not. (I had never seen it and soon found out that it was a pretty tricky piece and I should not have much time to learn it - in fact it would not be far off sight reading!) I gave up my Highland holiday and duly drove back to town. The broadcast went satisfactorily - Alan had fixed a very good pianist friend who dealt with the very challenging piano part with considerable efficiency.

After this I was invited to join the Quartet permanently - the 2nd violinist who had had to cry off at the last moment, decided to quit - I think he suffered from something that did not seem to be improving. We got a number of engagements and even, one summer, went away for a week and stayed at a farmhouse near Plymouth where we had a "working holiday", rehearsing in the mornings for the forthcoming season, and relaxing in the afternoons. We used to get quite regular broadcasts at the B.B.C. - usually about tea time on the "Home Service".

Alan lost his life in the 2nd World War. He was flying with the R.A.F. over the North Sea when the plane suddenly disappeared and was never heard of again.

5. STRING ORCHESTRAS

The Boyd Neel

Humour, thrills, fine experiences and, very occasionally, boredom - not to mention life-long friendships - are all part of a professional musician's life and certainly have been of mine. It is in one's own interest to take advantage of them to the full. I have never made a great deal of money out of any of it, though, of course, currency was worth a lot more in my early days when £1 was quite a lot of money. Even so, I believe these days musicians are "compensated" to a very fair degree.

Twenty-five years of my life were spent in the London Symphony Orchestra and it was mostly in that time that I played under so many different conductors. This was from my final days as a music student. But the change from being a student to full-time professional was gradual, not sudden. When I passed my audition and became a full member of the L.S.O. I was already a member of the Boyd Neel String Orchestra, which was quite a different experience. We were a "select" group of 18 string players and were as near pioneers of the medium "as makes no difference", with the exception of a pre-War string orchestra formed and conducted by Anthony Bernard. Boyd Neel himself was a keen amateur musician who played the clarinet. He went up to Cambridge and there met my brother, Clive, as they were both studying to be doctors and they became firm friends. Although Boyd Neel went on to be a General Practioner in Camberwell his heart was much more in music than medicine.

Clive did actually play (viola) in one Boyd Neel concert. It was a concert of music by Ernest Bloch, a native of Switzerland, who was in the audience at the Wigmore Hall. The main work I remember was his *Concerto Grosso* for Strings and Piano - a very good work. I had purchased the music from America and I got Bloch's autograph on the full score at the end of the concert.

When I went from audition to join the orchestra, Boyd Neel said: "How many are there of you?" and I said: "Just the two of us". During my 11 years in the Orchestra I had some fine experiences. Reading some of the reviews of our concerts, we were obviously thought of as being the top String Orchestra of the time, and it is not an exaggeration to say we were really pioneers. We undertook quite a lot of travelling including concerts abroad, and we did a considerable amount of recording for Decca. I always remember the first record we made; It was of Holst's *St Paul's Suite*. The records were due to be on sale by Christmas. As it happened I had to drive up to the B.B.C. on Christmas Day for our annual broadcast and was told that, if I could pick them up myself, copies would be available from the Decca address near the Oval Cricket Ground. I did this on my way up and passed them on to the Boyd Neel Orchestra at the B.B.C. studios amid quite a lot of excited expectation - after all it was a new experience and was the precursor of quite a lot of recording. Records were the old 10 inch ones of those days, and when we recorded Britten's *Simple Symphony* they got the four movements on to five sides, the sixth and last having to be a fill-up of just one work. It was at about that time that I had found - in a volume of J.S.Bach's piano music - a single Fugue in A minor which I had decided would sound well arranged for strings alone. It was "unattached" - that is to say, it had no Prelude belonging to it, and was ideal for the sixth side. I had arranged it some time previously and the "Boyd Neel" had used it on a number of occasions as an encore and it proved popular, so much so that the Oxford University Press published it. I naturally bought my own score and the string parts.

One of the depressing sides of getting something published is not the worthiness of the music - I haven't noticed any lessening in the popularity of the music of Bach - but the number of copies sold over a given period, and *my* Fugue eventually went out of print. That's where commercialism takes over from art. I blame a lot of it on poor advertising. If people never hear of the availability of certain works they certainly won't buy them.

One advantage of belonging to a well-known orchestra is the chance it brings to travel - at someone else's expense. In 1938 we travelled to Portugal for a series of concerts. Nowadays you go to Portugal in probably less than two hours by air - in fact in far less time than it would take to go by train from London to, say, Edinburgh. It took the B.N. two and a half days to reach Lisbon by sea! And we experienced quite enough rough weather, especially in the Bay of Biscay. At one breakfast there were very few people around - for obvious reasons. The previous evening the dance floor was practically deserted except for one player - David Martin, the leader of the 2nd violins with whom I used to sit in the Orchestra. He was sitting by himself at a small table at the side of the dance floor with a pack of cards, playing Patience. There came a particularly big wave and I saw him suddenly glide right across the floor to the other side, complete with table and chair, quite unconcerned by his sudden change of venue.

In Portugal we played not only in Lisbon but also in the University City of Coimbra, at Estoril, and in Oporto, the wine-growing town, where, after the concert we were shown round the below-ground vats of the famous Sandeman's firm of wine-makers. Each member of the orchestra was then presented with a small wooden box with a string handle, containing a 40 year old bottle of Port, a small glass and a corkscrew.

Two memories are stirred up by recalling two completely unconnected happenings whilst we were over there. When we visited Estoril, a very popular holiday resort on the Atlantic coast, it was a lovely sunny day, so we spent the morning on a sandy beach with hundreds of similar-minded people. It seemed an obvious opportunity to have a sea bathe, but it was not an unmitigated success, for if you quickly went in the sea, you could not stay in for more than a minute or two because the water was bitterly cold, and if you stood on the sand you burnt the soles of your feet! The other memory was of the concert at Coimbra which took place in the afternoon. The evening was reserved for a "performance" by a menagerie - most of the wild animals being housed in tanks of warm water just off the stage.

When the music started we soon found that the Orchestra would be "accompanied" from time to time by the alligators who, when the double-basses played on their lowest strings, lashed noisily about in their tanks, and it was quite an alarming experience. One naturally made a quick note of the nearest exit to safety. This became quite a news item on the following day in the London Times!

On the journey home by sea, the elements had subsided somewhat so that the voyage was quite pleasant and we felt more like having a bit of fun - so much so that I got up to some high-jinks myself. I have photographs of myself as Sir Adrian Boult shaking hands with the leader of the Boyd Neel, Frederick Grinke - and the other one is quite a good likeness of the British Prime minister of the day. On board was a well-known solo violinist, May Harrison - one of the famous Harrison sisters - who for some reason asked one of the orchestra: "I do wish you'd get Mr Nicholson to *do* Neville Chamberlain - he's such a good friend of mine" (she was , of course, referring to the Prime Minister, not me!). This must have been after the 1938 "Munich Crisis" for in the photo I am holding up a piece of paper, re-enacting the scene at Heston (now Heathrow) Airport at which I had been present, on his return from meeting Hitler. This "piece of paper" was the famous "document" containing the signatures of both men, mentioned by Chamberlain in his speech on "Peace in Our Time".

The previous year, the Boyd Neel string orchestra travelled to Salzburg to play at their famous Festival, stopping on the way to do a broadcast in Holland. Their studios at Hilversum were not as soundproof as those in this Country, for over there one can "see the World go by", and if a window was open you could actually hear the traffic. The journey to Austria was of course undertaken by rail. The weather in Salzburg was not particularly good, and due to heavy rain in the previous weeks the river was very full and almost menacing as it poured through the city, though never in danger of flooding. It was a fine environment and one felt it an honour to be playing at one of the Halls connected with their greatest composer, Mozart. The concert took place in the great Mozarteum. The audience did not by any means fill the hall but the concert was very well received. The soloist who had travelled with us was the finest oboist in England, Léon Goossens. The concerto he had wanted to play was the very attractive and effective one by Gordon Jacob. Unfortunately, with the 2nd World War only two years away, there was a lot of nervy business over names which might suggest any Jewish connection or origin, of which, of course, there was none in this case. Léon was forced to play the much less attractive *Oboe Concerto* by Rutland Boughton. (What a pity I hadn't by then written my own concerto for Léon - which he was to play seven or eight times but which was still 20 years off!)

Léon played magnificently and "brought the house down". The programme itself contained not only an unfamiliar oboe concerto, it was also the occasion for a brand new work, written for the occasion by Benjamin Britten. It was called *Variations on a theme by Frank Bridge*, Bridge having been Britten's original teacher. There was one variation for each of the 18 members of the Orchestra. I cannot

35

remember what my variation was like but I was allotted one!

The appearance of the Boyd Neel Orchestra at these famous festivals was important for British music, and this was the first time an English orchestra had been invited to play at Salzburg.

For some people my long memory could be a disadvantage - even an annoyance - for they can only report events through hearsay or by second hand accounts, whereas since I was actually present, it is much easier to be factual, knowing what actually happened. What happened at Salzburg is a case in point and has recently been a bone of contention between the B.B.C. and myself. I have always been proud of being a member of the Boyd Neel and especially to have been with them as the first British orchestra to be invited to play at the Salzburg Festival, in 1937. I was, therefore, lucky to notice that the B.B.C. had started a series of six Saturday afternoon programmes of 2 hours each - that is to say 12 hours in all - and I naturally listened to most of the remaining programmes, entitled "Celebrating Salzburg". Regarding those I had missed, I did check with someone who had listened to all the programmes and so was able to confirm that the "Boyd Neel" was not even mentioned! I was naturally disgusted and took it upon myself, as one of the two surviving active members of the B.N. still around, to write and complain.

This did not elicit an immediate reply - in fact I wrote three times to the presenter of the programmes. The first two letters, correctly addressed, were returned to me - one having a ridiculous label stuck on the envelope stating "addressee unknown"! Eventually the third letter did reach the appropriate individual and I had an acknowledgement in the form of an apology - the first "on behalf of the B.B.C. for the fact that I received neither of your first two letters" and went on to say "Not mentioning the Boyd Neel visit was - your letter made me think - a fearful oversight. It was, as you say, a famous occasion, with a Britten premiere. The curious thing is, the Boyd Neel concert is not listed in the Salzburg Festival's official archive or in its concert and opera register. There can be no doubt that the event took place - you were there! - but there appears to be some doubt as to the concert's status as part of the official Festival".

At about the time of this somewhat one-sided correspondence with the B.B.C., I had another letter requesting some information regarding the music of Benjamin Britten from the librarian of the Britten-Pears library at Aldeburgh in Suffolk. I did not know his name, nor have I ever met him. He wanted to know if I had any recollection of the first performance in 1932 of his Quintet, the rehearsal and performance having been at the Royal College of Music. On his enquiry to the Royal College he was given the names of those taking part, which included mine. Unfortunately I had (have) no memory of it at all. But I was able to write back and told him of the Boyd Neel's visit to the Salzburg Festival when we gave the first performance of Britten's *Variations*, written specially for us. He was fascinated to learn of my long association with the Boyd Neel String Orchestra, "a group", he wrote, "for which I have an enormous affection as it was their post-war recording of the *Brandenburg Concertos* that introduced me to those marvellous works. I recently had a chance to sit down and listen to the CD transfer of the Boyd Neel recording of the Frank Bridge Variations, and I was absolutely staggered by the brilliance of the playing. No wonder Britten had such an admiration for the group, and wrote two such marvellous pieces for it". And the B.B.C., in their 12 hour review of Salzburg Festivals, didn't even feel it could just bother to mention our presence there!

In the evening, after the Salzburg concert, the Vienna String Orchestra invited us to a dinner party. Travelling separately from me, my parents and a lady friend from Newcastle - a Mrs Armstrong - joined me in Salzburg to hear the Orchestra. My parents and I were a bit late for the evening party. The dinner had already begun when I peeped in. I don't know why but I got "cold feet" about going in late and went on about it and told my parents so. They meekly agreed to join me elsewhere. It was very silly of me and I have regretted it ever since. It is one of the things in my life I look back on with disappointment. My mother rarely visited the Continent as she was a bad sailor (and her father was a Sea-Captain!). She would probably be sick just crossing London Bridge in a cab. They crossed the Channel going out; there was scarcely a ripple on the water and Mother survived without incident.

Returning home, we left the main party who would be going back to England direct by train. Father was a good traveller and planner of holidays, tending never to go to the same place more than twice running. It wasn't a fixed rule but a tendency, hoping to give us a broader outlook and more variety of scene, which was a real success. We had some very close friends who lived nearly opposite us when we lived in Sutton. For year after year they went to the same place every summer - Ventnor on the Isle of Wight. How very boring, I thought. It wasn't as if they had another house there to go to.

Our journey home from Salzburg was anything but boring. It was an unforgettable experience. My father, with his usual enterprise, had hired a car to take us into Italy. This was to be one of the most memorable car journeys I have been on, rather similar to one I took with my great friend, Laurence Hudson, years before, when I was on holiday with him at his home at St. Marychurch, Torquay, in Devon. His mother had an old 11 horse-power Alvis, a tourer and a quite remarkable vehicle which had only two doors but could seat 5 or 6 people quite comfortably with "Dicky" seats at the rear behind the folded hood. We drove to the Lizard, the Southern-most point of Cornwall. Being another hot, cloudless August day, driving due South all the morning with the sun blazing down on us it can be imagined what colour we finished up at the end of the day! The return journey was just as memorable, mostly in the dark and driving across Dartmoor with now a full moon shining on us. It was another magical day to remember and I have slipped it in just to show one doesn't always need to go abroad to obtain the finest moments in one's life. It was Laurence Hudson who was involved in the "dead rat" episode when we were at the R.C.M. together.

Getting back to Salzburg, we had first to take the train to a large lake not too far from Salzburg itself called Zell am Zee. From here, for the time being we would be travelling by road as we were joining the car which was not self-drive as a driver was included. It was a large Hispano Sweeza (that's how it was pronounced!). It was a tourer with the hood right back and tucked in behind the rear seats. We were quite a large party, for besides my mother and father and Mrs Armstrong, there were Fred Grinke, leader of the Boyd Neel, and myself, together of course with the Austrian driver. We had the blazing sun on our faces all day - and no-one complained - and by the evening I was the colour of the sunset. The scenery was impressive all day until eventually we reached the foot of the mountains which are opposite the famous Gross Glockener range which rise to about 11,000 feet. We reached the highest point of the road, which itself was over 6,000 feet. As it was a powerful car we negotiated the many hairpin bends without difficulty - in fact very fast so that we rose to the unusual heights with some discomfort. The worst affected was Mrs Armstrong who really felt quite ill, and I even found standing up quite difficult. When we reached the highest point of the road we found we could purchase from a shop at the top a small liqueur type drink - rather like a neat whisky - made from a small sort of grape which grew locally in heather-like undergrowth found on both sides of the road. Imbibing this liquid in small quantities did wonders for us all - especially Mrs Armstrong - but none of us felt like standing too long! But I did manage to take some quick photos of the very impressive mountains opposite. Being a very extended range I had to take two pictures to get them all in. I then "repaired" quickly back to the car. You can't expect to become acclimatised quickly to great heights after reaching them so fast, so it was some time before I discovered that I had taken - quite unintentionally - a panoramic picture, one of the finest of my life. Even, when later, I discovered the two snaps had almost overlapped, I still did not know that when official photographers enlarged pictures they covered the edges as they put the enlargement in a folder, and the photograph did not include all the negative and was smaller than it needed to have been. I then ordered further enlargements from the two negatives *unscreened* and was delighted to find I had a near-perfect join. The only disappointment was a slight difference of elevation so that the picture was rather elongated, losing something in height and depth, but it was worthy of framing. I did not have a tripod which would have made things easier, but it was a wonder I took such good pictures with my "ticker" thumping away rather uncomfortably, and I needed to sit down.

We got on our way again towards Italy pretty soon and I must say it was a perfect relief to reach lower levels. The time of year was August and the evenings were already "drawing in". As twilight approached we were to witness an unforgettable sight which remains among the most memorable moments of my life. The sun was setting and the sky had adopted a vivid red glow. As we travelled towards Cortina - our destination for the next few nights in Italy - on our left was the impressive mass of the great Dolomite mountains. It was reminiscent of a scene from one of Wagner's operas. It was almost unreal. We reached Cortina where we booked in at a hotel without difficulty for a night or so. Meanwhile we parted company with our excellent driver who returned to Zell am Zee.

The following day I again took a photograph which I still have, and which was worth framing. It was of a tall dark local woman in long black clothes walking up a steep hill with the background of high mountains. It was indeed photogenic country and I had by now discarded my small VPK (Vest Pocket Kodak) camera which was very limited with just two shutter speeds, though it had an excellent lens, and I had acquired a very nice Zeiss which I became very fond of and which was much more adaptable. Unfortunately I lost it in almost unbelievable circumstances. Gill had borrowed it to take to her old school for a reunion. One would normally not think of taking precautions against theft on such an occasion. Girls had left belongings including, unwisely, purses containing money - throwing them - including my camera - on their beds when they went downstairs for breakfast. Someone had quite a field day in their absence. I've always regretted this loss.

The weather remained fine in Cortina and we all decided to admire the view when a local man caught up with us to remonstrate in Italian, trying to point out to us that we were trespassing on private ground. Another small party were not far away and a man with them came up to me and, in good English, apologised for our being approached and explained that we should have followed the footpath which turned to the left up the hill a little way back and that we were now on his private estate. To identify public ground the trees had a blue band round them. I, of course, was quite ignorant of this rule. At this point - as so often has happened in my life - another coincidence was to occur. I said to the man: "Aren't you Mr Paul Czinner?" (I forget the exact spelling), to which he replied "Yes, why do you ask?" "I was playing in the London Symphony Orchestra which recorded the music for the film *Dreaming Lips* which you directed at Denham Studios, England, a few weeks ago!" He was just as intrigued as I was. He was very friendly and seemed pleased to meet my family. The Denham film featured as the "Star" Elizabeth Bergner, and Austrian-born actress. Our final journey back took us first to Bologna where we caught a train to Calais, followed by a smooth Channel crossing, and so home after a trip full of memorable incidents.

Another well-remembered event concerning the B.N. is probably not remembered by anybody and I think it should be. A year or two ago I heard an up-and-coming young conductor being interviewed on the radio and he referred to the very event I am about to describe. He made a very brief reference to it - almost dismissing it as if of little significance - obviously having only scant importance rather than being a most important moment in the history of music in this country - the birth of Glyndebourne Opera. This young man made a number of errors including referring to Sir "George" Christie in 1933, who may not have been born by then and even if he had he would still have been very young!

It is always annoying listening to someone holding forth on a subject you know is inaccurate. I think I can claim to be one of very few still around who took part in the first opera performances one year *before* the actual opening of Glyndebourne Opera - now of world-wide reputation - where to purchase a ticket for a performance is like seeking gold dust.

This is how it all started. A few years before, I was playing golf with a cousin on the Lewes course, high up above the River Cuckmere, which is tidal. The golf course itself was on the Downs, with no protection from the wind at all, on the West side of the village of Glynde. It was said that if the tide was full when it was raining in the morning, the weather would improve in the afternoon as the tide receded. This was often inaccurate! My cousin had a delightful cottage just under the South Downs which run across to Brighton. It is still used frequently by members of my cousin's family, one of whom now lives there permanently. I have many happy memories of week-ends there - especially from late on Fridays to the Sunday evening, where golf was the order of the day. One looked right across the valley to the course opposite.

This cottage was bought by the family in 1910 for about £100! On one week-end, in the early 1930s, my cousin read a local news item which announced that an organ builder from Tunbridge Wells - but who lived near the little village of Glynde, less than two miles from Lewes - was planning to build an opera theatre attached to his lovely 16th century house, in his own garden. Of course all the "know-alls" scoffed at this crazy plan and wondered where this odd person got this idea from. John Christie ignored these people and pressed on with his idea regardless. We all know now who was right! It must have been in 1935 that Christie invited the "Boyd Neel" down one Saturday in the summer before the official opening so that he could test the acoustics of the newly-constructed opera theatre. We were to play for three short intimate operas - all three requiring only three solo singers and no chorus. Two of the works were Bach's *Coffee Cantata* and Mozart's *Bastien et Bastienne*. The three singers were Margaret Ritchie (soprano) - at the R.C.M. with me and known as "Mabel" - Geoffrey Dunn (tenor) and Frederick Woodhouse (bass). The B.N. consisted of strings only, of course, so the wind had to be provided from elsewhere. John Christie, being an organ builder, had decided to use his own pipes for the woodwind! Strings and wind were all situated in the orchestra pit and it seemed to work quite well. It must have been quite a problem manipulating the organ pipes to synchronise the wind parts with the strings, but I suppose one man played the parts like an organ. I seem to remember the sound was effective enough, and I suppose to have adopted this idea universally would have saved a lot of money. Unfortunately this intriguing plan did not last long as far as Christie was concerned. The news soon reached the ears of the Musicians Union who immediately put a ban on any more experiments of this kind which would, of course, have deprived wind players of any employment at Glyndebourne. The audience for these one-off performances was provided by friends and family and workers on the estate, who were essential in an acoustical test.

That summer, John Christie invited the B.N. to camp out in his grounds for about a week in July so that we could rehearse for our winter season. Unfortunately I could not take part in this unusual experience as I had a previous commitment.

The B.N. was almost a pioneer regarding string orchestras and for quite a time "we had the field to ourselves". One of our occupations was recording, for which we were employed by the Decca Recording Co. The biggest venture was to record all the *Concerti Grossi* of Handel's Opus 6. I am surprised they haven't been re-issued in long-play stereo and that they are never played on the radio. We really set a standard for string playing, and some of the notices we received for our concerts and recordings were glowing in the extreme. We were all of music college age, with the majority from the Royal Academy, but the Royal College was quite well represented.

In keeping with our age group, we often behaved like children, and our behaviour was - at times - not always exemplary, but it rarely affected anybody else and was only when we were "out of school" and usually when we were travelling home, mostly in trains. One incident occurred while we were travelling in a Portuguese train. It was not so much a "rough house" as a bit of horseplay. Apparently in one carriage there had been a bit of a scrap and they managed to smash one of the windows. There did not seem to be much alarm or anger by the officials. When the steward came round for us to pay our dues for refreshments, he wrote out small bills like "2 coffees, biscuits, etc, and when he reached the carriage with the broken window he wasn't a bit put out but just wrote a ticket for the usual "1 coffee, biscuits - so much" and added, on one bill, just "and 1 broken window - so much!"

One other example of high spirits in trains occurred somewhere in the Midlands, on a return from a concert tour. Our carriage was full - mostly of B.N. members, but there was another couple, a man and his wife, who obviously had no sense of humour. I had got up to go into the corridor and as I stood up I saw a woman's hat on the rack and (wrongly) thought it belonged to the viola player, Nora Wilson, wife of the cellist Jimmy Whitehead, and I unwisely stuck it on my head. To my horror it was not Nora's but belonged to the aforementioned woman! She immediately took umbrage and was, in fact, extremely angry that I had dared to touch her wretched hat, and got up to leave the carriage. Her husband enquired: "Where yer goin'?" "I'm going into the corridor to cool orff!" she said.

We were travelling on another train on our way to a concert, when I met the celebrated solo pianist, Harriet Cohen - noted for her playing of the music of Bach - who was obviously going to be our soloist at the concert, and this was a somewhat less flippant occasion. In fact it was a quite interesting and unusual scene. Several of us were in the corridor talking to Harriet who was busy reading the palms of members' hands, telling them what she thought the future held for them and something of their characters - not knowing any of us before, of course. When it came to my turn, I was quite surprised at some of her reactions and predictions. I suppose you can get quite a long way in this business by guess-work and using familiar phrases. But she got quite a lot right about me, I seem to remember, "a sense of humour and considerate to other people". I didn't write it all down, but it would have been fun if I had! Harriet was a great personal friend of the "Master of the Queen's Musick", the distinguished English composer, Sir Arnold Bax, and she became known as the "Mistress of the Queen's Musick".

You can't be serious all the time and I remember, during one of our tours of the country we had a concert at Sheffield Town Hall, scene of an incident involving Sir Thomas Beecham. We were all staying at the (now defunct) Grand Hotel which had wide landings in the bedroom area. In one we saw a large fire extinguisher attached to a wall. Among the instructions was this - "In case of fire turn bottom end up". Like a lot of overgrown schoolboys we organised our own fire-drill, but it was a bit difficult going down the landing obeying the instructions literally! We must have looked idiotic but I don't think there was anyone about to witness our bit of folly! It is not a bad thing to "let your hair down" very occasionally.

I must say the Royal Navy "did us proud" with some very generous liquid refreshment after a very well appreciated concert at Chatham. In the train home - a fairly short journey back to London - there was quite a lot of "horseplay" in the corridor. I suppose it could be expected from a group, none of whom had reached the age of 25, and could be excused after being plied with more alcohol than one was used to just after the end of the war, and it never seemed to affect anyone else. And if you were to attend one of our concerts, the reaction would have been of a highly disciplined group of young people producing fine music at a high level. We could not have afforded to allow our enviable reputation to slip, it was guarded so jealously.

One of our achievements - if you can call it that, but it must be quite difficult to do - was when, during one of our broadcasts, we kept the Sunday night "9 o'clock News" on the B.B.C. Home Service waiting for 20 minutes whilst we completed a performance of Schoenberg's *Verklärte Nacht*. The whole nation had to wait until we had finished. Someone must have slipped up somewhere over timing.

There was one annual engagement we carried out for a number of years. The B.B.C. employed us to play suitable music on Christmas Day, both before and after the Queen's broadcast. This was recorded ("for safety") three or four days before Christmas, just in case anything should go wrong on the day - I can't think what. Anyway they never had to use the recording. Naturally we were paid for "both" performances, but though it was Christmas Day, the B.B.C. did not pay us any extra. The only "sop" was that they gave us a free turkey lunch. We would - as it happened - have been better off without it. One Christmas Day several of the Orchestra were ill. Apparently the turkey was bad! Perhaps it was a precursor of today's meat scares!

We always had our own party - after the event - which was held at the studio where we usually rehearsed. It belonged to our original secretary, Margery Moray, at whose house in Earl's Court the studio was. It was not exactly what you might call a "smart" area and we used to have our morning break for tea or coffee almost next door to a "Good pull-up for carmen". We, of course, renamed it "Good pull-up for Madame Butterfly".

Margery had a "country retreat" at the attractive village of Marlow, on the River Thames in Berkshire. She employed a man to do some cleaning one day a week at Earl's Court, and I remember him saying once: "I 'ope that there 'Itler never gets 'is submarines as far as Marlow, Miss Margery"! Before I was called up I had taken over the job of Secretary of the B.N.

The Jacques Orchestra

Another String Orchestra formed during the war, and which I also joined, was the preserve of Reginald Jacques whom I knew from early R.C.M. days. It was never intended as a rival of the Boyd Neel, and there seemed to be room for both. Jacques himself had become conductor of the very long established London Bach Choir who had had such eminent conductors in the past as Sullivan, Stanford, and more recently Vaughan Williams and Sir Hugh Allen. One of the annual commitments of the Jacques String Orchestra was to play for Jacques' performances of the great Bach *St. Matthew Passion* by the Bach Choir at the Royal Festival Hall. In their very early days, one of the Jacques Orchestra's functions was to provide recitals of string music for Training Colleges at various centres, of which the Leys School in Cambridge was one of many.

6. HOME GUARD AND 1940 PROMS

L.D.V. and Home Guard

My date for call-up to the Forces did not happen till the war was more than a year old and I was well over 30. Although I had been in the School O.T.C. at Eastbourne, and would have soon received a commission, there had been a lot of pressure to provide music in the R.A.F., mostly at the instigation of Wing-Cdr. R.P.O'Donnell, organising Director of Music in the service. He was conductor of the Central Band at Uxbridge, which had become one of the top bands in the Country.

During the year of waiting when I lived in Sutton, I joined the L.D.V. (Local Defence Volunteers). It was some time later that it was renamed the "Home Guard". We did not have uniforms but wore an arm-band with just L.D.V. on it. I joined this Unit a short time after the evacuation from Dunkirk. They became the darkest days of the war. Reports "on the wireless" began using the emotive word "grave" which rather too vividly underlined the pretty desperate situation we had reached in this Country Some of the precautions which were taken at the time - for the one word which was on everyone's mind was "invasion" which had become more of a probability than a possibility with every day that passed - were primitive in the extreme, such as poles stretched across roads to delay the advance of German troops! But somehow the immediate crisis subsided and we went about our duties, such as they were. One of mine was to guard the local waterworks which were literally just round the corner from where we lived, and where, alone, I spent the night armed with just a rifle and about six rounds of ammunition. At a previous get-together we were asked: "How many of you men have ever handled a rifle before?". There were about eight to share among about twenty of us! I, naturally, was one of those who put their hands up after my experience with the O.T.C. We did have some rifle practice, and on one Sunday morning we drove to Bisley for that purpose. I remember that on the outward journey we had called at a pub just beyond Leatherhead called The Rising Sun, no longer so named, being part of a large conglomerate. One of our party was giving us some anxiety and we discussed among ourselves how we could prevent him from shooting at all as we felt he would be a danger to his fellow men. He was obviously "well over the limit" before we set out and stopping at the pub was the last straw. He was watched very carefully until we were safely on the way home.

There was a lovely story which I heard when I re-visited the village of Withyham in Sussex - referred to elsewhere - at that time. There is a delightful pub called the The Half Moon, just short of Ashdown Forest on the far side of this typical English village. Gill and I used to enjoy popping in after the war and hearing the typical Sussex "brogue". There was a "local" who had joined the L.D.V.. He described how, one very warm night, he had to patrol a field beyond and above the pub and was walking along by a hedge when he stopped to take a short break. In his own words: "I 'ad just dropped orf to 'ave a little snooze when P.C.Jones come along and shines 'is bulls-eye light in my face. I woke with a start and then said - Good

44

God! You give me such a fright. 'Alt! 'Oo comes there?' ".

The "miracle" of Dunkirk was greatly helped by the weather. There was hardly any wind and the sea was absolutely calm. Had it not been, all those little boats which rescued so many of our troops would probably not have survived and would have foundered in a rough sea. And I am sure the almost endless sunshine helped greatly in maintaining people's spirits when it was so much needed. Weather obviously plays a big part in war regarding morale.

It was just after Dunkirk that I was on guard at the waterworks and I remember the stillness of the nights - just an occasional sound of distant gunfire against a prowling plane, probably at a great height. On a Sunday afternoon we were summoned to parade on a local tennis club's grass court, and we were lined up in two ranks as we were to receive and be inspected by a high-ranking officer from the War Office. We had to wait some time before this official arrived. He eventually appeared and was smallish in stature, had a white moustache and sported red tabs at the ends of his collar - one each side - to denote his high rank. The war itself had reached a critical stage. France had fallen, Dunkirk was over with much more success than anyone had dared hope - and altogether things were pretty grim. Had it been awful weather as well, we might have felt "this is the end". But it wasn't!

This officer - I'm not sure of his rank - addressed us and, believe it or not, actually sat on a shooting-stick as though he had come to a summer fête! He said we were a fine body of men and he was sure we realised that, after Dunkirk, we had lost a lot of equipment. "We need", he continued "clothing, guns, ammunition, and much else. But - I have come straight from the War Office - and I bring you some very good news." (We wondered what the good news was and were quite excited.) "We are getting 60,000 armlets!" I thought immediately - "How can we lose the war with an idiot like this running it!"

Meanwhile, in London, the 1940 season of Henry Wood Prom Concerts at the old Queen's Hall was well under way. And I was playing in the Orchestra - i.e. the L.S.O. So far the concerts had been running without incident, and proved pretty popular. Sir Henry was still the night-after-night conductor. On one particular evening shortly before I received my call-up papers, the "Alert" was sounded just before the end of the concert, at about ten to ten. (The "Alert" was the word used to denote an Air Raid Warning.) So far no bombs had dropped on London, and though German planes flew over the Capital, they were, at that time, reconnaissance raids, in which the enemy aircraft were "taking soundings" with a view to the future "blitz" which everyone realised was bound to happen sooner or later.

Directly the concert ended, the Manager of the Queen's Hall came on to the platform and made an announcement to the audience - by no means a full house. As it turned out, it was the most unwise piece of advice possible considering what was to happen some months later, but at the time it proved to be perfectly safe. It was to the effect that the audience should not try to go home. "You are safer where you are, ladies and gentlemen. I suggest you wait till the 'All Clear' is sounded." It was not an instruction but a piece of advice - and how unwise, as it turned out!

As far as the audience were concerned, quite a number did "stay put" and I suppose there was quite a sizeable orchestra around, though one or two essential players had gone home. Their absence was quite noticeable a little later and made what we got up to all the more amusing. There was no certainty as to how long we were likely to stay in the Queen's Hall, waiting for the "All Clear" - it might be quite a long while. (As it turned out it was going to be a matter of hours rather than minutes. On some nights we were to wait well into the small hours, not leaving the hall till 2 or 3 in the morning.)

What should we do - organise a concert of an informal character? A compromise was decided upon - not only did the Orchestra entertain the audience, they took part in entertaining us! And this plan was so successful that a lot of hidden talent emerged from "the floor of the House". I remember one of the earliest contributions came from a foreign lady who came up on to the platform and sang an unaccompanied folk song in her native tongue. And one of the nicest touches occurred which caused a lot of mirth. The great Russian pianist, Benno Moiseivitsch had played a concerto with the L.S.O. earlier in the evening at the Prom concert and was still in the hall. The audience were, of course, delighted and surprised to see him for the second time that evening coming on again. He walked on with a young man carrying the music, who immediately sat down at the piano, with Moiseiwitsch sitting on his left, ready to turn the pages for him!

Looking back after all these years - and it's already more than 55! - it is difficult to remember how I got involved in those frivolities, except in a general sort of way. How could I have known in advance that there would be an "Alert" to detain the orchestra and audience that evening and some sort of informal entertainment organised almost instantly, and who suggested - unless I did! - that I should do "my Beecham act"? Where were the props coming from? Had we been in an opera theatre there would have been no problem, but it was in a concert hall and no likelihood of finding any available make-up. Whoever did suggest I should "do Beecham" - as R.V.W. used to call my "act" - I would need certain items of make-up -only a few, but some were essential to bring off the disguise, especially some false hair for the small moustache and "imperial" beard, and most important of all - *spirit gum*. (I don't usually carry these things around with me!) The rest would have been easy. I was already in evening dress and had a baton in my violin case. A comb - "no problem" - and some white powder - it wasn't an entirely male orchestra - to give the impression of greying hair (there would be no problem today!), and, of course, a mirror.

The plan was to re-assemble the orchestra, which was by no means complete - which made a certain passage in the work chosen all the funnier where some instruments were "absent without leave" - followed by the two flutes who were present and suddenly had two bars of a rushing passage in thirds which seemed to come from no-where! The short work chosen was the overture to Mozart's *Figaro* which we all knew, and which the librarian was able to locate the parts for in quite a short time.

There were many accounts of what happened on that - and other - nights, in various newspapers and elsewhere, but none were completely accurate. I have usually found this is so when I have been present somewhere and then read the accounts next day, or whenever. Editors seem to like "doctoring" reports to make them sound more dramatic. One thing which was almost universally reported was that these events took place at Queen's Hall at the height of the Blitz, which was inaccurate. The Blitz did not happen till some time afterwards. No bombs had yet been dropped. Mind you, for all we knew, at any moment the planes hovering overhead might without warning cause mayhem.

There was in London at this time a remarkable little Jewish lady who had managed to escape from Hitler's Germany with her elderly mother before it was too late. Her name was Berta Geissmar. She had been Secretary of the famous Conductor of the Berlin Philharmonic Orchestra, Wilhelm Furtwängler, and came to England where she took over the same duties for Beecham and the London Philharmonic Orchestra. She wrote a book called <u>The Baton and the Jackboot</u>. It just happened she attended the prom when I took off Tommy B. Her account was the most accurate one that I have read - in almost all respects - and I don't think I can do better than to quote in full the three or four pages she devotes to "the happening" - it is so well written.

First I should like to mention one or two things Berta would not be aware of - things that happened after I had taken a bow. Sir Henry Wood used to have on his right on the rostrum a small stand, like an umbrella stand, holding his collection of batons. They were mostly nearly 2 ft. long with cork handles, and could be called "the untouchables". I must have decided - once I had reached the rostrum - that I was going to enjoy myself and make the best use of my brief moments of glory. The first thing I did, Beecham himself might have done. I called George Wood, a member of the double-bass department and also the Secretary of the Orchestra. He usually gave me the orders. I had the pleasure of telling him: "Kindly remove this impediment", referring to the conductor's music stand, as I would be conducting from memory. What he said to me - *sotto voce* - as he carried out my "command" is nobody's business! I then did the unthinkable. I picked up one of Sir Henry's precious batons, throwing it back in disgust, and again I sent for George Wood, saying: "Take these away and bring me a proper one". Unknown to me, Sir Henry had not gone home to bed near Amersham, but was, in fact, just behind the curtains at the side of the platform, through which the conductor and soloists emerge, and he saw all this! Apparently there was a first-class row - that anyone had dared touch his precious possessions - but this fortunately did not affect the performance. I knew nothing about this until after I had come off the platform myself. "Timber" - as he was nicknamed - was still there and I believe I said something facetious to him as I passed, like: "I understand you do a little conducting yourself, Sir Henry!"

This was not the end of this Queen's Hall affair. After I had returned to normal I ran into Sir Adrian Boult wearing full evening-dress, having been conducting a concert elsewhere. He seemed disappointed to have missed my act and asked me if I would do a repeat performance three nights later when he would be in the audience. I reluctantly agreed - a second performance could have been a flop - but I believe it was O.K. But I stipulated I would come on from the other side in case Henry J. was still around!

As for Berta Geissmar, I had yet to meet her and had no idea of her existence before that evening, and the first time I was introduced to her was some while afterwards when Gill and I were invited to a little party at her flat in London which she shared with her mother. She must have been well advanced in writing <u>The Baton and the Jackboot</u> at the time of that Prom, since, what she describes occurs quite late on in the book and is as follows :-

It was certainly an amazing and unique experience. Queen's Hall, the place of so many famous memories, has certainly never witnessed such scenes. The evening of August 26th has especially remained vividly in all our minds. The concert, which had been conducted by Sir Henry Wood, was over, and a heavy raid was still in progress. The police requested everybody to stay where they were. The resourcefulness and wit of English musicians is well known, but what they were to do in such a situation was still to be seen. Soon the Orchestra and members of the audience took in hand the task of amusing the public, from whom some hitherto undiscovered talent also emerged, assisting the good cause. All sorts of features were presented.

Sir Henry has disappeared - has been listening no doubt from behind the curtain in the wings. But who is this tall smiling figure in evening-dress standing at the side of the platform? It is Sir Adrian Boult, come as from conducting a concert of his own. The Orchestra begins amusingly to reverse the principle of Haydn's Farewell Symphony, and arrive late, one by one. For the opening bars, a *tutti* passage, only a trombone and a clarinet are in their places, to play the fitful notes allotted to them in the harmony. Then Sir Adrian Boult strolls up to the percussion desk and adds embellishments with cymbals and triangle, till finally a real, if slightly unorthodox, *tutti* is achieved for the closing chord.

Again the Orchestra assembled. Ceremoniously the librarian distributed the parts for the *Figaro* Overture. Who was going to conduct? A hush spread through the hall, while Sir Henry Wood peeped from behind the platform curtain to see what was going to happen. It was then pompously announced that "a famous British conductor now in Australia" was going to conduct the Overture to *Figaro*. The audience was amazed to see the living image of Sir

Thomas Beecham with the well-trimmed beard walk, with the famous *maestoso* gait to the rostrum, and go through the ritual of - in the words of the *Star* - "the sundry familiar and well-beloved wrist-flicks, hisses, and the stressful stamps of the first conductor of Mozart in the world". There is no need to say that the impersonator began by throwing away the score and disdainfully ordering the conductor's desk to be removed. Any uncertainty was dispelled when the audience was addressed before the performance, and reference was made to another orchestra "apparently up to some high jinks elsewhere with Mr Hylton" and also to broadcasting. *And* the conductor found it necessary to shout "Shut up!" in the middle. The stretched-out arms and the baton, down-pointed in the familiar way for the *Figaro* opening, began to evoke something astonishingly like the world-famous Beecham interpretation! As the impersonator reached the wings after the performance, Sir Henry, who recognised him as one of his own violins, said with kindly surprise: "I did not know you were a conductor". Still loftily in the part, "Sir Thomas" replied: "Ah, yes, Sir Henry, and I understand you, too, conduct sometimes!"

A member of the audience then made a speech suggesting that everybody would agree that they were getting much more than their original money's worth, and that they ought to contribute to the Musician's Pension Fund. Thereupon Sir Adrian was given a large wastepaper basket, lined with newspaper to keep the coins in, and was soon seen taking it round the hall.

I must reveal that the impersonator of "a famous British conductor now in Australia" was a Mr Ralph Nicholson, a young member of the London Symphony Orchestra, now in the Air Force. Since this incident, Mr Nicholson has become known for his impersonations, and when I had the privilege of being present at one of his private shows, I only wondered that this exceptional talent of his was not more exploited. He told me that since the Queen's Hall episode many people asked him to "do Sir Thomas" and that he has a special outfit for this purpose, including the well-known grey linen jacket and the world-famous goatee. He gave me a photo of himself in the rôle of Sir Thomas, and I could not tell it from the original.

The raid sessions at Queen's Hall quickly became publicised and added to the attraction of the Proms. The following conversation actually took place at the Queen's Hall box-office. WOMAN: "Do you think there will be an air raid to-night?" BOX OFFICE, politely: "Sorry, Madam, we can't tell you." WOMAN: "Well, I am only going to come if you think there *will* be a raid!"

However, the increasing seriousness of the blitz made the continuation of concerts in London inadvisable, and on September 7th, this memorable Prom season came to an end.

Having never met Berta Geissmar before she wrote her book, it was nonetheless not long after the Queen's Hall events that I got to know her personally. She gave a dinner party to a small but exclusive group of musicians at her house in North London and invited Gill and me, and we not only met her elderly mother, who had also escaped from Germany. Among the other guests were Felix Aprahamian and the distinguished Italian Conductor, Victor de Sabata. I remember the latter examining my wife's hands and pronouncing his reaction - "Your hands show you are very artistic!" It was a fascinating evening, especially when Berta showed us her visitors book which had been signed by Brahms himself when she was a young girl! De Sabata conducted the L.S.O. for at least one concert on the Continent. I don't recall much about him but I always remember his departure on a train - possibly in Italy - when we waved him off to other fields. Had I my camera with me it would have been a splendid picture as he was in the last coach on an open end of the train as he waved us farewell.

7. WAR-TIME IN THE R.A.F.

Having been to a Public School and received training in the school's O.T.C (Officer's Training Corps) one would expect to get a commission quite soon, and I did for a time consider volunteering for the Air Sea Rescue Service. From reports one read in the newspapers this seemed a worthy and necessary service. Otherwise there did not seem much activity in the first year or so of the war leading up, eventually, to the Battle of Britain and the heavy and disastrous air raids on our big cities, towns and military installations.

The date of one's call-up was based on one's age and I was probably a bit older than my contemporaries and certainly well past the age for flying duties, which was remarkably low. Meanwhile the Air Ministry had decreed to provide some sort of entertainment, especially to the more isolated air-fields where it was possible to become bored when there was any lack of activity.

It seemed sensible for the Services to enlist people who would not require a lot of training but to post them according to their profession into similar occupations in the Service allocated to them. For instance a professional cook would soon find himself working in the cook-house of a station, and a doctor would become a medical officer, etc. My own brother who was a doctor did exactly that, spending a lot of the war in India. He was eventually "demobbed" as a Wing-Commander. Musicians were needed in the R.A.F. especially, whose H.Q. was in Uxbridge, Middlesex, and housed the splendid Central Band of the Royal Air Force under the inspired leadership of Wing-Commander R.P.O'Donnell.

The Air Ministry was keen to provide this extra service with not only a band, but with smaller units to be posted to various areas according to needs - in fact for a start, in the form of string quartets. As the date of my call-up was approaching I was invited by Harry Blech - who after the war formed the London Mozart Players - to play 2nd fiddle in a quartet he was forming, the other two players being Keith Cummings, viola - a colleague from the L.S.O. - and Harvey ("Jim") Phillips, cello - one of my closest friends. Alas the last two are no longer with us! I was still playing with the L.S.O. in the Proms on the day our unwelcome call-up papers arrived.

Everything in one's life for the next five years was now in the hands of higher Authority. The actual date the papers came was, of course, thoroughly inconvenient, for we were required to attend immediately at Uxbridge Camp to "attest". The chance of our being able to get back in time to play at the Prom at Queen's Hall that evening, where Jim Phillips and I would have preferred to be, was pretty slim.

The act of attesting was quite memorable, and was conducted by a somewhat uneducated R.A.F. sergeant. The ritual consisted of our holding a bible in one hand and "saying after me: I sware to hallmighty God - to be loyal" (etc. etc.) "to 'is Majesty, King George VI, and to 'is hairs and successors . . . . ." and so on!

We were allocated to the area where we were to spend the night in a large dormitory, the first three beds to be occupied by Jim Phillips, myself, and someone else we did not know, but we noticed an oblong black box which he slipped under the bed. I don't know whether he had any idea who we were but he made a most surprising remark, especially in these surroundings, saying to us: "What chances do you think there are of making the numbers up to play through the Mozart *Clarinet Quintet*? It naturally took us somewhat by surprise. It turned out to be none other than the eminent clarinettist, Jack Brymer, whom neither of us had met before.

We were eventually posted to Uxbridge, in the building housing the Central Band, and Brymer became a P.E. instructor. Other already well-known and long-established quartets joined us and initially we were to be sent to various R.A.F. stations to provide entertainment. But there was someone else who had other ideas which were much more ambitious. He was Wing-Commander R.P.O'Donnell, Organising Director of Music, R.A.F., who felt that a much larger unit would give much more pleasure and bring with it prestige for music in the R.A.F., and incidentally give him a good opportunity to develop his own musical talents and break away from the more usual bands in the Forces With the quality of the quartets which were enlisting under his direction he decided he would retain them at Uxbridge and form a full symphony orchestra. He also had the ear and backing of the Arts Council, who were fully in favour of the project. After all, we had some of the cream of young musicians with which to build an outstanding orchestra. You couldn't do better than have such players as the inestimable Dennis Brain as 1st horn with Norman del Mar as his No. 2. Most of the wind players had "star" status. The strings, who were the foundation of the orchestra, had players of the quality of David Martin, Frederick Grinke, Sydney Griller and a number coming in as established string quartets. And a group who were destined to remain together as a unit for the best part of five years naturally developed a feeling of unity of purpose and a splendid feeling of camaraderie. And we needed it at times as we were not used to the ways of the Services, and with a combined sense of humour it was easier to take the rough with the smooth. One advantage, when not touring, was that we had "sleeping-out passes", and it was still possible to carry out extended engagements from time to time, like, for instance, Dame Myra Hess's famous National Gallery Concerts in Trafalgar Square. In fact we appeared at one of them as a unit.

O'Donnell himself was one of three brothers, all originally in the Royal Marines. One of them, B.Walton O'Donnell became well-known as a conductor in Northern Ireland and a composer of popular music.

We had the senior flight-sergeant of the R.A.F. in charge of the whole music assembly at Uxbridge - both band and orchestra. He was a character and a fine example of smartness and efficiency. He was strict about discipline, but if you "toed the line" he was your friend. He was invariably well-turned out, with a typical short "Service" haircut and spotless uniform. His name was Flight-Sergeant Sotheron and he realised he had a lot of raw civilians - unused to Service life - in his charge. He was very much on our side and knew how to keep in with - for instance - the C.O.

(i.e. O'Donnell). For example he knew when O'Donnell had a birthday on the way and made us collect a "compulsory " sum to pay for a nice present for him from the "Royal Air Force Symphony Orchestra". This, of course, went down well.

At roll call at 9 o'clock we would assemble in a double rank at "East Camp" - quite oblivious to the fact that, well underground was the most secret establishment regarding the war effort, known only to the likes of Churchill and Co. Anyway, there we were, trying to look the part - sometimes, at the rear, one or two breaking ranks to buy a pint of milk from a passing milkman - which would be handed through the railings which divided us from the road surrounding the camp. At one of these parades, my friend, Eddie Walker, was late, arriving on a bicycle. He rode down between the ranks, and as he passed the sergeant reading out the names, heard his name called, and immediately answered, "Sergeant", as he cycled by. It was at another of these parades that Flight-Sergeant Sotheron made one of his priceless and memorable edicts. It was something like - "Now, it's been brought to my notice that some of you living-out airmen have been taking meals at the airmen's mess. This constitutes a crime and comes under 'stealing a comrade's rations'. It ain't a crime to steal 'em - it's a crime to be caught stealing 'em." And then, as a delightful coda he added: "Anyone stealing them rations must be bloody 'ungry!"

Like many things I don't remember exactly how it came about but I soon found myself being the Wing-Commander's unofficial chauffeur. At the time I did possess a very reliable "Austin 10", which was to last me sixteen years! I soon began to enjoy the privileges attached to this job which, though it may sound a pleasant occupation was not always so because wartime motoring was quite different from what we call motoring these days. For one thing it was easy to lose one's way - unless you had memorised a map before setting out - for there were no signposts to help you as they had all been removed, like anything else that might be helpful to the enemy in the event of an invasion. But I think there was a more hazardous restriction - which I always thought was over-done. On leaving one airfield, after we had given a concert there, the "alert" had sounded, and we were commanded to turn out all car lights. This was really rather absurd since every car anyway had to conform to certain restrictions. Side lights had to be partially blacked out, and all the headlights were fitted with covers with slits which hardly lit up the road, but were a warning to a vehicle coming towards you. Very little light shone on the road, and as for being seen by aircraft flying above you, I doubt whether a car would be visible more than ten feet off the ground!

I must say that driving in pitch black conditions, especially on non-moonlit nights, was somewhat hazardous, but somehow we managed to come through it all without mishap. On one occasion we were due to give a performance at one of the biggest "bomber" air stations - Mildenhall in Suffolk. King George VI was due to visit the site and was travelling by air. At about the time he was due to arrive, there was an air raid warning as though the Germans had pre-knowledge of his movements. We were all seated on a raised stage in a large hall and had to wait some time before

His Majesty arrived. The C.O. was awaiting the King off-stage, and at last they both appeared. "Rudy" - as O'Donnell was called - knew him quite well, as they had been partners in the Men's Doubles at a "Wimbledon" a few years before. As they came through the door just below the stage, the C.O. was heard to be saying to the King: "Yes, Your Majesty, we have some eminent musicians in the Orchestra. We've got the Griller Quartet, the Martin Quartet and the Hirsch Quartet" - none of whom I suspect he had ever heard of! - to which he replied: "I see you've Scooped the Pool, O'Donnell."

On another occasion we were, for some reason, travelling by train - and had been waiting for a long time on the long platform at Cambridge Station - second only, I believe, to Platform 1 at Rugby - and I was having a number of drinks in the company of that splendid character, Jim Merrett, who, like his father, was a fine double-bass player and principal of the B.B.C. Orchestra. After the long delay on Cambridge Station - occasionally coming out of the bar to see if a train was coming, it became a permanent joke between him and me when we had a drink together. He used to ask me: "A small port?" I was his No. 2 throughout the war, for I had trouble with my neck - I actually had an operation to remove a cyst and couldn't play the fiddle. Once, when we were playing at the Colston Hall, Bristol, the concert ended with one of the Tchaikovsky Symphonies where the double-basses play the final bars with a *pianissimo* fifth. Jim and I were the only two basses - and it was in tune!

We were concerned in quite a number of important - and memorable events - between 1940 and 1945, usually involving a section of the Strings of the R.A.F. Orchestra. On two of these, the venue was No.10 Downing Street. It was all very friendly with little obvious security. On the first occasion, several of us were in a room in the basement, and Churchill's youngest daughter, Mary - who is now of course Lady Soames - showed us various treasures in a show-case. I remember her proudly showing us what she called "Papa's favourite scoop." It was a medal Mussolini had had struck to mark his triumphal entry into Rome - which never took place!

We found that, in the room upstairs where we played from time to time, we could move around quite freely among the guests, among whom was that great South African, General Smuts. I was standing quite near him and noticed how his eyes brightened up as he spoke with enthusiasm, with those little "crows feet" each side of his face. During the evening Jim Phillips was walking downstairs and passed the P.M., Churchill, with a whisky in one hand and a large cigar in the other, coming up. He said to Jimmy: "Thank you for your fine playing." Actually he hadn't played a note as there wasn't room for another cellist in the rather confined space!

The biggest undertaking by the whole of the R.A.F. Symphony Orchestra and Central Band occurred towards the latter part of the war, which was a three and a half-month tour of the United States. It lasted for just over the final three months of 1944 until the end of the first month of 1945, when the war was still at its height. The main object of the operation was to raise money, chiefly by the sale of what were called War Bonds in aid of the war effort. In those three and a half months we covered about 25,000 miles of the U.S.A. entirely by train! The trip left Liverpool to cross the Atlantic unescorted - that's to say - not in convoy. The sea journeys were each taken by the two longest and fastest passenger liners in the world - and both British! The two ships were the Queen Mary and Queen Elizabeth, and the crossings took about five and a half days in each direction. With the speed of the liners and by zigzagging we were able to avoid the German submarines prowling the Atlantic, waiting to pounce.

The sea journeys and other forms of transport by land were far from luxurious. All trimmings and other items associated with a peace-time cruise, had been removed, and both ships had been reduced to absolute basics. To accommodate the enormous number of troops to be transported, the cabins were somewhat overcrowded. For instance, our cabin, built for two passengers, had to be shared by at least seven of us! There were two meals a day for which we had to queue for anything up to two hours in the long corridors, and with any luck you might have breakfast by 10 a.m., with the same process being repeated in the evenings. There was no possibility of drinking too much, the two concoctions being Coca-Cola and Pepsicola (I preferred the latter). The number of troops on board, apart from ourselves, was about 5000 in one direction, mostly consisting of casualties from the various fronts, and in the other direction, about 16,000 American reinforcements for further action on the Continent. In the mornings, there would be a call for boat drill, which was pretty farcical for it was almost impossible to get up on deck. I dread to think what would have happened if there had been a serious emergency. After over five days of discomfort, it was quite a relief to be confronted by the Statue of Liberty with the distant background of New York's "Skyscrapers". And later, it was quite a proud moment when we eventually "tied up" in New York harbour, to survey the scene of berths Nos. 90 and 91 occupied by the world's two largest Ocean liners - the "Queens" - and both ours!

After relaxing for a while in New York itself, we set off on our mammoth journey, the first stop being Washington, a much more gracious city where we were to sample the first example of generous American hospitality, followed by much variation of weather, from the winter of New York and the first taste of real summer in Florida, especially Miami beach where we were able to enjoy a dip in the warm Atlantic, which usually prevails all the year round at places like Miami.

In case anyone should get the idea - we had already made quite a number of stops as we travelled down the East Coast of the States - that we were beginning a romantic journey round the U.S.A., I would like to mention the form of transport used to convey us across this vast continent. It was entirely by train, and we covered something like 25,000 miles in five months or so! Again the actual journeys left something to be desired. I had bad luck again. The sleeping bunks had to be rationed as there weren't enough to accommodate everybody, so a rule was made that anyone of 6 feet or over could have a bunk to themselves and the remainder had to be shared, two to a bunk. I was 5ft. $11^1/_2$ ins!

After four years or more of food shortages at home, it was a pleasant change to be in a land of plenty. The meals on the trains were good but after so many years of deprivation it was a pleasure to eat chicken again, but we did find, while on the trains, that there did not seem to be much alternative. It seemed awful to find - very edible as it was - even in war-time one can have too much of a good thing! I remember the luxury of seeing eggs again, and the great pleasure of going into a "PX" (a U.S.A Service canteen), and ordering two fried eggs, "sunny side up" (i.e. not turned over). And another pleasant surprise - on a dark night at midnight - lights were blazing away with no curtains necessary, there being no need for black-outs in America.

Briefly the itinerary was from New York, right down the East Coast, taking in East and West Virginia, to Florida, then right across the Southern United States, crossing Texas - which took a week, and naturally included Houston and other big cities - "thru" to Phoenix, Arizona, and eventually reached the Los Angeles on the West Coast. The four-hundred mile train journey up to San Francisco must have been through some lovely scenery but sadly we did not see any of it as we travelled by night. San Francisco was memorable for its very steep roads - up which trains travelled - and seemed rather like switchbacks - and, of course, the Golden Gate Bridge across the estuary.

The journey back, eastwards, was memorable for many things, which included the magnificent Rockies through which the train passed, and we took in many notable cities on this Northern route, such as Salt Lake City, and about half way across, Chicago. There was one bad hold up when a train ahead of us had stopped. Apparently its engine had broken down and, being in open country, there was no hope of immediate assistance from any break-down services. There being no immediate solution to the problem it was decided that our train would have to resolve the impasse, and our engine would have to pull both trains - a considerable challenge for what must have been a pretty powerful locomotive. The two trains were eventually attached together with our engine at the front and being given a test which it probably had never faced previously. The result was the whole train was probably the longest ever, consisting of at least twenty-five coaches!

It was somewhere in the mid-west that we gave six concerts in three days, with the same programme at all three venues At every concert a "3 star General" gave a welcoming speech half way through, and after the first one we were suitably moved by his complimentary remarks and thanks, though there was a touch of sentimentality and over-dramatic references to our representing "the boys in blue - the white cliffs of Dover - the Battle of Britain" and lots more, somewhat overdone so that there was hardly "a dry eye in the hall." But when, at the very next concert, the General repeated his speech word for word, and having to listen to it another four times, it was almost more than we could take. In fact we probably hoped for a sign of hesitation so that we could "prompt" him!

One of our stops was at New Orleans, where, one free afternoon, we were given the choice of either a steamer trip down the Mississippi River or a visit to the Latin Quarter of the City. Unfortunately my choice was not the better one for it was one of the most boring river trips I've ever undertaken. There was no scenery to speak of - in fact it was particularly unattractive on both banks and the progress slow - while we heard that those who chose the Latin Quarter had a fascinating afternoon.

Naturally, having travelled such huge distances in those $3^1/2$ months, there were considerable variations of climate and temperature. Right from the very beginning of this tour we noticed considerable differences. We left Liverpool in the height of winter and on the first night, with everything blacked out, we began to feel very warm. On making enquiries why this was, we were informed that we had been travelling South as well as West and had passed near the Azores as part of the process of zigzagging across the Atlantic to avoid the German submarines. On reaching the U.S.A. we immediately noticed many differences from the U.K. Apart from no black-out, there were few restrictions but, of course, there was plenty of food. By the time we reached Washington we had already received a taste of American hospitality. After one of our earliest concerts we were all invited to two simultaneous parties. The reaction to one of these was not good for, it seems, those attending it left something to be desired, their behaviour being hardly exemplary. I think that some of the trouble had been the availability of free alcohol after years of privation at home. This caused certain restrictions on future behaviour which was somewhat annoying to say the least.

I found myself, not necessarily through choice, at the other party which took place at a rather refined ladies' club, where normally good behaviour was expected and respected. It was here that I fell in quite a big way for a very attractive girl, which was the start of a lasting and firm friendship. She was quite young, but already divorced. I was not yet (quite!) engaged to Gill, and it rather reminds me of the wartime story where a serviceman had been posted to Canada. He wrote home to say he had fallen in love with a local girl, to which his English girl-friend replied: "What is it she has which I haven't got?", to which came the reply: "Nothing, but she's got it over here!"

In my case the "Dorothy" and I seemed to get on very well and agreed to meet again at the conclusion of the tour, which happened. After this we kept in touch over the years. A son spent several days with us when we lived in Esher, and Dorothy twice took Gill and me out to a meal at a hotel near Gatwick on her way home after a trip to Europe. She, like far too many people, succumbed to the horrible affliction of cancer.

There were other moments of hospitality during our visit. I can remember a bachelor man - rather serious and quiet - inviting six of us back to his house in Phoenix, Arizona, and taking us out for a meal where I had my first experience of eating oysters which, as far as I was concerned, wasn't a rousing success.

One Sunday morning, after we had reached Los Angeles, we were in the

Hollywood area and we met Gracie Fields' husband. He was rather a "rough diamond" and looked rather like a motor mechanic, which he probably was, judging by his appearance and greasy hands. Anyway he was very friendly and asked anyone who would like to to visit him and his wife in their home above Hollywood in the afternoon, but I don't think anyone did, which was a pity.

There was one open-air concert planned where the weather was brilliantly fine and very hot. There was nearly a riot here, and about half the string players - many with really valuable instruments - refused to play in the hot sunshine. As far as I can remember there was a deputation to the C.O. and it was a very unpleasant incident. I forget how it was resolved, but somehow the tour continued. My "Uncle Harry" - i.e. my double bass, seemed to be immune to the extremes of heat and did not suffer from the very hot sun! It was known as "Uncle Harry" since it had stood like a statue in the hall-way of my father's brother's house in a village in Essex for many years, unplayed. My uncle gave it to me and it was ideal for me being on the small size and more suitable for a violin player (which, of course, I really was). I've always regretted selling it to a member of the band who wanted to play in a dance band at the end of the war. I received £18 for this transaction!

Small things still remain in my mind. For instance, in Chicago the railway ran down the main streets on rails exactly above the roads themselves! In large cities like Washington, pedestrians had to obey the lights as well as road traffic. When it changed from red to green, the word came on with the green light with the single instruction "Walk". It was said that if you disobeyed the light you could be fined, but I never saw a case of disobedience!

Engine drivers were called "engineers" and I've no doubt railway guards are now named something like "passenger service representatives", just as our own dustmen have been redesignated "waste disposal executives"! When we eventually returned to New York after our extensive tour - and I remember a G.I. (American Serviceman), saying to us: "Gee, I guess you've seen more of America than we'll ever get to see" - as we were given a fortnight's leave. I went to a broadcast quiz programme one evening, and one of the questions was: "What is a fortnight?" and nobody knew! The answers varied from "two days" to "three weeks", but no-one had, it seems, ever heard of it.

One other memorable example of hospitality occurred which was in Atlantic City. It was a party several of us went to at lunch time, invited by a very affable man named Carter, at his house. He plied us, as usual, with refreshments and unlimited liquid fare and suggested we came back again that evening. Some of us did so, but when we arrived there was no sign of Mr Carter or anyone else. It seemed they were all asleep, or more likely, after an over-indulgence of alcohol at lunch-time were perhaps walking it off.

For the week or so before we sailed home to England, when we were free to do as we liked, I was lucky for I had a very nice and generous great aunt (after whose husband I was given my second name), who knew a lady who lived in New York who wasn't - as they say - "short of a penny or two". She - a Mrs Huyck (pronounced "Hike") - had been given my name by my great aunt, and she invited me (and my friend Jim Phillips) to stay with her for the duration of our stay in New York, at her sumptuous flat. Though it was in the centre of the City, it was very quiet, being in the back of a large block of flats. I must say it was a pleasure to sleep in a real bed again after three and a half months of discomfort.

One morning we were woken up to be told that a car would be picking us up at 10.30 a.m. to take us shopping in 5th Avenue to buy presents "for our wives and girl-friends" at home. (I think Jim was married but my wedding was to be at the end of the year.) We were allowed to send short telegrams home but restricted as to the information we sent which was probably censored anyway. We weren't for instance allowed to mention the weather, whichever way the telegram was travelling. The sort of wire might be: - "I'm well. Hope you are", and the reply would be "in code" - that's to say, it might contain numbers like "16.12.15", which referred to the size of undergarments which weren't available at home!

We returned from our shopping trip with all sorts of exciting things. It was a lovely gesture of Mrs Huyck's. She herself used to send us food parcels after we got back. She made an unfortunate miscalculation on one occasion. I had an urgent message from the postmaster of Esher, where we then lived, to collect some eggs which had arrived by air from America and were causing rather a mess to other parcels. I was not surprised when I reached the Post Office. There were - or had been - two dozen eggs of which about one had remained unbroken in the flimsy cardboard box she had sent them in!

The war continued for several months after we returned from the U.S.A. and we kept up our various commitments until May 1945, when hostilities ceased in Europe. We had one more historic occasion to take part in. A very special event took place just after peace had been announced at the end of the war. This was at Potsdam, the conference between the three nations - Great Britain, the U.S.A. and Soviet Russia - in a building named temporarily 10 Downing Street, Potsdam! There were about sixteen of us (strings only) under O'Donnell. The three leaders were Churchill, President Truman (Roosevelt having recently died), and Stalin. It was interesting to see, from an upper window, the arrival of two of the leaders. Stalin was rushed down the footpath from the road with guards every side of him, whereas Churchill walked down from his car with no-one in particular accompanying him!

There was a dinner which took place in the adjoining room to where we were going to play. Every now and then, during a break, we would peep through the partly-open door, especially when speeches were taking place. At one point when a speech was being made in English - the guests were seated alternately round the table, English, American, Russian - and a joke would be made and all the English speaking guests would laugh. It would then be translated into Russian and every third member of the assembly would dutifully laugh too!

After the dinner and speeches, some of the high-ups came into our room and stood together on a small stage. They consisted of the three leaders with a few others, including Mr Byrnes, American Foreign Minister, and Anthony Eden from the U.K. We then played the well-known waltz movement from Tchaikovsky's *Serenade for Strings*. Stalin then said something in Russian to which Churchill took it upon himself to interpret for us - having obviously been prompted, saying: "The Marshall says your playing is very good." This was, rather predictably, followed by Stalin - who still had a glass in his hand - again speaking, and Churchill still felt he had to say: "He is now drinking your health!" After Stalin had left the building - and probably Churchill too - there was quite an informal atmosphere. President Truman came down to us whilst Denis Matthews, a fine pianist, was playing the piano. Truman waited till he'd finished and then said: "Gee - I play the piano a bit", and then sat down and played part of a Mozart Sonata. It sounded rather odd as he did not use the sustaining (i.e. "loud") pedal! Air Chief Marshall Portal, who had heard the whole Orchestra, said: "Now the war is over, I suppose this great orchestra will soon be disbanded, which is very sad." Anthony Eden was about the last to leave the hall, but in fact he came back in to thank us for our playing, which I thought was a very nice gesture.

After everyone had dispersed, we all went into the dining hall to see what we could pick up! I took an empty wine bottle, which I took home as a memento. As I wasn't able to oversee my move to Somerset, I'm afraid it remained in the wine rack of our cellar, where it had been for all those years!

8. LONDON SYMPHONY ORCHESTRA

Although the L.S.O. is mentioned in many different aspects in this narrative, chiefly in the chapter on Conductors, I have not dealt with the Orchestra as a whole, where the "band" itself is the feature and not the conductor. The L.S.O. was formed in 1904 - three years before I was born! - really as a result of controversy with Sir Henry Wood over the business of deputies. The name of the Orchestra has been familiar in our family for, I suppose, the best part of a century, as the L.S.O. started a winter series of Queen's Hall monthly Monday night concerts soon after it came into being. In fact it could not have been many years before my parents became regular subscribers to the concerts. My father always bought seats in the "area" part of the hall. They were the cheapest but not the most ideal for sound. The seats were behind the downstairs stalls and were immediately below the grand circle seats, not quite "in the open".

I can remember my parents going up to the Queen's Hall even when there were air raids on during the Great War. I would be left alone with a maid or nurse who would be in our kitchen, and with the sound of distant gun-fire and Zeppelins., I would - as a little boy - bury my head in her lap to get away from the noise!

I joined the L.S.O. in 1937, and for over six years I was a Director. Apart from the unforgettable concert at Ypres, described in the chapter on Conductors (Sir Arthur Bliss), the most extensive foreign tour was when we flew to South Africa in 1956 as part of the 70th birthday celebrations of Johannesburg. (I was surprised it was such a young city.) I - along with many others - was disappointed that we were not flying on to the more attractive city of Cape Town, but the somewhat misguided Secretary of the Orchestra (who is still around, working in the U.S.A., so I won't mention his name), said he was against our going there as it would stop people coming to our concerts in Johannesburg if they knew we were going there afterwards. Thic was a rather silly remark considering Cape Town was a further 1100 miles further South!

We did the usual sightseeing etc., from watching native dancing a little way from the City to playing a round of golf with little shoe-less black boys caddying for us. I played with one of Gill's late next-door neighbours from Gerrard's Cross - where we were married - who worked for E.M.I, but the most moving experience was a special concert we were asked to give. The Musician's Union weren't too keen on us going at all since all our concerts were for "white" audiences. The difficulty was overcome by our agreeing to give an extra concert for a "coloured" audience only. No-one was paid and no charge for entry was made. The concert was given in the University, and after the performance we were nearly overwhelmed by the audience who practically embraced us and were emotionally overcome. They had never been to such a concert before. One woman told us she had travelled three hundred and fifty miles to be there. We really felt we were doing something of untold good.

While we were in Johannesburg I visited the Wanderers Cricket Ground. It was still a few years before any Test matches were to take place there, and the ground was still incomplete as far as cricket was concerned, the buildings still being under construction. But it is fun, when listening to broadcasts from there, to be able to picture the scene from experience.

On the return journey - the total time in each direction was about twenty - seven hours - we stopped at the old Nairobi airport (which was almost primitive), and I met a family of relations of my wife, who had come to meet me at Nairobi, the father being head of the Farmer's Union in Kenya. It was sad that they were all planning to return to England when, just before they set off, the father, Gill's uncle, died and was deprived of the pleasure of returning. After stopping at Khartoum, which was very hot and sticky, with nasty little "wiggles" crawling up the airport walls, we had one less stop than we had on the outward journey, for we flew then straight to Rome, avoiding Cairo this time since the Suez crisis was coming to a head.

Calling at an airport on a long flight for a mere hour does not really give you much idea of a place, but when we stopped on both journeys for that brief time we were, quite surprisingly, struck by one stop-off which was at Salisbury, in what was then Southern Rhodesia (now Harare, Zimbabwe). The climate seemed ideal, and the generally relaxed feeling of everybody and everything was quite remarkable and unforgettable, even to this day. Flying over Switzerland, it was quite a thrill to look down on the top of Mont Blanc. We were all queuing up to take a quick snap with our non-flash cameras through a port-hole.

During the earlier days of the L.S.O., when I first joined, there were often quite small audiences, but I remember Constant Lambert saying the L.S.O. always had a special string sound derived from what was known as the "Elgar sound". Elgar himself used to conduct the Orchestra in the 20s and early 30s at Three Choirs Festivals - at Worcester, Hereford and Gloucester - and the Orchestra seemed to retain a sort of legacy from those days.

Fortunately every overseas tour by the L.S.O. has ended successfully, but it could have been otherwise. When the Orchestra was a mere 8 years old, they might have literally disappeared without trace. They were booked for a tour of the U.S.A in 1912, but the liner on which they hoped to travel was fully booked for its maiden voyage. The name of the liner was the "Titanic". Happily for the L.S.O. their booking had been transferred to the "Baltic".

The Orchestra at play!
In the somewhat sedentary occupation of music-making - though conductors might not agree with that statement - it is a good thing to take healthy exercise when possible. It had been said that, years ago, the L.S.O. ran a cricket team and there was a very keen cricket enthusiast in the orchestra during my time with them named Eddie Walker, second flute to his father, Gordon, who was not only principal flautist but Chairman of the Orchestra. Eddie and I decided it would be fun to form a team again and we discovered that many Public Schools, within a reasonable distance of London,

ran the sort of sides that we were likely to produce - that is to say teams consisting of a few Masters and mostly boys whose main sporting activities were probably rugger or football in the winter terms and whose prowess at cricket would probably qualify at about Grade Three level which was about our own level too.

As ever, the actual details of how it all began are somewhat hazy but it did soon get going. Eddie was to be Captain, and I, the Hon. Sec., which, of course, entailed quite a lot of correspondence, mostly with various schools - and it worked surprisingly well. We managed to have a fixture list with something like ten matches during the summer, some games having return matches later in the season. Some villages were included too.

We had our own notepaper or printed cards with our own "Coat of Arms" which one of our first violinists - who was also an artist - designed, creating it from the initials L.S.O. His name was Bertie Lewis, another character, who had been leader of the Bournemouth Symphony Orchestra. He was a more than passable artist - I still have one of his paintings - and he used to make his own furniture. It was he who told me the story of the trombone player at Leeds Town Hall, playing with the Hallé Orchestra under Sir Hamilton Harty, and which can be found in the chapter on Conductors.

The teams we played had some delightful titles such as the "Charterhouse Maniacs"; our very first match which took place on the School's playing fields - and I think they still exist; and then there were the "Harrow Outcasts" - they claimed to have the largest area of mown grass in the country! - the "Eastbourne Erratics" (my old school), the "Epsom Platipods", and a number of others including the "Aldenham Addicts". On one occasion we played the B.B.C.'s Second XI at their fine ground at Motspur Park - and beat them! I think they were a bit peeved when they discovered that two of our best players were not genuine playing members of the L.S.O.; they were brothers who were loyal supporters of the Orchestra, and when you read, these days, of footballers being paid millions of pounds to become members of a team who may never have been near the Country before, let alone played with the team, I don't think we did anything underhand or to be ashamed of.

One annual fixture which we all looked forward to was a game we played entitled, "Strings v Wind" at the Three Choirs Festivals, whenever we had the afternoon off, which became rather rare. However we managed to fit in quite a few matches, sometimes on very nice grounds; for instance, the Hereford Choir School pitch which was next door to the County Ground. One year it was not available and we had to travel a little way out into the country. We had a delightful character who was travelling with the L.S.O., a fine accompanist and possessing a nice sense of humour; he was Wilfred Parry. He was married to the viola player Eileen Grainger - the only woman player, at that time, in the L.S.O. - apart from Marie Goossens, the harpist. Wilfred decided he would like to come to the match, though he was not quite sure where the ground was. Anyway, he caught a bus out of Hereford and when the conductress came round to collect the fares, she asked Wilfred where he wanted to go

63

and he answered: "The Cricket Match." She was obviously not going to be amused or helpful and answered, rather crossly: "What cricket match?" "Strings versus Wind", replied Wilfred. By this time the humourless girl felt he was - as they say - "taking the Mickey" and continued to be unpleasant. When Wilfred felt he had reached his destination he called out to the girl, as he left the bus, a final "I'll let you know the result!" If there were more people like him about the world would be a happier place!

Another year, when the Festival was at Gloucester, we held a match on the Wagon Works ground which was at one time one of Gloucester Cricket Club's first class grounds. I was quite pleased with my own performance. Their side was captained by the Captain of Gloucester City's Cricket Club, who had also played for his County itself. He was batting when he hit a high shot in my direction, fielding at deep mid-off. I had to run in quite a long way to reach the ball and as I reached it, it jumped out of my hands - in fact twice - but the third time I made sure I caught it! I do not think that it won the match at that point but I gave myself a pat on the back!

Another memorable occasion was when I achieved something that had probably never happened before in the Orchestra's history - when I got an Albert Hall L.S.O. rehearsal put back half an hour to fit in with a cricket match. It was a Sunday. The L.S.O. had a three hour rehearsal called from 10 a.m. to 1 o'clock for a 7.30 p.m. concert the same day, and we had a match against a village team in the delightful Surrey village of Holmbury Saint Mary, some way out. The conductor for the concert was Josef Krips and he had made an announcement at an earlier rehearsal. "Next Sunday's rehearsal will start at 9.30 instead of 10 o'clock because of 'ze crickets'." (I do not think he ever knew what a cricket match was but I successfully persuaded him to make this change of time!)

Holmbury Cricket Ground is not the easiest location to reach. You have to leave your car down below and walk up some way via a footpath through wooded surroundings before it opens out on to an attractive ground not far from Leith Hill, high above the village. One corner of the ground tended to fall away quite steeply and the line of the boundary could not be seen from the middle. It reminded me very much of that delightful book: "England my England" by A.C. Macdonnell who wrote a priceless description of a cricket match in which the village blacksmith had to chase a ball that had been hit into one corner of the ground which fell away so steeply that he practically disappeared from view. Having retrieved the ball, the first sight of him occurred when the top of his bald head came into view!

Holmbury St. Mary at that time still had no running water and in some ways it was delightfully primitive. In order to have boiling water in time for the tea break, a log fire was lit behind the pavilion and large kettles would be placed on it at about 3 p.m. and, with luck, would be boiling by about 4.30. A little time before 6 p.m. we had to leave the field and reappearing at about 6 o'clock would be eleven cricketers dressed in dinner jackets like a group of waiters, and, after a quick beer, would be on the road for the Royal Albert Hall! The traffic was fairly light in those days. I'm sure we could not have risked what we did then, today. We eventually arrived at the Albert Hall in time - and in good form - but there was one scare - there was no sign of the principal horn, and it was 7.30 p.m.. All was well when it was discovered that he had been consuming fish and chips in a nearby restaurant - quite unruffled! He was one of the cricketers, of course.

One particular fixture I used to enjoy very much - we tried to make it two fixtures a season - took place not one hundred yards from our house in Esher, Surrey. It was played in the adjoining village of Claygate where there was a "pocket handkerchief" of a ground, and to look at it would seem to be the most unsuitable place on which to play cricket. There was a road on two sides of the "village green" leading to a cross-roads - one of the roads was a bus route - and on the third was a stream (into which the balls often entered). You could only score ones and fours - there was no time to run more than a single. I was delighted on one occasion to hit what would normally have been a six but on this ground nothing higher than four counted. But my disappointment was countered by my shot which landed on the adjoining house the other side of the stream and I had the satisfaction of seeing two tiles of the roof sliding to the ground! There was another amusing incident when one of our players, fielding in the deep - if you could call it that - who, I think was Principal Second fiddle in the L.S.O., whose forte was obviously not cricket, and, after fielding a ball near the boundary, with the intention of returning the ball to the bowler, unfortunately let the ball go on the back swing of his arm and nearly broke a window in "The Swan", the pub just behind him!

The local side was called "The Leverets" - named after the road running between the pub and the ground, which was called "Hare Lane". We had a lot of fun playing there and it was a very popular venue - it had been going many years. It was amazing, on such a miniature ground - it was a "matting" wicket - how many sides were bowled out for under one hundred. One Sunday, at the end of one of our matches, we heard the bolts being lifted on the door of the pub at 7 p.m. indicating "opening time" and the umpire would call "Last Over!" After one match the whole team came back to our house, just up the road and we had a "rollicking" evening, playing darts etc. Our front downstairs room was about to be decorated, so there was no carpet and no necessity to keep it either tidy or clean - which it certainly was not after they had all left!

One Sunday I was walking down to our nearest pillar box - just across the road from "The Swan" - to post a letter, and just ahead of me was a rather thick-set man in a white shirt - it was a hot day - and sleeves rolled up, but not very far - a habit I have noticed with cricketers - and I thought he looked familiar, even though it was only a back view. When he turned back to return home I was right, it was "Wally" Hammond, the great English cricketer, Sir Walter Hammond! I had no idea he had come to live in Esher, just round the corner from us. At the end of their road was the Esher Cricket Club, which he was persuaded to join.. He was, of course, a great "draw" but did not make very many runs - I once watched him for a little while and

I think he scored three! I know he complained that people expected him to make a century every time he went out to bat. He explained that it took some time to acclimatise to completely different conditions. I remember it was a pleasant ground but definitely not an even surface throughout with quite a dip in it at one point. (I don't think Hammond lived there very long).

Finallly, on cricket, I must report on a remarkable occasion, all the details of which I must admit I do not really recall clearly. The match in question took place during an Edinburgh Festival. How it all began I cannot remember, as usual, but I must have been quite involved.   Who thought of it? How was it organised and advertised? - I know not, but I recall the occasion most clearly.

The teams consisted of the L.S.O. who challenged as their opponents conductors, music critics, soloists, composers etc. and we managed to organise two teams. It puzzles me which Edinburgh ground did we play on, but I do remember it was well equipped cricket ground with a proper Club house. One small incident I remember well was that one of our players - our harpist Ossian Ellis - was on the field, when we were fielding, wearing white shorts - rather unusual at a game of cricket! But I am still at a loss to know how it was that I was doing a sort of running commentary on the match to, of all unlikely people - whom I had then never heard of, called Magnus Magnusson! He was at the time a reporter for the Scottish Daily Press. There was a telephone in the corner of the Club house, with a good view of the pitch, and we were fielding, and he wanted up-to-date reports of the progress of the game. I had been describing play on the phone just after the music critic, Noel Goodwin, had been out for "a duck" and remember Magnus saying: "Any more wickets down?" and my answering: "None at present" then quickly correcting myself by saying: "Yes - Colin Davis also just out for a duck!" I think we eventually won quite easily but I would love to have more details of the "whys and wherefores" of this quite unusual occurrence. I have contacted Magnus Magnusson and received a charming letter from him. Alas, he has no recollection of the actual match but he was able to confirm for me which paper he worked for.

As a footnote to our exploits on the cricket fields, one of the pleasures of these outings was the "follow ups" after the games, usually a gathering with our opponents (at least the grown-ups!) at the "local" for a pleasant chat and liquid refreshment. At Epsom College - a little way out of town - the venue was the Masters' Common Room and it was also an extremely pleasant get together. The Eastbourne visit was memorable for at least two things - our best batsman was needlessly run out in the first over (rather a long way to travel and not face a single ball), and the glorious weather of the afternoon - in keeping with their having one of the best sunshine records on the South coast - while we could hear, and see, violent thunderstorms raging only two or three miles inland. Sunshine can do a lot to obviate the woes of life. Our wicketkeeper, by the way, was none other than the Principal Second Violin - Neville Marriner. I always thought it was a risky position to hold for a string player, but Neville came through without injury and was a very reliable keeper. It was about that time that he was second fiddle in David Martin's string quartet. David led the second fiddles in the Boyd Neel and I was his Number Two and sat with him for the eleven years I was in the Orchestra.

David was also in the L.S.O. with me for a while. I must mention that he was a great practical joker and one incident happened when on a Sunday - again in connection with the Boyd Neel - we had a concert at Rugby School and had travelled up from London by train. Rugby station possesses what is believed to be the longest platform in the country! One is so long, I believe, that about halfway down, the number changes but not the platform! Anyway, the school is some way from the station but straight up from it. We were all walking up together and, as with large groups of people, talking as we walked with our heads down. Nearing the school the road divides into two forming a crescent with gardens in between. As we reached this point a man was playing a violin, standing in the gutter with his case open on the pavement, and as we passed him, still looking downwards, several of our players threw coins in his open case. As the man's hat was pulled well over his eyes it was not till a little while afterwards that we realised that we had been paying David to play the fiddle in the street! We had not noticed that he had hurried on ahead of us!

9. GLYNDEBOURNE

I have described the very beginning of Glyndebourne and the Boyd Neel Orchestra's accoustical tests in the mid-Thirties. Just before the outbreak of war I played at two seasons there where the Orchestra for the opera was the L.S.O in all but name. It was based chiefly on the London Symphony with George Stratton leading, and with many Principal players filling key positions. I was engaged as a viola player for these two seasons and, as it turned out, I had quite an advantage as I could just see straight up the auditorium to the private boxes at the back, whereas the violins, facing across the orchestral pit probably saw about a third of the stage. In 1938, the most important and lengthy opera was Verdi's *Macbeth*, requiring the largest orchestra. Other operas alternated with ours, so I, along with several others, was not on every night. It was a great experience playing opera under Fritz Busch.

On one night in 1938, we were given the tip that things might be happening later in the evening. *Macbeth* is in four Acts with two each side of the interval. We had heard that the Prime Minister, Neville Chamberlain, was expected to attend, and would be sitting as John Christie's guest in the main box at the rear of the auditorium. If Chamberlain was absent for the last two Acts we could presume there was trouble, either that war had been declared or was about to start. There was general relief when the Prime Minister reappeared after the interval and we could all relax. In fact we were spared the precious time of another year to prepare ourselves for war.

Soon after the cessation of hostilities in 1945, Gill and I, on a Sunday afternoon - in fact I was still in uniform - took a train to Lewes and had a very pleasant walk across the Downs and on to Glyndebourne. There we found a number of American servicemen being shown round the theatre by a soprano with a lovely voice and a very attractive personality - none other than Mrs Christie herself - known professionally as Audrey Mildmay. She invited us most warmly to join the party. It was a lovely way to spend a sunny Sunday afternoon. When I reached home I wrote to Mrs Christie thanking her for her courtesy to us and, most unexpectedly, had a very sweet reply. It was one of the saddest things when, such a lovely singer and person, died so young when at the height of her career. She really was a jewel in the crown of all Glyndebourne singers.

To attend an opera at Glyndebourne, especially after the war when things were gradually getting back to normal, was something very special. The most obvious attraction was the unique and lovely setting of the opera house; the country around is completely unspoilt, with the Downs sloping up almost at once to the north. The gardens at the back of the buildings are quite beautiful, where guests can wander, either during the long intervals or before the opera starts. Looking south towards the coast are level fields where cattle are grazing. The lawns of Glyndebourne appeared to be part of the fields beyond and one at first wonders why the cows never seem to enter the grounds, as there is no hedge until, after further inspection is disclosed a fairly wide water-filled ditch between the lawns and the fields beyond.

One of the special attractions is the choice of either taking dinner in the indoor restaurant during the interval or having your own picnic supper in the grounds, having brought everything with you. Some people provide themselves with most elaborate repasts from cold salmon salads and champagne to simple picnics. In summer weather it is one of the joys of this special trip to Lewes. I once took the organist of our church in Sutton as my guest. I remember him saying that he wouldn't mind if he didn't even see the opera, it was worth going just to enjoy the atmosphere of the setting. In fact I once said that you could go to Glyndebourne just for the cost of the car park!

10. ON COMPOSING

In my early days I did not seem to have any urge to compose myself. I think my earliest effort was when I was still at school. I wrote the music for the Responses for the choir to sing at Chapel services. (I wonder if they are still in their archives?) I made rather a pompous statement - many years ago - that I felt enough music had been written without my adding to it!

People teach and learn Composition, and I wonder what that entails. Having learnt the theory of music as a student, what else can be taught I wonder? - certainly not inspiration. I think a lot of experience of performing and listening to good music is half the battle. Personally I could never just write something, but "doodling" at a piano sometimes sets one off. I remember being very encouraged when Ravel the great French composer said you cannot invent chords without a piano! I find you must have a person or object as the reason for writing anything - or indeed to be inspired, in a small or much bigger way. I must have a goal which is the object of the operation, and people to keep in mind while writing. Ravel's remark I found most reassuring as I had always thought that using a piano was "not the done thing", and that most great composers just sat at a desk - not a piano - and composed - whether in full or short score, straight off or in, say, four parts or so, and then orchestrated it. I still don't know, but must admit I can only compose in the latter manner - i.e. at the piano.

As I have said, I must have an object or person in mind for me even to start operations. Since I started quite late in life, I really did enjoy it, and I think I've written 50 to 60 works, or pieces. For instance, I have written quite a number of wedding marches, including for my own daughter, and numerous songs - admittedly usually for attractive sopranos - attractive in voice of course! I have been lucky so far in not having had anything turned down, and I have naturally felt greatly honoured when such great artists as Léon Goossens or Archie Camden have accepted concertos I have written for them for oboe and bassoon respectively. Not only that, but they played them a number of times, including on a B.B.C. broadcast. I had a little joke with Léon - which he always enjoyed - when, in connection with a festival of some years ago in which he was involved (and the joke was on him), I had introduced two bars of *Le Cygne* (The Swan) into the slow movement of my *Oboe Concerto*. When I happened to be conducting, Léon always looked up at me and winked. I will not disclose the rest of the story, but just to say that it was during a Music Festival at Tunbridge Wells in which he was soloist, and the hotel near the hall was called "The Swan".

Apart from two part songs and two arrangements for orchestra, I have had nothing published in this country. I once composed a piece for Contrabassoon and Piano - this has so far had fifteen performances in the U.S.A., with Susan Nigro as soloist, the top woman contra player in the States - and that peice has been published in Fort Lauderdale, Florida; and a piece for four bassoons was published a year or so ago in Berlin, which seems to support the well-known saying "A prophet is not without honour except . . . etc". It is strange that I, as a string player, have written works almost exclusively for wind instruments!

A few years ago I wrote an Introit for four-voice choir, with the title *I said to the Man*. When George VI gave his - as it happened - last Christmas Day broadcast, he read a poem by someone called M.L.Haskins, and I was always intrigued by the words starting "I said to the Man who stood at the Gate of the Year", and I decided to set it to music. This I did, setting it for four-part choir and organ, and it has become very popular (publishers please note!), with at least five performances recently.

I often wondered who M.L.Haskins was, and I had a guess that she was a maiden lady living in Tunbridge Wells. Some years ago, a very well-got-up magazine found its way into our house and I found quite a long article, over about four pages, with excellent photographs and most interesting details of the whole poem and how it had attracted the King. Some of the article was naturally devoted to who the author of the words was. She apparently was a maiden lady, but hailed from East Grinstead, so I wasn't far out with my guess - a mere ten miles or so!

I also wrote a four-part carol for women's voices together with Ursula Vaughan Williams who wrote the words. The occasion was the 50th anniversary of the Surrey Women's Institute. I conducted the first performance with a choir of about 400 - there is just piano accompaniment - at the Guildford Civic Hall. The carol, called *A Winter Birth* - was printed and published very quickly when they heard how many voices would be involved, even though it had not been seen or heard. The criteria seems to be, not the quality of the product but the number of copies likely to be sold. I have found this elsewhere. I once arranged a Bach fugue for String Orchestra and it was published by a well-known firm and it became very popular. That went out of print. I happened to meet up with one of the firm at a concert in London. I tackled him about it saying: "I hadn't noticed Bach had gone out of fashion", and he just said: "The sales have dropped." I blame the publishers for poor publicity and lack of "push". People are unlikely to buy something they haven't even heard of unless it is well advertised.

One of my latest efforts, in 1994, came from an invitation to write something for choir and orchestra for the tercentenary of the Bank of England. The venue was Gloucester and the participants were the members of the Registrar's Department who were stationed in Gloucester, the Conductor and Musical Director being an excellent cellist whom I knew, Peter Harman, son of Charles Harman who gave such splendid support to the Croydon Youth Orchestra in its early days - of which more later. I took on this commission, inviting Ursula Vaughan Williams to write the words. Together we concocted a short work in three movements for choir and orchestra, under the title *Reflections*. It was well received - and excellently performed by a choir from the Bank of England and a very good orchestra led by the leader of the B.B.C. Symphony Orchestra, Stephen Bryant, a school friend of the conductor. My daughter, Diana, played Oboe in the orchestra.

71

11. ON EXAMINING

I came to be an examiner quite late in my career, but I was taken on by Trinity College of Music and enjoyed a number of years in this capacity. Having, in my early days, gone through the quite emotional and sometimes anxious "ordeals" myself, I know what it is like to be a "victim". I soon realised how necessary it is for an examiner to possess a touch of human kindness. Without ever lowering one's standards, there are ways of putting a candidate more at his or her ease by the odd word of friendship - even a light-hearted quip to help a performer do himself justice. One should not pressurise a candidate or make him flustered and *never* say things like, "Get a move on. I haven't got all day," or other facetious remarks; even if it is true, one's time is not limitless of course.

I have always thought that the human touch is essential and a candidate should feel you are helping them to relax. It always gave me much pleasure when, as quite often happened, an entrant, as he left the room, passing my table, would say: "You won't remember me but . . ." and I would interrupt and say: "Come on - Croydon Youth Orchestra. What year?" and they might say: "1959" - and this happened a number of times! Examiners are usually well looked after, and I remember once a young girl at a school asking me what refreshment I would like at the morning break, and saying: "Tea or coffee?" - adding: "The coffee's awful!"

One always had to be careful to make sure the remarks on a performance tallied with the total marks you were awarding. It would be unacceptable, for instance, to give a candidate 18 marks out of, say, 20, and then say something like: "Very weak on sight-reading". And it is good to remember that - for the most part - one is not necessarily recording a fact, that can be proven, but an opinion of the quality of a performance which is entirely one's own.

The venues for examinations - often in schools - varied a lot. I remember a large room - probably used for concerts - at one girls' Public School in Kent, where I had to sit through a very cold day. It did not help that one of the large windows was being repaired and had been taken completely out. I felt sorry for the girls who had quite a long walk to cross the room to the grand piano and my table. I called it (to myself) "the Walk to the Scaffold" - rather like a contestant in "Mastermind", walking to that forbidding black chair - but considerably further!

The name of the school, now sadly - and for what reason I know not - closed down, was "West Heath", near Sevenoaks. I went there two years running and I remember the very pleasant lady Director of Music, telling me at the end of my first visit, that had I come one year earlier, I would have examined Lady Diana Spencer - I think it was for Grade Six piano! I've often regretted missing this opportunity. I asked the Music Mistress what she was like and she said: "Very nice, but very naughty!"

Examining was a pleasant episode in my musical career and I made a lot of friends. One rather surprising assignment, which in fact turned out to be also quite enjoyable, was when Trinity College asked me to examine a candidate at Maidstone Gaol in Kent! I was warmly received and escorted to a room where a piano entrant was waiting to be examined. He was a colonial man who, it appeared, had been convicted of murder! I believe there had been a certain amount of uncertainty as to whether his crime was unpremeditated or not. In any case I was left alone with this man who had a very pleasant manner and turned out to be keen on music and played quite well. He wondered whether I could help him, which I was quite willing to do - to find him some book or other which would help him study composition or some other form of music making - which he was not likely to find in the prison library.

One of the nicest things occurred when, some years after I finished my examination "stint", I had an extremely nice letter from Headquarters, i.e. The National Federation of Festivals, apologising for not writing sooner and thanking me for my work for the Board, which they appreciated very much.

I once asked someone in charge of music at a school, for no particular reason, just out of interest, why they used Trinity College for their music exams rather than a much larger organisation (which shall remain nameless): "Because we like their examiners better!" was the reply. I did not demur!

12. COINCIDENCES

I have always been fascinated by coincidences and some of those I've been involved in have been so incredible as to be almost beyond belief. One of my favourites happened during the last war and concerned a great friend of mine, the cellist Harvey Phillips, who had his own string orchestra. Jim (or Jimmy as he was to me), and I, were in London one early afternoon, both of us in R.A.F. uniform. There wasn't much choice of drinks in those days and anything special had to be sought after. But I did know one very nice wine bar in Marylebone Lane - nearly opposite Trinity College of Music. It was a Hennessey house and they sold Harvey's Amontillado sherry - a favourite of mine and very appropriate since one of Jim's first names was Harvey since he was in fact related to the famous Harveys of Bristol, where he himself used to live.

Having ordered two glasses of sherry, the rather care-free and "blousy" bar-maid became very chatty with us and, as far as I can remember, for no particular reason, she suddenly said to Jimmy: "I'm the daughter of the vicar of South Petherton." I knew what was coming for I knew Jim very well, and though I never knew his father, I knew his occupation so I wasn't in the least surprised by his reply, which was: "And I'm the son of the vicar of North Petherton!" Now if he'd spoken first she could have felt cheeky and made up her reply but it was the other way round.

Both the villages are in Somerset and not long ago I drove through North Petherton for the first time, as it is fairly near where I now live. I should have liked to have called in at the church to check up the records but unfortunately the church was closed. I also remember this girl saying to Jimmy: "I was the "black sheep" of my family. Were you?" Rather taken aback he answered, a bit shyly: "I don't really know!"

Another quite amazing coincidence occurred when I was still a student at the Royal College. I was at the time the conductor of a village choir in Withyham, Sussex - referred to more under Malcolm Sargent in the chapter on conductors - and one Tuesday, our practice night, I had another engagement and had to find a deputy to take my place. A friend of mine at the College called Brian Fitzgerald was always glad of an opportunity to do some conducting. He was a delightful chap and well spoken. I rang him from the R.C.M., having ascertained his number which was something like Maida Vale 4233. A voice very different from the quality of Brian's usual refined tones answered the phone: " 'allo," which rather surprised me since he hadn't had time to ascertain who was speaking and, anyway, would not try to be funny. I decided to continue, so I asked him, "Can you take my choir at Withyham next Tuesday?" to which came the reply: "I beg yer pardon?" and I repeated my question and he said: 'Oo do yer want?" and I said: "Brian Fitzgerald." "This is Brian Fitzgerald speakin', greengrocer, Maida Vale 4239" !

I could hardly believe it - to dial correctly but to get the wrong number but someone with the same name! The young girl at the switchboard at the College but in the same small room as the public phone, had heard all that had been going on, and, for a bit of fun, wanted to follow this up, rang this bloke up on the "wrong" number which I gave her and when he answered she said: "Would you come to the College for your singing lesson next Monday. . . " and rang off!

Another coincidence happened before the war concerning my own family. My father and I had been on holiday together, as often happened, and were returning one summer after a visit to Scotland - more than likely mostly to play golf at a favourite resort of ours - Pitlochry, Perthshire - where it cost two shillings all day. In high summer with the long evenings it would be possible to play three rounds if you started early enough! In this hilly, almost mountainous course I found two quite enough!

In those far off days one would never try to drive to Scotland from Surrey in one day - more likely three. Even to the North of England, one would allow two days. On our journey home we had decided to call on some first cousins who lived at a village called Riding Mill about sixteen miles west of Newcastle-on-Tyne with really delightful wild open country with no sign of any industrial eyesores. A few miles farther west is Hexham and the beginning of Hadrian's Wall. My brother, Clive, was staying with the cousins, recuperating from a minor tonsil operation. As usual when staying with them I would be "put out to grass" - ie. to mow their very nice tennis court and then have a game with some of their large family.

At about 5 p.m. I said to my father it was time we thought about continuing our journey South. The evenings had already begun to "draw in". We eventually set off with no idea at all where we would stay the night, except that we would head for the Great North Road. When we reached one town in Yorkshire, called Richmond, we decided to stop, first driving the full length of the town. I remember it to be somewhat "one-sided" - that is to say, most of the buildings were on the right, the left side being practically clear of anything. There were about three largish hotels and we decided on one which looked promising. Leaving the car outside the entrance, we made enquiries and they had accommodation for us for the night. We were then handed a key for the line of lock-up garages which were situated behind the hotel and told which one to take. That was another thing one would never dream of doing in those days - leaving one's car in the street. How tidy we must have been! We drove back in the direction from which we had come and taking the first turning on the left, we soon found the garage allotted to us. As soon as we had put the car away, another car followed us and took the garage next door. By then it was pitch dark, with not even a moon to help us. When the car lights were switched off, one couldn't see a thing. We thought we ought to be sociable and waited for the other people, who turned out to be a man and his wife. They were staying at the same hotel as ourselves, so we walked round with them. They had left London, also with no plan of where they would be stopping the night. I told the lady we had earlier left Northumberland, having called on some relations at a small village called Riding Mill. "That's where we're going, " she said, "people called Sanderson." "They are my cousins, " I said.

"Is the house called Underwood?" she asked me. "Yes!" I said. Again I could hardly believe it.

Before we had reached the light of the Hotel - I could still not see her face, and we had not yet got back to the hotel - I had discovered this lady had been at school with my mother at Ilkley Moor in Yorkshire!

Another coincidence of sorts concerns the lives of the family of some of my first cousins, the Heaths, and their remarkable similarity with the Goossens brothers and sisters. The elder Goossens brother, Adolf, an outstanding horn player, was killed in the early stages of the Great War in France while still in his teens. My own cousin, Geoff, who loved Army life, was also only 17 or 18 when he too, was killed in action - possibly in the same battle. (He was already showing promise on the violin.) That left two boys and two girls. One of the boys, Rex, survived the war and after suffering from "trench feet", eventually went on to a reasonable age if not exactly "old age". This matched Eugene Goossens, who started as a violinist but switched to conducting. He too lived to a reasonable age after a successful career in Australia.

Cousin Rex was an excellent pianist and a first class sportsman. He played hockey for Southgate and made friends and played with Keith Falkner, the distinguished singer and cricketer who later became Director of the Royal College. Alan, who started on the fiddle, developed a very pleasant baritone voice and was a member of the Philharmonic Choir. He was the first of the family to reach the 90s. He was not fit enough to serve in other than the Army Pay Corps. He was an Air Raid warden in the last war. He was my favourite cousin and one of the funniest men I knew. He was joking two days before his death. It was wonderful how he faced up to many adversities in his latter years. Both "girls" lived to their late 90s - one married to an amateur "scratch" golfer. Her younger sister, Elsa, became a P.E. Instructor and had four children. They "matched" the Goossens sisters.

Another recent coincidence concerned my daughter and her husband who live in Pitminster, less than three miles up the road from where I now live. Their Silver Wedding date was coming up and they thought a few days in Paris would be nice. Diana looked up advertisements in the magazine, "The Lady", and finding there was a small flat to let in Paris which sounded just what they wanted she rang the number. A very pleasant sounding lady's voice answered the phone in English. Yes, this flat was still available and this lady then asked Diana her address. "The Coach House", she started, - "That sounds nice", interrupted the lady - "Pitminster," continued my daughter. "Is that in Somerset?" "Yes," came the quick answer. It then transpired that they had once lived next door - in fact, Diana thinks they also owned their house as well! Not only that, but they themselves were coming over for Christmas to stay at Corfe - a village just over a mile from Pitminster - cue for the usual: "It's a small world"!

A year later the coincidences continued. Diana, with at last a few days off before Easter, and a break from teaching the oboe etc. in Somerset, decided along with her husband Mike to have a two day break - with one night away - going off without a plan. They finished up at St. Ives, South Cornwall to start with. They found a very nice hotel right on the seafront and had the place to themselves with no other guests staying there. It transpired, during the course of conversation, that the father of the proprietoress had cut the hair of Mike and his brother when they lived at Reading, many years ago!

Possibly the most amazing and unbelievable coincidence occurred towards the end of one of Harry Isaac's Maida Vale parties - described elsewhere - when I happened to be talking about gramophone recording with one of the guests whom I had not met before. In the earlier days of recording, the records themselves were the old "78s" and quite heavy. A Brahms Symphony, for instance, would take five or six records in an album which in itself was quite heavy to carry, and a cupboard housing, say, three or four volumes of different works would have a very heavy weight to bear.

This particular guest to whom I was talking was obviously a distinguished scientist whose name escapes me (he was knighted) and worked at an Institute between Chelsea Bridge and Victoria Station. I can't recall how the particular conversation arose but I know that there was one recording I particularly wanted to trace, and, if possible possess. "What work is that?" this gentleman asked me. "Walton's *Belshazzar's Feast* recorded by the Huddersfield Choral Society conducted by Malcolm Sargent." I could hardly believe his reply. "I've got it in my car, " he said! He could tell I was almost unbelieving and added: "If you don't believe me I'll go and get it," which he did and it *was* the exact recording I had been looking for. I then asked him if he had all his recordings in the back of his car and he answered: "No, just this one which you mentioned. I was going to give it to my daughter. We were having a bit of a clear-out at home!"

13. MUSIC CAMPS AND SUMMER SCHOOLS

In the 1920s, when my brother was at Cambridge, he met up with three other excellent string players with similar interests in music making and they formed themselves into an ensemble which was named the Cambridge String Quartet. This was led by Alan Richards, a fine player who could easily have become a professional but, like my brother, had chosen to become a doctor. He came from a remarkable family who lived in the Croydon area and could boast a string sextet in the family, for his mother played the fiddle and his brother and three sisters all became professional string players.

The Cambridge Quartet had an interesting time while they were at University and their trips included a visit to the United States where they gave a number of recitals in 1924 and they also played, by invitation, to Thomas Hardy at his home near Dorchester. Neither of these events seem to have been recorded anywhere which I find surprising.

During his time at Cambridge the viola player, Bernard Robinson, formed an annual gathering of amateur musicians, in late July - of both instrumentalists and singers - for a Music Camp, held in various venues over a couple of weeks. It never had any other title and has remained, almost anonymous, even to this day. It is quite amazing how it attracted people, far and wide, among them very well known names such as Archie Camden, the famous bassoonist, and in later years Norman del Mar and Colin Davis. It was a great place for making lasting friendships and also learning fine music. I remember playing in Sibelius' *Fifth Symphony* for the first time - and could not get it out of my head for some weeks afterwards!

The Music Camps were started in a large field in a Hertfordshire village called Furneaux Pelham and most of us were accommodated in tents with some of the more elderly or squeamish in a nearby barn. There were at least two "official" cooks in charge and many helpers. The whole concern was always very well organised and the Music Camps had a deservedly high reputation and should have had support and recognition from the highest in the musical world. It should take its place as a unique institution in the history of music making in this country. I always thought it odd that they never seemed to wish for any other name than, "Music Camp"!

The venue of the first Camp changed after a few years. There was, I believe, another held at a different site in Hertfordshire, before it eventually moved to a completely new location in Berkshire, not far from Newbury. I only went to a few but eventually found professional engagements preventing me from devoting enough time to committing myself to the camps. I do remember visiting the Music Camp once before the fortnight began and found Bernard Robinson hard at work in his shirt sleeves and he said to me: "This must be the only known case where the conductor has dug his own orchestral pit!" (He was putting on Beethoven's only opera, *Fidelio*, that summer).

One year I was at a summer school held at the famous Berkshire Girls'

School near Newbury, Downe House, at which a number of later well-known musicians were educated, including Evelyn Rothwell (Lady Barbirolli). The "Music Camp" was not too far away and we challenged them to a cricket match which was accepted. For us it became an "away" game and took place in a far-from-suitable site which was no more than a field, recently occupied by some cattle. The weather closed in before the match finished and I remember a very "gallant" act on my part. We had reached the lower order of our "batsmen" when the next to go in was a girl. I felt quite sorry for her as the drizzle had become heavier and the field itself had a number of hazards, including several "cowpats", so I drove her up to the wicket in my elderly Austin 10! It would take some pretty horrendous conditions, an earthquake perhaps, to prevent a cricket match with a determined group of players - intent on going through with it!

Among those taking part, and thoroughly "with it", with some quite skilful bowling and a very good eye when he had the bat in his hands, was Bernard Robinson's partner in running the camp and conducting the orchestra and choir, a most delightful man who became another close friend. He was Edric Cundell who was to become Principal of the Guildhall School of Music in the City of London. He was a most accomplished musician who once played the cello in the Covent Garden orchestra and played Brahms' great *Piano Concerto No.2 in B flat* with consummate ease. And Edric had a great sense of humour. Some years before, the Daily Telegraph ran a competition for a new string quartet for which the 1st prize was £1000. Just for fun - you might say "a sense of devilment" - Edric Cundell decided to enter the competition. He wasn't a great believer or lover of "modern music" and did not really like what he had written. To his amazement he won the first prize!

When the war was over, amateur music making was at a low ebb and music schools and courses, not to mention youth orchestras, sprang up like mushrooms. Music lovers living, especially in Surrey in the Dorking area, were lucky in having Ralph Vaughan Williams who, though born in Down Ampney in Gloucestershire, had lived for many years at Leith Hill Place, very near Leith Hill itself and the home of the Wedgwood family, the famous makers of fine china, to whom Ralph Vaughan Williams was himself related.

"Uncle Ralph" was always keen on competitive festivals where local choirs spent the winter months learning specific works, most of them of the highest calibre and many quite difficult, the choirs being of varying size and experience, the only stipulation regarding eligibility was that the choir had to be situated within ten miles of Leith Hill Tower itself, the measuring point being the Dorking Halls. The Leith Hill Festival had long been established when the Second World War ended, as it had been at the end of the Great War, having, of course, been established in 1905 through the enterprise of Miss Vaughan Williams, sister of Ralph Vaughan Williams. He was by no means a figurehead and he conducted the concerts, which took place on the three evenings during the Festival, the orchestra consisting of professionals supplemented by good local amateurs, and continued over fifty years. During the winter months Vaughan Williams frequently visited village choirs, offering advice and encouragement. He often travelled to the choirs, on the darkest of nights, on his bicycle!

Well known musicians used to conduct a choir for a season with people like Gordon Jacob, Boyd Neel and Robin Milford, the latter being a composer who wrote very attractive music. He was tragically killed on a main road near Newbury, where he lived. He had a daughter with a lovely soprano voice.

Ralph Vaughan Williams fought in the Great War, in the Army, and was one of the few who survived, thank God. During the second war he could often be seen driving a horse and cart around Dorking collecting metal, like pieces of railings which could be used in the war effort, such a desperate situation had the country reached.

Some of the performances from the Leith Hill Festival became of national importance and the B.B.C. broadcast one of his very individual annual performances of Bach's great *St. Matthew's Passion*. One of the instruments he couldn't abide was the harpsichord which is often used as "continuo", and where sometimes two "oboe d'amore" were indicated he would use two violas. He was not, however, averse to using the piano, which was played by the ever reliable (and local) Eric Guritton.

It was not only for the Leith Hill Festival for which Surrey folk felt gratitude to Ralph Vaughan Williams and his personal encouragement. He, in conjunction with Norman Askew the Surrey Music Adviser, started the Surrey County Music Association (S.C.M.A.) which began in a small way in 1945 with keen young instrumentalists who met together for a week or fortnight at the end of the summer term to form what became the Summer School. The venues varied from schools in the Godalming area of Surrey to a school on the other side of the county, St. Michael's, Limpsfield. These late summer events, when most schools were largely inactive, must have been a welcome source of income when the school can be let to such worthy and reputable organisations. Although in the early days of the S.C.M.A. those who attended the Summer Schools tended to be young school children, it was not long before the overall age grew considerably. In fact a minimum age was established and today, over fifty years later, a typical English institution is here to stay and is as popular as ever, with people booking from year to year.

After a somewhat spasmodic existence, with the school rarely held in the same venue twice running, a more permanent home was found for it at Gipsy Hill College, Kingston Hill, the road running down to the end of Kingston by-pass and the entrance to Richmond Park. This was an ideal location with plenty of rooms, a good size hall for full orchestra and a smaller hall for string quartets and lots of practice rooms. A great asset, which they still don't have these days, was a rectangular dining room with one large table from which, at any meal, announcements can be made which everyone can hear. Nowadays, with more people attending the course at Charterhouse, there is one sitting for each meal which means using the dining hall which is shaped like a huge horseshoe, surrounding the kitchens. Any special announcement would have to be given out three times for everyone to hear it.

At both Gipsy Hill which was financed by Surrey County Council and Charterhouse the sleeping accommodation is excellent with single rooms only at Kingston and a number of double rooms at the latter. One big difference between "then and now" is that the original plan was to hold the Summer School for a fortnight, the first week being exclusively for instrumentalists and the second for singers. I did hear, that in the early days - before I became involved - they tried having singers and players under the same roof in one week and it was as near a disaster as it could be. In fact it nearly resulted in open warfare! I've never heard of feuding of this nature between similar groups. I know there has always been a standing joke between the two "sides" with references to "singers and musicians" but nothing worse than that. What a pity that there was a divergence of attitude as there could have been golden opportunities for performing great choral and orchestral works together. Nowadays the final evening concert is the climax of the week's work. The standard is high as there is a staff of established soloists and teachers who undertake the coaching of the singers during the week. The same goes for the wind and string players and there is a resident string quartet who not only coach but give evening recitals during the week.

It is all very friendly and happy and definitely comes under the category of "a good thing". There have been of course, like everything else, many changes since the S.C.M.A. started. The main thing must be the cost of attending a music course. Nowadays I suppose it might be invidious to talk of finance, especially with anyone who comes these days and has to pay the full amount, but it is almost unbelievable that when I first became involved, the charge for residents for one week was about fourteen guineas and for non-residents, five pounds! Nowadays the total cost is several hundred pounds per head (double for a married couple). Inflation is, I often feel, used as a good excuse for many rising costs but I should love to challenge someone one day to give "chapter and verse" to justify some of the huge rises we have to suffer and see the number of red faces and hear some of the excuses!

The other main difference is that the Summer School occupies just one week, usually in the Chapel, with everyone - or nearly everyone - coming together on the last night for the performance of the main choral work after which a Cabaret, containing a surprising variety of talent, "ends the entertainment".

But it might have all been so different. Gipsy Hill College belonged to Surrey County Council and a committee of six or seven members were responsible for the grant we received from the Council annually. The modest fees we asked from students, it seemed, was not enough to meet the cost of running the Summer School and there came a time when they were running out of funds and the "School" might have to close its activities. Apparently the main cause of the crisis was when the individual members of the committee discovered they would each have to pay something like forty pounds out of their pockets if the impending crisis suddenly faced them and it looked as if the Summer School was finally at an end.

81

However, all was not lost. Charterhouse School, high up above the Surrey town of Godalming, with its own extensive grounds with fine views, also ran holiday courses and had a cancellation and had heard of our plight and offered us the chance to take over the very week that the Surrey Music Association, having apparently done everything it could to survive, and decided it would have to fold. They accepted this offer with gratitude and relief and, of course, to the joy of everyone concerned.

Since then things have never looked back. As a forum for forming friendships, making music - including perhaps less familiar but thoroughly worthwhile works - of a high standard with the excellent coaching of a professional musical staff of considerable experience - all with a holiday atmosphere and in a delightful setting, where the food is as good as any first class hotel, it is highly recommended. Although Charterhouse can offer in its own grounds, among other things in the matter of recreation, an open air swimming pool, tennis courts and golf, there is usually little time for such relaxation!

Charterhouse are now well past their 21st anniversary and, with the S.C.M.A., the Combined Summer Schools have now been in existence for well over 50 years. The title was adopted after a few years and is now known officially as "Charterhouse Summer School of Music". How proud Ralph Vaughan Williams would be to know that his inspiration of 1945 had progressed and grown into such a healthy and permanent organisation. A great deal of the credit for its inception must always go to this famous Old Carthusian! Students are now coming from all over the world for the week's music course.

14. ARTS COUNCIL AND C.E.M.A.

I doubt whether anyone has the first idea of how the "Arts Council of Great Britain" evolved. I am probably the only person alive - a phenomenon which often seems to happen when one has passed what is called "one's allotted span"! - who knows quite a lot about this subject. In the early days of the war, with the object of encouraging music-making, especially where there was little or none, an organisation was formed called the "Council for Encouraging Music and the Arts", or "C.E.M.A." for short. I was invited to join a small committee making up four in all, the other three being Dr. Reginald Jacques - Conductor of the Bach Choir and a life-long friend (who never quite got over the horrors of the Great War in which he was shot through both knees while being rescued after being wounded), Ivor Brown who worked for the Manchester Guardian, and a very distinguished lady named Mary Glasgow, who lived near High Street Kensington and died not so many years ago. The four of us worked in a small office, very near Charing Cross Station with Jacques as Chairman. My job was to get in touch with well-known musicians and invite them to give recitals etc. at various venues. I can remember ringing the well-known baritone, Roy Henderson - who is still alive and I believe nearly 100 - and asking him if he could go to Bournemouth to give a recital. Fee? £5! (He more or less told me what I could do with it!) As I was still playing in the Jacques Orchestra, some of our concerts were sponsored by C.E.M.A. and I always recall our giving one at the Leys School, just outside Cambridge. C.E.M.A. lasted a few years, and it did a good and much-needed job providing first rate music where it was really appreciated. There was another organisation formed during the war which provided a more popular brand of light entertainment, particularly for troops in camps etc. stationed around the country. This was called E.N.S.A.

 C.E.M.A.'s work was eventually recognised as something of considerable importance, requiring national support and expansion and it was not long before it became "The Arts Council of Great Britain" and the "rest" - as they say - "is history". Everyone knows of this colossal and multi-million pound organisation and not only of great importance in the Nation but of world-wide reputation. But it is fun to look back, with some feeling of pride and satisfaction, and to know that I was in "at the birth" - so to speak - of this enormous enterprise which had such modest beginnings. I think it is most important that these things are remembered and recorded for posterity. The average person might naturally presume that the Arts Council had always been there and just take it for granted. They would be surprised to know how it all started!

1. Fritz Kreisler at Winter Gardens, Eastbourne in 1930s.

2. George Bernard Shaw, a keen L.S.O. supporter, at Three Choirs Festival, Worcester 1935.

3. Beecham at the re-interment of Delius at Limpsfield - 1935.

4. *Léon Goossens with Boyd Neel rehearsing before Salzburg trip.*

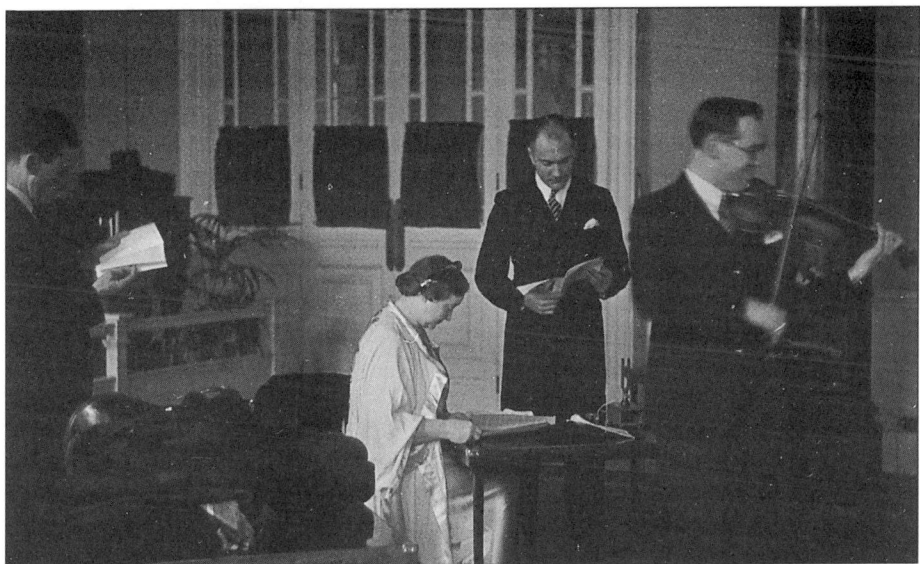

5. *Boyd Neel, Isobel Baillie and Frederick Grinke waiting to go on - Cheltenham.*

6. *In the car at Zell am Zee - 1937 (left to right) Mrs Armstrong, Mrs Nicholson senior, Fred Grinke and Mr Nicholson senior.*

7. *Poster for Boyd Neel Salzburg concert.*

8. *Boyd Neel on the boat to Portugal - 1937.*

9. *The author as Sir Adrian with Fred Grinke on the boat returning from Portugal.*

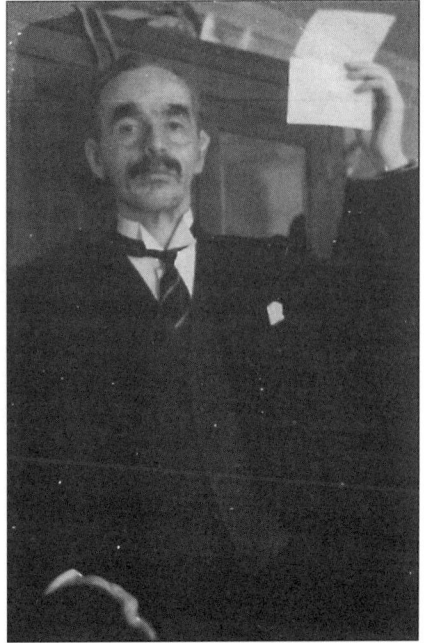

10. *The author as Chamberlain with 'the piece of paper'.*

11. *The author as Beecham at Hoffnung Festival Concert at the Royal Festival Hall - 1957.*

*12. Group in Elgar's garden at Broadheath in 1938 (from left) Hon. Clare Wortley, W.H. Reed,
Lady Hamilton-Harty, Troyte Griffiths, Mrs Blake (Elgar's daughter), Mrs Reed,
Mr Blake and Mrs Steward Powell (Dorabella).*

13. Dorabella and Troyte in Elgar's garden - 1938.

ROYAL ALBERT HALL

(Manager : C. S. Taylor)

PROMENADE CONCERTS

Forty-eighth Season

1942

Conductor

SIR HENRY WOOD

Associate Conductors

BASIL CAMERON
SIR ADRIAN BOULT

THE BRITISH BROADCASTING CORPORATION

PROSPECTUS PRICE TWOPENCE

(By post Threepence)

14. *Programme for 1942 Proms.*

89

15. W.H. Reed and G.B. Shaw at Worcester - 1938.

16. Ralph and Ursula Vaughan Williams at Hereford.

17. Group at Hereford Three Choirs in 50s, including Vaughan Williams, Herbert Howells and Leslie Woodgate

18. *Dr Gordon Jacob in court dress before travelling to Westminster Abbey to conduct his orchestration of Zadock the Priest at the coronation of Queen Elizabeth II - 1953.*

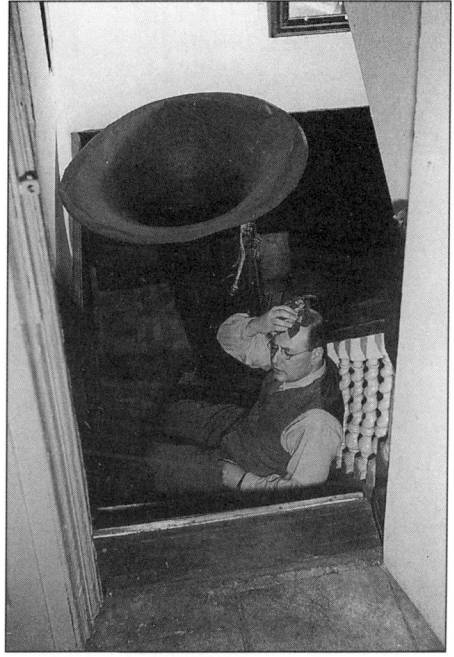

19. *Hoffnung with tuba having a rest on the stairs.*

20. *Hoffnung with two members of the L.S.O.*

21. *Sir Arthur Bliss (centre) with the Leader of the L.S.O., Hugh Maguire (left) and the Chairman, Harry Dugarde (right) on the steps of the Cloth Hall, Ypres - 1958.*

22. Before lunch at Epsom Golf Course - (left) Lady Falkner, (2nd from right) Sir Keith Falkner - Director of the R.C.M., (centre) Sir Anthony Lewis - Principal of R.A.M. with Lady Lewis.

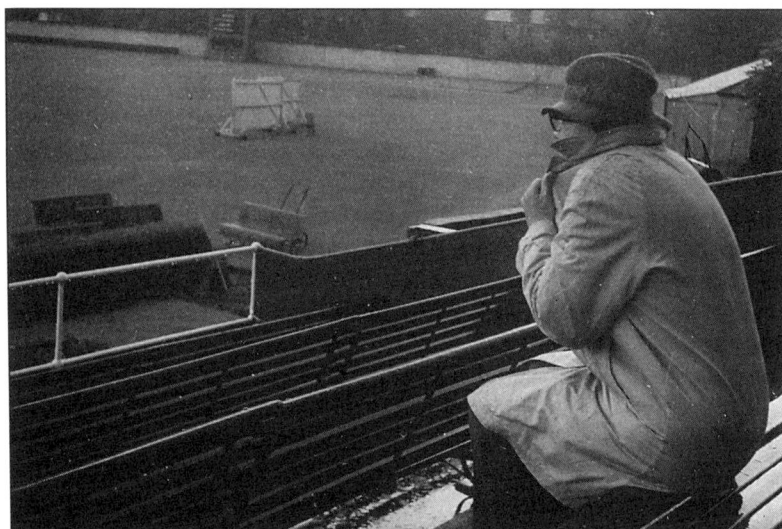

23. Lone spectator (Harry Lester - continuo) at L.S.O. Cricket, Edinburgh - 1962.

24. Pierre Monteux and his wife outside Bath Abbey - 1962.

25. Barnes Wallis (right) and his wife (centre) with the author's wife Gill (left) at a Bookham Choir Dinner.

26. *Dorothy Owen (centre), co-founder of the Guildford Symphony Orchestra, with members of the Orchestra on the occasion of her 100th birthday - 24th October 1989.*

27. *The author with his elder daughter Diana (right) and two members of the Croydon Youth Orchestra.*

GSO

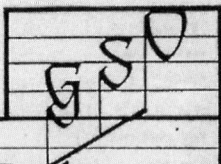

Guildford Symphony Orchestra

Bernstein – Cimarosa
Tchaikovsky – Vaughan Williams
Nicholson – Delius – Chabrier

Conductor: RALPH NICHOLSON
(retiring after 30 years with the GSO)

CIVIC HALL, GUILDFORD
Saturday, 21st April, 1990
at 7.30 p.m.

sponsored by

Gerry Lytle Associates

Architects ⧄ Guildford

in aid of St John Ambulance, Guildford Divisions

Programme 50p

28. Programme for the author's last concert with the Guildford Symphony Orchestra.

CROYDON
YOUTH ORCHESTRA

President: JOHN ODOM, Mus.B.

(*Founder:* Marjorie Gill)

Joint Leaders: Alan Tooke
Derek Booth

30th Anniversary Concert
by
Past and Present Menbers

Conductor;
RALPH NICHOLSON

Guest Conductors:
RONALD BINGE
RONALD GILLHAM
GUY WOOLFENDEN

Soloists:
LESLEY WILSON — Contra Bassoon
ALAN TRAVERSE — Violin
RICHARD ELLIOTT — Trumpet

TRINITY SCHOOL
Shirley Park, Croydon
(by kind permission of the Headmaster)

Saturday, July 12th, 1975
at
7.30 p.m.

29. Programme for Croydon Youth Orchestra 30th Anniversary Concert.

96

15. ON CHOIRS AND PLACES WHERE THEY SING

There is quite a difference in approach when it comes to conducting amateurs. A good singing voice in training a choir is an asset but is not essential. One cannot recall many well-known conductors of the past who were also outstanding singers. I can think of two - Malcolm Sargent, conductor of the Royal Choral Society, and Reginald Jacques, conductor of the Bach Choir. Sargent had a slightly quavering voice with a fast unattractive vibrato while Jacques had a very pleasant and quite attractive singing voice. As for Beecham, he produced the most extraordinary sounds, especially in intense passages when he got quite worked up as he approached a climax. I believe Toscanini, while conducting an orchestra, would sing most of the time but usually far from in tune!

I have never thought it necessary for a choral conductor to mouth the words all the time. Who gains, say, in a complicated 4-part passage, with everyone singing different things. Sargent never did and sensibly relied on each singer to learn his own part properly. Whoever saw an orchestral conductor trying to sing the first violin part!

When conducting a choir, it is useful to possess two assets - a sense of pitch - the more easily to point out wrong notes - and a sense of humour. The occasional short story or anecdote does not come amiss. Choir members have only their vocal scores to interest them whereas although not having the advantage of his vocal colleagues of having all the other parts of the choir printed in front of them, the orchestral player only has a single line, which just concerns him, but he may have other problems and complications because of his particular instrument. It is up to the conductor to draw the best from him. It is not necessary for him to be a player himself but he needs to have a working knowledge of the instruments confronting him. If he does happen also to be a player, so much the better.

It is rare for a conductor - especially in these days of competition and displays of intensity and, sometimes, over-commitment - to have a sense of humour, but what a difference it makes. It can often affect a performance in a positive way. One almost inevitably thinks of Beecham, where every rehearsal was an event. I am probably lucky in that I grew up in less urgent and intense days and one could name quite a number of people who could qualify for the accolade of "A Bringer of Jollity!" - with no lessening of standards.

I was involved in both forms of music making - vocal and orchestral. For five years I conducted a choir at Brighton with rather an elaborate and non-informative title: "Brighton and Hove Harmonic Society." They kept going nearly 150 years. Before I left them I suggested inserting "Choral" somewhere - to show what they did and I think they eventually adopted this idea before they closed their shutters. I don't think it helped that there was a professional choir in the Borough.

Again I made quite a few friends while I was there. At Christmas time we gave a Carol Concert in the Dome and we invited well-known personalities to compère the concerts for which we had an excellent orchestra. Although Richard Baker was unable to make it we did have - among others - Alan Melville and Roy Plomley. The latter, Roy, ended the evening by introducing a touch of "Desert Island Discs" into the proceedings. He asked me: "What music would you like to have with you, Ralph?" to which I said: "A recording of the Amen Chorus from The Messiah." "Sung by whom?" he asked me. "The Brighton and Hove Harmonic Society." This, of course, went down very well! Afterwards my wife and I, Roy and his wife and a member of the orchestra had a rollicking time in a local pub near the Hall.

During my final year at Brighton we gave a performance of a new work by Donald Swann called "Requiem for the Living" in which there is a prominent part for solo piano. The composer was due to play the piano part - he was, of course, the other half of the famous "Flanders and Swann" duo, but unfortunately he was taken ill and could not make it. A piano professor from the R.C.M., John Barson, took his place with his usual skill and efficiency.

Another choir I conducted was the Bookham Choral Society, Bookham being a village not far from where I lived near Dorking, and the choir was one of those formed as a result of Vaughan Williams' great musical presence in Surrey, and the Leith Hill Festival. The Festival itself was formed in 1905 and Vaughan Williams conducted at it for over 50 years. The choirs themselves practised in the winter months and came together in the spring to compete against each other, and then combine in the evening for a concert with a full symphony orchestra of basically amateur players. Only recently has a professional orchestra taken part. I have mentioned other details of Ralph Vaughan Williams and the Festival elsewhere, but I must just mention at this point that during the winter months, R.V.W. used to visit the village choirs personally to encourage them during their practices, usually travelling by bicycle. He used to recall, with some pleasure, certain stories. One was the occasion when transporting heavy instruments, like double basses, could be a problem, and there were no instruments for the players at the rehearsal for a concert of the Leith Hill Festival. A telegram arrived one afternoon saying: "The two double beds are being despatched by train." The other one of Vaughan Williams' stories concerned a story of someone receiving a present of cherry brandy and the recipient saying: "I'm not too keen on cherries but very much appreciate the spirit in which they were sent!"

My own connection with the Festival must have covered nearly 60 years, for I was not only one of the choral conductors but played for a number of years in the orchestra, usually in the viola section, but also percussion. Quite a number of well-known musicians have conducted one of the choirs over the years. They include Gordon Jacob, Boyd Neel, Robin Milford and Robin Gritton.

My connection with the Bookham choir went back 27 years. We had one famous member of the choir for a while, and my first encounter with him occurred in quite an amusing way. I had arrived at the village hall as usual, on a Tuesday evening, and as I opened the door there was quite a hubbub just inside among a group of men who were in some state of excitement. I was greeted with the news that we had a new tenor that evening. "Do you know who it is?" they asked me. "I've no idea," I replied. "It's Barnes Wallis," they said with some glee. "Oh yes," I said, "Is hc first or second tenor?" (I wasn't going to allow myself to be *too* impressed!) Actually, at the time he wasn't all that well-known as the inventor of the "bouncing bomb" during the war. He had not received his knighthood by then. The Wallis family were loyal supporters of Bookham (they lived about two miles away) with Mrs. Wallis one of the sopranos, a son who sang bass and Elizabeth contralto. After *she* was married I always referred to her as the late Miss Wallis! After her father was knighted Mrs. Wallis had already become Chairman of the Choir, and at the first rehearsal after the Queen's honour, I referred to her as Lady Wallis. She snapped back, "I'm not Lady Wallis," to which I asked, "Who are you then?" and she replied: "The late Mrs. Wallis!"

During my time at Bookham I formed the Surrey Festival Choir when choral societies from all over the county came together once a year to perform one of the great choral works in Guildford Cathedral. It was a thrill - and a privilege - to conduct these works, from Handel's *Messiah* to Berlioz' *Childhood of Christ* and many others. I did Ralph Vaughan Williams' great *Sea Symphony* twice and inevitably Bach's *B minor Mass* and Mendelssohn's *Elijah*.

I had a lovely "send off", a few years ago now, after about 19 years, with a party at the Cathedral, chaired by the mayor of Guildford. I treasure a book I was presented with containing names and appropriate comments from many people from various choirs who had sung for me. My final performance, by the way, was of another exciting, popular and suitable work - which I had conducted before - Verdi's *Requiem*.

The orchestra for these annual Surrey Festival Choir performances was always the Guildford Symphony Orchestra - which, at the time, I liked to call *my* orchestra - and rightly so, since I held the post for 30 years. I retired in 1990 having celebrated the G.S.O.'s 70th anniversary with a special concert. I was only the second conductor they had had at that time!

At the same time I was also conductor, for about ten years, of another amateur Surrey orchestra - one of the five Dr.W.H.Reed used to conduct before the war - which was called the Redhill Society of Instrumentalists. There was a well-to-do maiden lady, who was also a great benefactress who was concerned with the founding of the Orchestra - Phyllis Vigers - and played sub-principal herself. She gave the impression of being a bit fierce and difficult to please, but she was nothing of the sort - she was most kind and generous but she expected people to be like her - loyal and dedicated to the cause of the Orchestra. She ended her days living in a delightful house right on top of Reigate Hill, with its superior views to the South.

I was quite sorry to leave the Redhill Society but I had to choose between continuing with them or taking over a Brighton Choir which rehearsed on the same evening and I chose the latter. A few years ago I went to Redhill to hear a concert as part of the celebration of their 90th anniversary. I was extremely impressed by the high standard they had achieved and the enterprising programme. After the Overture, they performed the Mozart *Clarinet Concerto* with Jack Brymer as the usual worthy soloist and, after the interval, a most admirable performance of Holst's *Planets* suite. I don't think there was any instrument missing - not even a bass oboe! - and of course there was an off-stage unaccompanied ladies choir. Who was it who said that England was a land without music?

I am glad to hear that Redhill now has a modern, suitably equipped concert hall among many other improvements in the town. In my day we gave concerts in the old market hall, a very unfriendly and unattractive building, with its cold stone staircase leading up to the first floor. It was in the same road and not very far from Redhill railway station. There was an occasion when a late traveller dashed up the uninviting staircase, passing members of the orchestra, who were assembling to take part in a symphony concert and called out to one of them, "Can you direct me to the platform for Brighton?"

16. RALPH VAUGHAN WILLIAMS

"Uncle Ralph", by which he was affectionately known to people (particularly at Dorking), comes under so many categories - composer, conductor, friend et. al. - that he really deserves a chapter to himself. He was a big man in every sense of the word. He, of course, was one of the greatest British composers of this century. If I were to be asked to put the three top ones, in my order of preference, I should name Ralph Vaughan Williams, Delius, and Elgar - with not much to choose between the first two. In fact they differ so completely that it is hardly fair to compare them. I derive almost as much pleasure listening to either, whereas with Elgar, while recognising the greatness of some of his large scale works, I must admit I do find some of his lesser works don't bear too much repetition, and some of it is definitely "dated".

I had more opportunity of getting to know Uncle Ralph well, mainly - initially - through environment, that is to say, we both lived in Surrey and my home was first at Sutton and then at Esher. So I rather naturally became involved in the Leith Hill Festival at Dorking every year. And when we eventually moved to Capel, I was even nearer - a mere 5 miles. R.V.W., whose sister started the Festival in the early part of this century, lived in Dorking for 20 years. I once asked him why he eventually moved to London. His immediate reply was that there was a greater choice of cinemas in Town!

Although born at Down Ampney in Gloucestershire, it was not long before he came to live at Leith Hill Place - high up on the Surrey hills, and the home of the Wedgwood family, of china fame, to whom he was related. To qualify to take part every choir had to be not more than 10 miles from Leith Hill tower! One of the choirs which I conducted for well over 20 years - Bookham - which must have sung under R.V.W. for many Festivals, I took to Down Ampney Church to give a memorial concert of his music, which included his *Benedicite*. The soprano soloist was Marion Milford, daughter of the composer, Robin Milford. We had a small orchestra of friends from the Guildford Symphony Orchestra, and we played in the Parish Church.

Some years before this event - in fact, very soon after the end of the War, there was another concert in the West Country of a very different nature but again involving V.W. It was a celebration of the music of Gloucestershire composers, and besides V.W. were Herbert Howells and one or two others. We were a small group of string players from the L.S.O., conducted by Muir Mathieson, who was in the same conducting class as I was at the College. We were actually the guests of a well-known film producer who happened to be the Lord of the Manor - his name was something like Lord Courtney - who lived in a splendid country house on the fringe of the village of Bourton-on-the-Water. He did not actually put us up for the night, but he did invite us to a most sumptuous meal. Few people in this Country had enjoyed a square meal for more than six years, and rationing continued for a number of years after the end of hostilities, especially of such commodities as potatoes and bread, so that what confronted us as we entered our host's super dining room was indeed "a sight for sore eyes".

It must have been an afternoon concert as so many other things happened later in the evening, no-one enjoying it all more than V.W. himself. The repast which was set before us was unbelievable, especially with so much rationing elsewhere. Among many choices was not just one helping from a joint, but as much as you liked, not only from, say, cold chicken but also turkey, with unlimited salad, followed by plenty of sweets and, of course, wine. With so many restrictions on food at the time, we wondered how our host "got away with it". You would think he wasn't aware there had been a war, and had always lived in such conditions of luxury. I doubt that he could have done, but there was no "show" at all, and everything seemed perfectly natural and we obviously enjoyed the occasion to the full.

Bourton is a charming village and was obviously a tourist attraction, with a little stream running down the side of the main road. After our meal we were entertained by the showing - in some room or small hall or other - of a very funny, privately produced film with a priceless commentary by Alvar Liddell, the well-known and immaculate announcer, frequently to be heard "on the wireless". I found him a real charmer with a keen sense of humour. We became very firm friends. Ralph joined in all the fun to the full. I made one very unfortunate choice regarding a drink - I forget what I started with, either wine or beer - but I was then persuaded to try the driest of dry cider, possibly scrumpy, though I think it was called something else. I soon regretted it!

We spent the night - my wife and I - in a little cottage in which the bed was hardly compatible with sleep. On examining more closely the amenities, we discovered the "mattress" consisted of bales from the corn-fields tightly held together in solid blocks with rope! In the morning we had a look at one of the village's main attractions - a model village. The whole occasion was one of different surprises, and generally speaking it was very enjoyable. One could anyway say it was "different".

To return to more serious business, I enjoyed playing in the orchestra at the Leith Hill Festivals as I played viola for R.V.W., which meant sitting almost literally facing him and nearly under his conducting stand, and heard all his comments, both public and other more intimate ones. He occasionally got really cross, especially if the choir were slow on the up-take and did not respond quickly enough to his requests, but he would regret almost immediately having shown his displeasure. The principal viola in the Orchestra was Jean Stewart, a fine player for whom Uncle Ralph had a great respect. He once composed a string sextet and dedicated it to her. At one rehearsal at Dorking, Jean was missing from her place in the Orchestra. She had recently given birth to one of her children. R.V.W. enquired: "Where's Jean?", receiving the reply "In the Martineau Hall" (the smaller hall of the Dorking Halls) "feeding the baby", to which he angrily responded by saying: "Tell her her place is in this hall, rehearsing with me. We can't turn the place into a creche!" At one particular Prom at the Royal Albert Hall, V.W. conducted one of his later Symphonies himself and elicited a fine performance from the L.S.O., and naturally, with the great man "at the helm", there was extra interest and enthusiasm, especially from the young "Prommers" who gave him a tremendous reception. At the end, after he had gone through every permutation - from getting the Orchestra to its feet to shaking hands with the leader, George Stratton, he leant down and said something to him. In the bar, in the interval, we asked George whether the old man said how pleased he was with the performance. George said: "Oh, nothing like that. He just said - Why do they keep calling me back? Are my fly buttons undone or something?"

I happened to see V.W. one day after I had been playing in the *Sea Symphony* at the Royal Albert Hall with the Royal Choral Society under Sargent. I couldn't resist mentioning to him something which occurred - or rather didn't occur - when Sargent had conducted the *Sea Symphony* the previous evening, and quite incredibly, omitted the Scherzo movement - "After the sea's ships" etc. I never discovered why - lack of rehearsal or what? I couldn't imagine Sargent doing that or even having a dislike of the movement. V.W.'s only comment - "Interfering fellow!"

V.W. once made a rather nice remark when he said: "I never know how you chaps (i.e. other conductors) know exactly at what speed you're going to start a piece. I suppose it settles down after about ten bars!" Apart from there being books on his life and work, he often appeared in books of reference. I was at the R.C.M. one day, when I went upstairs to the Orchestral library to borrow some music. While I was waiting to be attended to I noticed a book on Vaughan Williams, on the counter, by Michael Kennedy (not the violinist!), and thumbing idly through the index at the back, I was surprised to see "Nicholson, R." What a coincidence, I thought modestly! (I did remember seeing in a London Telephone directory years before, the name of Ralph Nicholson. His trade was as a tailor in Albemarle Street, W.1. I wondered if I would have received any concessions if I ordered a suit from him. I rather think not - in the West End!)

This reference related to something I wrote in the R.C.M. Magazine. I had the honour of being invited to write an appreciation of the great man in company with four or five others, and I chose to recall a performance, which V.W. conducted at Dorking at one of the Festivals, of *On hearing the first cuckoo in Spring* by Delius, and I wrote that - as it was a lovely Spring day, R.V.W., by his own personality, produced the ideal sound, evocative of the prevailing weather.

Another reference to R.V.W. occurred in another book which some friend of mine was browsing through, and he too turned to the index and came across just three words - "a good mind". This intrigued him as he had always regarded him with great respect and wondered what had been written about his great mind. Turning to the relevant page, he read: "As Vaughan Williams was walking down Dorking High St. one morning, he turned to his wife, Ursula, and just said: "I've a good mind to go to London tomorrow!" When he had turned 70, the Leith Hill Festival was arranging to give him a birthday party. The hard-working secretary, Margery Cullen, who obeyed his commands to the letter - and woe betide anyone not toeing the line according to the way she thought right - asked Uncle Ralph what sort of music he would like on his birthday. He snapped back: "Music? I don't want any music! I want a conjuror!" - and a conjuror he had.

Many years before all this, when I don't think I had ever met Uncle Ralph, there was a performance of his incidental music to the *Wasps of Aristophanes*, performed in the grounds of Epsom College (where my brother was educated), and we all sat in deck chairs, with R.V.W. in the audience. The boys wore rugger jerseys which by good fortune were the colour of one House which happened to be yellow stripes on a black "background", and with artificial "stings" on their backs they darted about like wasps!

Another "character" and a man of many parts, one of whose tasks was to make a fair copy of R.V.W.'s Symphonies - was Roy Douglas. He was familiar with his idiom but there was just one bar of one of his newest works which he could not really decipher and he had to write to V.W. for clarification, saying something like: "8 bars after letter G in the 2nd movement - is it B flat or B natural?" The reply came back on a postcard - "Yes!" Roy was a delightful, friendly and unassuming man. Though he was a professional, he was not averse to playing tympani or percussion in his local amateur Tunbridge Wells Orchestra - unpaid, of course.

On the final night dinner at one of the Summer Schools, V.W. had been invited as a guest, and I sat next to him. He had been rehearsing that morning his quite new *6th Symphony* at the Royal College of Music with the L.S.O. in preparation for the Three Choirs Festival the following week, and there would be no further rehearsal before the concert since the three days of London rehearsals were devoted to any new, and other works for orchestra alone, so that the Conductor could spend most of the time in one of the three Cathedral Cities concentrating on the large scale choral or orchestral works. Whether that arrangement still pertains I know not, but that was how it occurred in my time. It was a typically English compromise, but seemed to work perfectly well. V.W.'s *6th Symphony* is possibly the most complicated of his eight, and probably quite difficult to conduct. Anyway, in the evening - the Summer School that year was held at a girl's school in a nice setting at Esher, called Claremont - V.W. said to me during dinner: "I'm a bit worried about my 'time' ", to which I said: "I don't think there's anything to worry about, Uncle Ralph. I thought it was going pretty well at the morning's rehearsal." But he still had his doubts, adding: "It's all right for you chaps. You've played it before, but I've never ever conducted it. There's one place where you're all apparently doing one thing while I seem to be conducting something quite else." Then as a final more optimistic rejoinder he added: "I think the best way is not to listen - don't you?"

One of V.W.'s greatest joys - and triumphs - was to conduct Bach's great *St Matthew Passion*. It was the final work he conducted in Dorking as part of the Leith Hill Festival. I remember it well as I was playing in the Orchestra. Not only that but the B.B.C. broadcast the performance on the Third Programme (now Radio 3). It was a deeply-felt performance, and though he might tell you he was an agnostic, there was no sign of this being true in his reading of this great work.

It was a very personal performance. He could not abide harpsichords and "continuo" parts were played on the piano by Eric Gritton, and he eschewed the oboe d'amore and replaced them with two violas. One thing he was absolutely adamant about was applause, which he forbade - either at the beginning or end. He even introduced a trumpet in the opening chorus - played by Bernard Brown. Bernard was a lovely trumpet player. He married a niece of V.W. when they lived in Chelsea. She was killed by a "doodle bug" while he was at Chelsea Barracks. Bernard, who was a super man, married again and had three sons. He was riding with his wife down a tarmac road one day when his horse suddenly took fright and galloped off, throwing Bernard to the ground, landing on his head - a great tragedy.

I well recall another performance in which I took part, at Redhill, not more than 5 miles from Dorking, which V.W. also conducted. He had given a directive, as before, with regard to applause. Twice this edict was not observed. There was no excuse for the audience to ignore this request since there were large printed notices on the walls of the hall saying "No Applause". As V.W. walked on at the start of the performance applause immediately broke out. If looks could kill, as the great man glowered at the audience, they would all be dead as he walked off again in a state of high dudgeon. After a few moments, he returned in silence - but only momentarily. Just as he raised his baton to begin, a large policeman standing at the back of the hall, in a stentorian voice, bellowed out: "Would the owner of the car XR 1987 kindly remove it as it is blocking the entrance to the 'all." V.W. gave up and got on with the music.

He was a most approachable man, and although you felt in the presence of "greatness" he never gave that impression himself and made you feel his equal, and talked to you as man to man. I hope all these facets of the great man show him to be a thoroughly normal and uncomplicated man who enjoyed the good things of life. He really relished the occasional holiday with Ursula in Greece where the warm waters of the Mediterranean strongly appealed to him. He did not receive a knighthood but probably a much higher honour from the Queen herself - the Companion of Honour (C.H.), of which there are only twenty-five at any one time.

To sum up, Ralph Vaughan Williams was not only a great figure - in both senses of the word - and a fine composer - he was also a most natural human being. Sometimes even self-effacing, he was friendly and modest. It was a pleasure to be in his presence and a privilege to have known him. He enjoyed the better things of life to the full, and he was not averse to asking one's opinion.

There were two activities in his life which must never be forgotten - in fact they may not be generally known. Vaughan Williams was, of course, an individual of international standing, known the world over, yet it was just as important to him to be thoroughly involved in what one might call "parochial matters". In the years between the wars, on cold dark evenings, he would cycle from one village to another criticising and encouraging village choirs as they had their weekly winter practises in the local halls in preparation for the Leith Hill Festival in the spring. I wonder how many professional conductors would go to such lengths - not for any personal gain but for the greater good of music.

During the Ist World War, V.W. joined the R.A.M.C., seeing active service in France. There were sometimes light-hearted references to his less than soldier-like puttees! In the next War, he was to be seen driving a horse and cart round Dorking collecting scrap metal such as railings etc. for the war effort - such was his patriotic desire to become involved.

17. GUILDFORD SYMPHONY ORCHESTRA

In about 1984, someone wrote the following short history of the Guildford Symphony Orchestra whose sub-title for many years was the Claud Powell Concerts Society:

The Guildford Symphony Orchestra was founded in 1919 by the late Claud Powell and by Miss Dorothy Owen, M.B.E. - now living in retirement in Dorking. It is now in its 66th year, having given symphony concerts without a break, in Guildford, and during the last war also at the Theatre Royal, Windsor and at St. Albans. During this time there have only been two conductors. Mr Claud Powell, O.B.E., conducted the GSO for their first 40 years until his death in 1959 and Ralph Nicholson has held this position for the past quarter of a century.

The founders pioneered the establishment of orchestral music in Guildford with dedication and enterprise. Much stress was laid on the importance of promoting British music, with many native composers represented in the Orchestra's programmes, so much so that in the "Morning Post" of some years ago, the GSO was called "the friend of the British composer".

The very first programme for October 8th 1919, stated that "the programmes will be seen to consist of good music only, both serious and light. Gloomy and depressing music is avoided . . . There are many Beautiful British works needing only repeated performances to give them a place in the affection of the public".

It is interesting to note, also in their first season, that "Mr Adrian C. Boult, the well-known London Conductor, who conducted the Royal Philharmonic Society's Concerts at Queen's Hall with distinction, has promised to assist at the last concert". (Sir Adrian later became a Director of the County School of Music at Guildford). "And Major (later Sir) George Dyson, Director of RAF Music, will conduct his own work at the second concert".

Many well-known conductors have been guests at the concerts, some conducting their own compositions. They include Sir Edward Elgar, Arthur Somervell, Dame Ethel Smyth, Dr. Gordon Jacob, Sir Charles Villiers Stanford, Sir Arthur Bliss, Sir Percy Hull, Dr. Ralph Vaughan Williams, Sir Charles Groves and many others.

Among singers the great tenor John Coates - who helped to make famous "The Dream of Gerontius" sang with the orchestra as well as George Baker and Dame Maggie Teyte.

Solo pianists have included Yvonne Arnaud, Adeline de Lara, and more recently Harry Isaacs, Phyllis Sellick and Cyril Smith, Howard Shelley and Hilary Macnamara, Bernard Roberts, Frank Wibaut, John Barstow and Philip Fowke.

Instrumentalists have included Leon Goossens (Oboe), Archie Camden (Bassoon), Gervase de Peyer (Clarinet), Alan Civil (Horn) and John Wilbraham (Trumpet).

Among string players, Alfredo Campoli gave memorable performances of the Mendelssohn violin concerto and Vaughan Williams' "The Lark Ascending" and last year Hugh Bean, one-time pupil of the great Albert Sammons, gave an exquisite performance of the Violin Concerto by Delius as part of the Orchestra's commemoration of the 50th anniversary of the composer's death. Shortly after the last war Dame Myra Hess honoured the Claud Powell Concert Society by giving a recital in Guildford.

The strings of the orchestra are mainly good local amateurs and the wind is augmented by well-known professionals. The GSO receives little in the way of grants and relies on good audiences.

Last year, for the first time, they received some sponsorship from Lloyds Bank which helped towards paying the fees of a number of young soloists, and a legacy from a one-time member of the viola section of the Orchestra - the late Judge Lionel Jellinek - brings in enough to pay the fee of a young soloist to perform with the Guildford Symphony Orchestra once a year.

The beginnings of the Orchestra are detailed in the foregoing which has fairly recently come to light and to which I have just added some embellishments.

In 1919, the Great War having ended, some sort of normality was beginning to emerge. Miss Dorothy Owen who had studied the piano at the Royal Academy of Music and was a good pianist - especially for accompanying young students - was friendly with Capt. Claud Powell who had served in the Army during the war, and the two of them decided to fill a gap in the musical life of Guildford by forming a Symphony Orchestra in the town. This they did and together they also started the County School of Music.

Dorothy originally lived in St.Albans, and it was there that she met and befriended Samuel Ryder who gave quite a lot of help towards the foundation of the

Guildford Symphony Orchestra. He was, of course, the founder of the famous Ryder Cup which takes his name.

A cutting from the "Morning Post" of November 22nd 1922 makes interesting reading:

"Guildford Music : The Mastersingers"

A typical and successful example of decentralisation in music is found in Guildford. There it is evident - and audible as well - that there is keen interest in music by all sections of the community. But the interest would be of little use were there no means of satisfying it save by occasional visits to Town. Guildford, therefore, is to be accounted happy inasmuch as it possesses the means of gratifying its musical inclinations. As the outcome of the enthusiasm of Captain Claud Powell who since the war has conducted in Guildford a persistent campaign directed to the development of the gifts and tastes of the inhabitants; there is plenty of good music for the inhabitants of the delightful and busy town. The subscription concerts which have been in being since 1919 have done much to help towards the making of good music.

This year's autumn season which has supplied orchestral and chamber concerts and a brand new Symphony, was brought to a close today with a programme consisting of a concert performance of the salient points of Wagner's "Maestersingers". The choice was happy, for the music-lover always deserves to be informed concerning this masterpiece of comic opera whose overture at least is as well-known in the concert room as in the theatre. . . . appreciation of the enterprise was shown today, and the County Hall was crowded in every part by a keenly interested audience.

Incidentally the town itself provides an excellent setting for the "Mastersingers" with its many old houses, not omitting the Abbott Hospital, dated 1619, and other buildings that go back to the early 16th century, though they are youthful affairs compared with the "Mastersingers of Nuremburg".

"Appreciative Listeners"

The strong force of Guildford music lovers present showed themselves to be perfect Wagnerites by their interest and comprehending attitude. They were well rewarded by an excellent representation of the . . . "

At this point the rest of the concert review was no-where to be found but it gives some idea of the sort of concert notice which was written about 75 years ago.

Claud Powell conducted the G.S.O. for its first 40 years. He died in 1960 at which point I took over. During my 30 years I had the pleasure of working with some of those on the top rungs of the musical fraternity, being honoured, as we all were, by the visits of distinguished musicians such as, for instance, the Master of the Queens Musick, Sir Arthur Bliss, who conducted his *Piano Concerto* with Frank Wibaut as soloist. That well known duo, Cyril Smith and Phyllis Sellick, played a concerto for 2 pianos but only 3 hands. It was the Concerto written specially for Cyril and Phyllis by Gordon Jacob after Cyril had suffered a stroke which left him with one sound hand, but it did not prevent him from continuing to perform in public, with a number of works being rearranged by expert orchestrators from four hands to three. He was fortunate to be spared for quite a number of years more in the musical profession.

Another musician of distinction to visit was Sir Percy Hull, for many years Organist and Choirmaster of Hereford Cathedral. His wife, Lady Hull, played viola in the G.S.O. in my early days. I shall always remember how my wife Gill and others helped to get his white waistcoat to do up at the back. It had been several years since he had worn full evening dress. No-one ever likes to admit to putting on weight but Sir Percy could not get away with it! He came to conduct *Pomp and Circumstance March No. 5.* Elgar had written it specially for him at a Three Choirs Festival when it fell upon Hereford to act as host. In connection with this, on September 2nd 1930 Elgar wrote the following letter to Sir Percy, of which he gave me a copy:

> My dear Percy,
> There was a little thing which I hate mentioning to you now. I meant to ask you last week whether you would allow me to dedicate the new "Pomp and Circumstance" to you. I meant to ask you, if you accepted the dedication, how you would like it worded. But I had to send the proofs back without consulting you, so I have put,
> "To my friend Dr. Percy C. Hull, Hereford."
> Will that do?
> With love,
> Yours ever,
> Edward Elgar.

Two distinguished wind players did me the honour of playing concertos I had composed for them - Archie Camden, the bassoon player supreme and Léon Goossens who seemed to like my Oboe Concerto for he played it three times at Guildford, and in all, seven or eight times. The third and last time he played it at Guildford was after his dreadful car accident in London when another car drove at him head-on and his steering wheel cut him right across his face, almost like a razor. Most people would have predicted the end of Léon's career, at least as a player, but

110

not Léon whose spirit helped him to make a remarkable recovery. He had a very skilled Indian surgeon who did a fantastic job in getting his mouth back to as near round as possible. This, initially, meant stitching almost from ear to ear, right across the front of his mouth. He then had to teach himself how to play again, playing with the reed "off centre" until he found he could overcome this horrid temporary disability and through his great skill and determination, was able to play again. From then on I always felt every performance was a "challenge" for him.

On his third appearance at Guildford, he played two concertos, first mine, which was not, perhaps quite up to the refinement of previous performances (including a BBC broadcast, not long after I wrote it in about 1960). But the other concerto on that occasion was a much greater test, the one by Strauss. I remember Léon saying *sotto voce* to me while still on the platform, "I was absolutely terrified for the first fourteen bars that I wouldn't get through". But, of course, he did and showed again, with skill and determination what can be achieved by will-power and genius. The Strauss concerto starts from the very beginning with the solo oboe playing for the first fourteen bars without a rest, with hardly time to breathe.

I always enjoyed what the Surrey Advertiser critic said in his review of the concert: "I felt that the applause for Mr Nicholson's concerto was rather greater than that for the Strauss" - adding, rather delightfully - "but I don't think Strauss would have minded". I wrote a small 'encore' piece for Gervase de Peyer which he played at the County Hall where he was soloist, and another friend of mine did me the honour of playing a work I wrote for him. He is the bassoonist, Val Kennedy, whom the L.P.O. retained as their principal contra-bassoonist until he was 75. That, I thought, with so much redundancy everywhere, was worthy of high praise in my profession. The piece was an *Impromptu* for Contra-Bassoon and Orchestra. It reached the notice of the only known woman soloist on the 'contra' in the U.S.A. She lives in Chicago, and "at the last count" has played my piece fifteen times. So far I have not received a penny in royalties, but it is nice to get it performed. Her name is Susan Nigro. She really is a fabulous player.

Campoli, the violinist, came down to Guildford and played two works with us, first the Mendelssohn, the second being R.V.W's *The Lark Ascending*. At one point he played a short passage 'col legno', i.e. as near the bridge as possible. I had never heard this effect before in this particular work and was rather taken by surprise. But, after a while, I came round to thinking it was quite effective.

Sir Arthur Bliss's beat was always clear and expressive, and his intentions positive, resulting in thoroughly enjoyable performances. Another guest who came down to hear one of his works was Sir Lennox Berkeley. We played his *4th Symphony* - a difficult and challenging work, well worth the effort to bring it off satisfactorily. One of my great pleasures towards the end of my stint with the G.S.O. was when that delightful violinist, Hugh Bean, played the lovely Delius *Violin Concerto* with us. Just before the rehearsal began I mentioned that one of our bassoonists was a great-niece of that great English violinist, Albert Sammons. Hugh had studied with him for nearly twenty years. When I mentioned this to him, he was so thrilled that he shot like a bolt to greet her in the bassoon section of the orchestra. I remember Hugh - during one of our lighter moments at the Royal College - doing one of his tricks, which was to play the violin behind his back.!

We had one "family ensemble" who contributed largely, with various ensembles, to our concerts. John Francis (flute) and Sarah, his elder daughter (oboe) often played in the Orchestra. (Sarah is still giving most pleasing and expert solo performances on the radio.) Before her sister Hannah took up singing, she used to play the harp and on one occasion, with her father, performed Mozart's *Concerto for Flute and Harp*. When the whole family performed together, John's wife, Millicent Silver, was the pianist and Lionel Bentley played the violin. For one concert, when a *Brandenburg Concerto* was in the programme, with a very prominent violin part, Lionel was not available to play, so I was invited to take his place. This was, for me, a very pleasurable occasion.

There were two occasions when there was a crisis at the last moment regarding the appearance of soloists; the worst one was when not one, but two works were due to be played by the same soloist. The works concerned were Rachmaninov's *2nd Piano Concerto in C minor* and Gershwin's *Rhapsody in Blue*. I had arrived at the County School of Music where we had a preliminary string rehearsal on the Friday evening, the night before the concert, in the usual way - full of enthusiasm and relaxed, feeling well prepared for the forthcoming event - only to find the office in some state of panic and turmoil. Unbeknown to me, our soloist, Frank Wibaut, who lived in the Birmingham area, had been taken ill the night before. A replacement had to be found immediately, but there was the problem of finding a soloist who knew two very dissimilar works and who would be willing to perform them both at very short notice.

A very great friend of mine and a very sweet person, who was the very efficient hon. secretary of the R.C.M. "Union" had already been contacted and had started a very large number of phone calls - most of them, so far, to no avail. But she was working splendidly and by the time I had arrived had managed to engage someone who knew the Rachmaninov but had not played it for about six months. However she agreed to take it on. Her name was Hilary Macnamara. But the *Rhapsody in Blue* was quite a different matter and no-one seemed to know it. All was not lost as this remarkable "saviour of the situation" - whose name was, and is (but more of that later), Sylvia Latham, knew of one excellent pianist - another product of the Royal College, who might be able, and willing, to help out. Unfortunately he was giving a joint piano and oboe recital somewhere in the North of England and wouldn't be back till late, but she gave me his parents' number in London. When I got home at about 10 p.m. I rang his father who told me his son would be home at about 2 a.m. and he would get him to give me a ring in the morning (I had told him why I wanted him so urgently).

At about 10 a.m. the telephone rang and a rather sleepy voice answered - his name was Howard Shelley - and he said: "What's all this that I'm supposed to play at Guildford this evening - the Rachmaninov and Rhapsody in Blue." "No, not the former - only the Rhapsody. Do you know it?" I asked. "No!", came the reply. "Have you ever seen it?" "No", again was the discouraging answer. "Have you ever heard it?" said I, almost in despair. "Yes", came the slightly more hopeful reply. "Well you're playing it tonight at Guildford. Will you catch the mid-day train at Waterloo and I'll meet you at Esher. You can then practice it on my piano for the first part of the afternoon, catch another train to Guildford in time to get to the latter part of the rehearsal with the orchestra." Looking back at these events after some years, it all seems like a bad dream and one begins to wonder if it all really happened.

Not that everything went smoothly before the concert. For one thing, Howard found my Steinway "boudoir" grand piano very heavy going, being badly in need of attention. (Bought in 1923 this has recently been overhauled and is now back to its best - in appearance, sound and touch.) And Howard Shelley also said he would not have taken the job on if he had known that he was going to be confronted with such a solo piano part. It was one of those "Piano Conductor" scores - not very well printed, with small notes and lots of cues of the orchestral contribution and not what you would call a solo copy at all.

With such an unpromising preparation for this somewhat dramatic occasion the result was an unqualified success. No-one could possibly have guessed what drama had taken place in the 24 hours or so leading up to the concert itself, and nothing indicated that things were other than normal. While Hilary Macnamara was giving her quite excellent performance of the Concerto, Howard Shelley was frantically practising the Gershwin on a piano backstage. During quieter moments I could once or twice hear him!

Howard Shelley has since become one of the finest pianists in the Country - and probably one of the busiest. Although he specialises in some composers, especially in satisfying the demands of recording companies, his repertoire and favourite works are far from narrow. Never having met either Howard or Hilary before, I often wonder whether this was a "first time" for them too, and my curiosity even causes me to wonder if this concert was the precursor of them now being Mr and Mrs Howard Shelley, with a rising family! Whether this is so or not, it would be difficult to find a more delightful couple.

The other soloist mishap also involved Frank Wibaut who played with us several times, and was due to play the John Ireland Concerto, but I did on this occasion have three days in which to replace him. The concert, as usual, was on a Saturday, and on the Wednesday he was giving a girl pupil a piano lesson at Birmingham Conservatoire. Frank was playing a passage to her of a piece she was learning. She stood up to turn the page for him but unfortunately caught the piano lid with her hand as she sat down. It crashed onto his hands, badly damaging one of his fingers. This put Frank out of action for several weeks and, of course, I had to find a deputy pretty quickly. Once again there was the problem of finding someone who knew the work, and it was surprising how difficult it was to find anyone who had the Ireland in their repertoire. I tried the obvious player - the acknowledged expert on Ireland's music - Eric Parkin - but he had a previous engagement. Success eventually occurred when I managed to engage Philip Fowke - a most successful replacement. I had not known his name previously, but I frequently hear it announced on the radio nowadays.

I referred earlier to someone who gave so much help in resolving what could have been such a disastrous situation. Her name was Sylvia Latham. She was everyone's friend and did so much to help in various ways, especially in connection with the Bach and St. Paul's, Knightsbridge, Choirs, and with her work at the Royal College and Alexandra House by the Royal Albert Hall. She is godmother to my elder son who lives in California and I was best man to her late husband, Dick, who was for many years organist at St. Paul's, Knightsbridge, and played for my own elder daughter's wedding.

Some time ago, Sylvia had driven her daughter to Paddington one morning but no-one could have believed that the same afternoon, at her flat, she would have suffered a debilitating stroke. She is the last person in the world you would imagine, after all she has given, to end with a life that no longer has any meaning for her because she is unable really to enjoy anything any more. It is one of the saddest things to have happened during my life, second only to the tragic death of Princess Diana, and one's feelings must be with her loving family.

I hope that what I have said shows how much pleasure can be derived from working with a local orchestra and from meeting and making music with some of the finest artists of our time. I end this chapter on a happy note by mentioning one of my closest friends who gave so much pleasure to Gill and me, not least when we were invited to one of his inimitable parties at his Maida Vale Studio. He was Harry Isaacs, who was a most popular Piano Professor at "the other place" - i.e. the Royal ACADEMY of Music.

He used to give these parties from time to time, perhaps inviting a dozen or so guests of various interests, though usually musical ones, often also inviting young promising students of his from the R.A.M. to play a piano solo, or sometimes a duet with himself, to give them an opportunity of playing in front of a critical audience.

They were delightful occasions, leavened by Harry's infectious humour and wit. He would have a charming way of devaluing his hospitality, usually, immediately on arrival by offering you a drink with the words "Cooking sherry?" and then pour you out a glass of the most high class sherry known! He would then provide a most delectable meal - after the last guest had arrived - prepared by a helper who obviously looked after Harry's material needs. Conversation would always be lively, the tone of which would be set by our genial and humorous host. Harry, who never married, was a lovely mixture of infectious humour with high ideals with regard to the performance of music. His parties were quite memorable occasions and at times also hilarious. Towards the end of the evening the party tended to get thinner as guests left in twos, leaving quite a few of us switching from one topic of conversation to another. And we met some very distinguished people from other walks of life. One very "high up" in the world of science was the one concerned in perhaps the most amazing of coincidences of all my life regarding a gramophone recording, which I have mentioned earlier. At one party was the Principal of the Royal Academy, Sir Thomas Armstrong and his wife. It wasn't until he died a few years ago that I discovered we shared the same birthday! And after one of these memorable evenings, Harry asked me if I would give a lift home to the distinguished Soprano, Dame Eva Turner, and, of course, I was delighted to do so.

In March 1962 I invited Harry to come to Guildford to play a concerto with the G.S.O. He accepted with alacrity and played not one, but two works with us! It was Beethoven's *3rd Concerto in C Minor* and the César Franck, *Symphonic Variations*. In the interval, after a most deeply felt performance of the Beethoven, he said to me: "I've got something I want to tell you, Ralph." He then quickly changed his mind and said he would tell me at the end of the concert. I was naturally intrigued by this and wondered what he was keeping to himself. After the final applause at the close of the concert for our performance of the *Marche Joyeuse* by Chabrier, I tackled Harry and asked him to disclose his great secret. "I thought you would like to know that it is 9 years since I played in public!" From the way he played, with his musicianship at all times underlining his artistry, you would never have guessed it. I'm sure he enjoyed the evening as much as everyone else did.

It was sad that his life ended in the same way that too many people's do. If only medical science could find a cure for cancer, just as they have largely eliminated tuberculosis. Harry's life came to an end in the same manner as he had lived it - with humour and optimism. He never lost his sense of humour, and he bore his final illness with courage and humour, and never let anything get him down.. After he had reached the age of 70, the Royal Academy gave him a special Concert, held in their Dukes Hall. A number of distinguished people had been invited to what was really a celebration but became a farewell. Among the guests was Cliff Michelmore. I once asked Harry how he got to know him - a personality of sporting inclinations best known for his radio commentaries of events like Test Matches - and he had told me that they had met when they were both staying at the same hotel in North Devon one summer, years before, and the weather was so awful they had spent a lot of the holiday indoors and had got to know each other.

Harry was obviously a sick man but managed to get on to the platform at the end of the concert, and he made a typical speech, full of humour. He recalled how his father tried to discourage him from taking up music and did not want him to go to the Royal Academy. "Why not?" asked Harry of his father. "Suppose the Academy closed down," replied his father quite seriously. This story naturally, and quite typically "brought the house down!" A lovely man whose friendship made the world a better place.

My final concert with the G.S.O. after 30 years as their conductor, was for me a happy and memorable evening, with a number of distinguished guests from the world of music, including Ursula Vaughan Williams, Sidonie Goossens - principal harpist of the B.B.C. Symphony for about 60 years - and Malcolm Smith, a most knowledgeable musician from Messrs. Boosey and Hawkes. The programme itself included a number of my favourite works, including *Brigg Fair* by Delius. Harry Blech, whom I had known for many years, first when he played in the L.S.O., and then as 2nd fiddle in his quartet from the early R.A.F. days, was there too. After we were "demobbed", Harry formed the London Mozart Players, which has flourished with the highest success ever since, although he has retired from actually conducting himself. One of my greatest feelings of pride at my final concert was to have my elder daughter, Diana, playing oboe in the Orchestra.

18. CROYDON YOUTH ORCHESTRA AND
YOUTH ORCHESTRAS IN GENERAL

I would never go so far as to claim being the pioneer of Youth Orchestras but I would tell myself I was jolly near the top. They really got under way shortly after the war was over in 1945, but there was someone who had a Youth Orchestra before the war. This was Ernest Read, a very dear man with whom I always got on famously. He became Vice-President of the Guildford Symphony Orchestra while I was there. He was, though, a product of "the other place" - i.e. the Royal Academy of Music, so I saw rather less of him than I did of my own colleagues at the R.C.M. I think it would be no exaggeration to say he was a part of the R.A.M. and much loved by all.

He had a young people's orchestra before the war, known as the London Junior Orchestra. After the war he ran more than one such orchestra and I remember taking a rehearsal for him at the R.A.M. one Saturday. Youth Orchestras were otherwise very much a new phenomenon and initially did not acquire that much importance or interest. How little did we realise at the time what a tremendous impact the very talented young musicians of this country were about to make on music nationally - and in a comparatively short time. And how glad I am that I was in almost at the very beginning of this new venture which, surprisingly, soon became a much respected and valued part of the Country's musical life. Who would have thought, in 1945, that before the end of the century the "National Youth Orchestra of Great Britain" would be appearing at the Proms on equal terms, not only with such as the B.B.C. Orchestra, the L.S.O. and the R.P.O, but also some of the other great orchestras of the world!

But first things first; these things do not happen overnight, and I was lucky to be around when a small Youth Orchestra began its life in Croydon, the details of which are worth recording. Croydon was not alone in being very deprived of amateur music making during the war. There were two keen violinists, a Mrs Gill and Mrs Spackman, both members of the largely inactive Croydon Symphony Orchestra. Mrs Gill was the leader of the C.S.O., which was conducted by the ubiquitous Willie Read, who was himself leader of the London Symphony Orchestra. They asked me if I would form a Youth Orchestra in 1945 and I willingly agreed. We advertised, saying that auditions would be held on two consecutive days. The response was encouraging and altogether we had thirty-one young people play on various instruments, and there was already a sign of talent available. From then on, for another thirty-three years, we never held another audition. We certainly didn't waste time, with rehearsals starting almost immediately. Before Christmas we were even able to give an informal concert to parents and friends. The Croydon Youth Orchestra was on its way. Actually, according to some of the early music folders we originally called ourselves the "Croydon Junior Orchestra", but this did not last long and we converted to "Youth Orchestra".

Looking back, it is remarkable how quickly it all happened, and the whole concept was most definitely "a good thing". So fast did we progress that within three years of our inception we had the confidence to enter the Harrow Competitive Music Festival, travelling by motor-coach from Croydon. With a certain amount of self-assurance we had almost cheekily put ourselves down for the open orchestral class - and won it! (And the National Youth Orchestra hadn't even been formed at this point.) We weren't quite the first Youth Orchestra in the Home Counties, for Stoneleigh Youth Orchestra from Surrey "pipped" us by two or three months. It wasn't long before we found ourselves rivals, the event being the London Music Festival which took place in the Westminster Central Hall. The adjudicator was Ivor James, the cellist, an outstanding musician, being one of the pillars of chamber music, though I never thought of him as an orchestral player or adjudicator.

I was naturally very disappointed when Ivor put Stoneleigh first and the C.Y.O second, but, of course I was prejudiced! But I genuinely felt, and others shared this view, that we gave a better all-round performance, and had I been adjudicator I would have reversed the verdict. But you cannot prove anything since it is one man's honest opinion. (A glaring error is another matter, but decisions have to be made instantly and I expect the young players took it all in good part and would have gained something from the experience. As an examiner myself I know how difficult quick decisions can be.)

For anyone who has never experienced the pleasure of working with young people in their formative years, I can assure them that it is a great pleasure to see and hear of their progress and successes in wider and more distant fields where their skills and industry earn them their just rewards. An early and useful forum for members of the Croydon Youth Orchestra, as they reached the required age and acquired the necessary ability, was provided through attendance at the Saturday morning sessions at the Royal College, which I know a number of them did, gaining further experience with the Junior College Orchestra. I always hoped that this was of mutual benefit to both sides. I don't expect the R.C.M. had any idea of the existence of the C.Y.O. or of any possible benefits we might have been able to provide. I had no connection whatever with that side of College life although in later years, when he was Director of the R.C.M., Sir Keith Falkner did come to one of our concerts in which a College student was a soloist in Croydon.

One of the pleasures and surprises in a Youth Orchestra, which tends to draw its personnel from the locality, is that one has to take what is available and make do. I had many fortunate periods while I was at Croydon. It was only five miles from my original home at Sutton, and not too much further on to Esher where I lived after I was married. It has always tended to be a musical town, especially with such people as W.H.Reed, who not only lived there but did so much for music both there and in other nearby towns. At one time we had in the C.Y.O. no fewer than four or five more-than-useful horn players, and at another, four bassoons - all of which would be counted almost a "luxury" in a similar orchestra.

Mention must be made of at least a dozen players who went on to higher things and carried out their new musical ventures with distinction, being a credit not only to the C.Y.O. but also to their old schools, especially Croydon High, and teachers in the Croydon area. There was one violinist who joined the Orchestra at the age of 8 who I shall always remember with respect and affection, whom I shall refer to later.

From the very start of the Orchestra, there was one young player without whom we would probably only have existed for a few weeks and then we would have had to have packed up and never be heard of again. Her name was Etaim Lovell, an already most promising cellist whose presence we relied upon for the first two years of the Orchestra's existence. All harmony is gauged by the lowest note in the chord and is understood by it. An orchestra without cellos, double-basses and bassoons would sound ridiculous, and this applies to choirs without basses - and similar groups - and it is not a cliché to say that apart from anything else "the bottom line" is essential. So it will be seen how valuable Etaim was to our very existence in those early days, and it came as no surprise that she eventually went on to become a useful member of the musical profession. It is also not surprising that music runs in families, as in my own case. Etaim has a brother, Keith, also a string player, who joined the C.Y.O. as a violinist at about the same time as her; I am not sure he wasn't the leader for a while. In later years he joined the Dartington String Quartet as their viola player. Sadly, after a number of years of success, with a high reputation, this ensemble disbanded. Another good fiddler joined us and led the 2nd Violins. He too has gone on to higher things, including forming his own Quartet with his own name - Roger Coull. They are now one of the top String Quartets in the Country. They have in fact built up a most enviable reputation and have obviously reached the pinnacle of the world of chamber music. Not only have they, for many years, been Quartet-in-Residence at Warwick University, they do a great deal of travelling, and not only in this country. They claim that their "numerous appearances in the U.K. have taken them from Shetland to the Channel Islands and most points between!" They travel abroad a great deal, including playing on cruises with P & O's popular classical music concert cruises which they have done for the past ten years. On top of all this they have been doing a lot of recording which has included the Opus 33 set of Quartets by Haydn, and they have recorded the complete set of the quartets of Mendelssohn. These were recently the recommended choice on B.B.C. Radio 3's "Record Review".

The Quartet itself was formed while all four players were students at the Royal Academy of Music in 1974. Not long ago they celebrated their 25th anniversary and there is obviously no slackening in their popularity and reputation - or work-load. A few months before this was written I had the great pleasure not only of hearing but of meeting this delightful ensemble, not a mile from where I live in Taunton. Queen's College, just up the road from me, put on (or provide the venue for) some splendid concerts each year - some professional and some amateur - all of which are well worth going to. It was there that I heard the Coull Quartet. Before bidding farewell at the end of the recital, I had a word with their viola player, David Curtis, and was both surprised and delighted to discover that he, for a short time, had also been in the Croydon Youth Orchestra.

There is one other string player I must mention, but not through any distinction in the profession, and I'm not sure whether to consider him a professional or not - perhaps as a player - No - but since he teaches still in the Croydon area, definitely a pro. But it matters not; it is as a person, a friend and a most reliable, valuable and indispensable adjunct to "orchestras and places where they play" - if I might describe him thus.

He is Charles Harman, who still lives and teaches in the Croydon area. He was "in" at the start of the C.Y.O., and what he did I still remember with gratitude, and amazement. He would come to a rehearsal with a fiddle, prepared to play 1st or 2nd. One evening he came along to the school in South Croydon where we rehearsed and said, "No violas tonight? I'll go home and get one". Going home and getting one was not as simple as it sounds. We didn't all have cars in 1945, and he certainly didn't. He did not live in Central Croydon but a mile or two outside in Sanderstead, where he still lives, and this little operation must have taken at least half an hour, relying entirely on the bus service. And on the rare occasions when there were no cellos, the same thing would happen. Charles was adept on all four members of the "string fraternity". I can't imagine what would have happened if he had thought it was time we had a double-bass in the Orchestra, as we didn't at that time.

The above episodes needed to be described, for it is the unsung heroes of this world and the voluntary actions of people who have not only enthusiasm but specific interests at heart who can translate small and possibly slightly discouraging beginnings into something really lasting and worthwhile.

Two players of long and loyal service were Alan and Wendy Tooke. Wendy was once a violin pupil of mine at the Royal College of Music but played viola in the C.Y.O, while her husband, Alan, led the Orchestra. Another couple in the Orchestra fell in love and married, so I felt perhaps I should advertise that the C.Y.O. was not only an orchestra but also a marriage bureau. Alan and Wendy made what turned out to be a successful decision - to try out a similar form of music-making with young people on the other side of the world. They decided to "give Australia a go" and emigrated on a three year trial. With their two sons - both useful fiddlers - they are obviously making a success of their "new" venture - now well over 20 years on. Now in Melbourne, they seem to have instituted a school of music, and an orchestra, and must be establishing similar activities to those already well-recognised in the "Mother Country". Such news - gleaned from Alan's parents in Sussex - is gratifying indeed.

A Croydonian who was loyal to me and most helpful throughout my thirty-three years was Ronnie Gillham who conducted when I had to be away. He also took over the Pearl Assurance Orchestra from me after I had conducted it for a number of years. They used to rehearse once a week at 6 p.m. on a top floor of their fine

120

building in High Holborn. They later moved to near Peterborough and I believe the move has not been a great success, especially since their Holborn H.Q. is a listed building where they used to give concerts to members of their staff from time to time. I understand that a nucleus of their orchestra still meets once a week at Ronnie Gillham's house near Hammersmith. It is this orchestra for which Colin Davis (now Sir Colin), took the odd rehearsal for me, presumably in his early R.C.M. days, when he began to realise that the baton was going to give more joy and a sense of fulfilment in life than the clarinet. I used to pay him, and other stand-ins also on the quest for higher things, a guinea per rehearsal.

I have referred to a number of string players I was lucky enough to have over the years in the C.Y.O. Certain wind players also need a mention. At one time we had an excellent oboist, Maurice Checker. He eventually played cor anglais for the London Philharmonic Orchestra. I've rather lost touch with him but if rumours are to be believed, his hobby - and I've no reason to doubt the truth of this one - was to keep bees on the roof of the Royal Albert Hall! I should like to follow that one up. Guy Woolfenden was one of our excellent horn players. He later became musical director at Stratford-on Avon, which not only entailed organising the music but also conducting and composing, and his name often occurs on the radio as he still holds that post. His delightful father used to run a very pleasant and successful music shop in Cambridge which I once visited. Among bassoonists, Charles Miller went to Ireland and became principal bassoon with the Dublin Symphony Orchestra, while Lesley Wilson had a similar position with the B.B.C. Scottish Symphony Orchestra in Glasgow.

Quite recently I was invited to a private party at the Fairfield Halls in Croydon for the Diamond Wedding of the parents of three players who played in the C.Y.O. in the early days. The two sisters were oboe and strings, while the brother played clarinet. All three played as a trio with a piano at the party - the family name being Macfarlane. John now lives in Belgium where music still plays an important part in his life, for, not only does he keep up his clarinet playing but he also conducts. He is a radiologist by profession. Among the guests at the party was Jack Brymer, whom it was a pleasure to meet again after so many years.

It is salutary to look back merely half a century and realise what a tremendous revolution has taken place in that short time. There were many young people in that Orchestra who may not have been old enough to order themselves "half a pint" in their "local" after the concert, yet one can pick up a Radio Times many a week and see an item among the main programmes of the day, in large print "Youth Orchestras of the World". Youth Orchestras are no longer a phenomenon requiring excuses or explanations, but a matter of course where the performers are judged along with the best in the world. I defy anyone switching on the radio by chance and not knowing to whom he was listening, to identify the age and experience of the players. To those who have had any connection with the training of these young groups, it is both rewarding and gratifying to watch and listen to them.

On at least four occasions, well-known composers wrote special works for the C.Y.O., three of them coming to the concert itself, and two conducting their own works. Alun Hoddinott, the Welsh composer wrote us a short Overture but was unable to travel up from Wales to hear it. Ernest Tomlinson came down from Yorkshire to conduct a Suite he had written, and Ronnie Binge - who became a warm friend of ours, and probably made his name (and fortune) as composer of *Elizabethan Serenade* - seemed to enjoy conducting a delightful work he had written specially for us, and my old friend Gordon Jacob and his wife were in prominent seats at the Fairfield Hall to hear the first performance of a work he dedicated to us and published by the O.U.P. on an old poem called "A Noyse of Minstrelles", in which he treated the strings and wind as separate entities and then brought them all together in a grand finale with the skill of a master of orchestration.

I was also involved in starting Youth Orchestras in South and West Wales. The first one, at Llanelly, when we started was an off-putting experience, and I remember wanting to ask one of the officials if he had a timetable of trains back to London because it was so awful - but I resisted. It is remarkable what can be achieved in a week if the will is there. Among the somewhat discouraging sounds emanating from around my stand was that of one excellent viola player who gave me hope that all was not lost almost before we had begun, and it was not at all surprising to learn that, when the National Youth Orchestra of Wales was formed some years later, this young player was quickly appointed Principal Viola and later went on to become a full professional.

It did not take long for those young people to realise what orchestral playing was all about, and it made me happy once more to find what could be achieved with a modicum of faith, hope - and a certain degree of latent talent. And personally I was also to witness a good example of Welsh friendship and the ability to enjoy the better things in life. When the "School Day" was over one had the pleasurable prospect of a good sociable evening. I remember there were four male members of staff who were there to help in various ways, so in the evenings the five of us used to climb into the largest of their cars and drive off into the country and refresh ourselves in some local hostelry, and I was responsible for introducing them to a drink which none of them had ever heard of - a "Whisky Mac"! One can imagine that by the time each of us had "stood a round", we were well away. I am glad to report I was *not* driving!

One of the party - a very affable character - kept one of his arms in a very odd position, and, on the quiet, I asked one of our staff for the reason for this. He explained that he had been a Welsh International Rugby player who had broken his arm in one match and it had to be set in this position. Somehow I don't think such a thing would be allowed to happen today.

At the end of this memorable and successful week, we were able to give a concert of some of the works we had been studying, to parents and friends of those promising youngsters. There was one memorable event which took place during the course of the concert - a surprise for everybody, and almost to the person concerned himself, through an oversight of one of the local Music Advisers, who had advised me that there was to be a small "happening" after the interval. I had got on especially well with the Adviser during the week and we quickly became firm friends. He had told me he had a particularly bright musician of 12 or 13 to whom he was going to give a test during the concert giving him only a short time to digest and think about it. The plan was to give him a slip of paper on which would be written the test he was to undertake. The interval of the concert arrived but no test. The Music Adviser himself had found himself involved in one or two other things and unfortunately had forgotten to give the slip of paper to the young man. He gave it to him with about five minutes to produce what was expected of him.

The second part of the concert was soon on its way with the young man sitting at the piano having had very little time for serious thought. The actual test was "to play variations on a well-known theme by J.S.Bach from a suite for solo violin" (which I had learnt as a music student) " in the style of various composers" (giving about six well-known names such as Handel, Mendelssohn, Mozart, Delius and others - one quite modern). It was a really brilliant treatise - for a mature student even it would have been outstanding - but for one of such tender years it was amazing. All this took place before the days when anything and everything was put on tape so that it has to remain as a fading memory and nothing remains for posterity. Even so, those of us who heard it were duly impressed by such spontaneous brilliance. It came as no surprise to learn that it was not many years later that this unknown schoolboy had quickly risen in eminence to become "Professor of Music in North Wales, William Mathias", stationed at or near Llandudno where he remained for the rest of his young life. He succumbed to the horrible and unsolved disease of cancer not many years ago - another waste of a more than promising career.]

I was always sorry I did not follow up my connection with Mathias, though I did benefit from one of his early compositions - a delightful three-movement *Suite for Orchestra*. It was published during my time at Croydon. The Youth Orchestra purchased the work and we had some most enjoyable concerts in which the work was included. It was as popular with the audience as it was with the "band". Unfortunately Mathias broke away from writing music which was "easy on the ear" and his later works were, in my opinion, not all in the "I'd like to hear that again" category. Mind you, it is easy to form an opinion of a new work too quickly - one must give it a chance. I remember, years ago, saying I could not stand a work by Stravinsky which, later on, I looked forward to hearing again! But there are some works that are so awful - and I have no hesitation in condemning them out of hand - that they should never be allowed "air time"! I see nothing whatever to be ashamed of in writing a really good tune. Was there something wrong with Ralph Vaughan Williams that caused him to write such stirring themes, even in his later works?

I spent another week on a further music course in Wales, at a place called Newtown - not far from Aberystwyth - which was a rewarding and enjoyable experience during the build-up of Youth Music in the Principality.

Before ending this chapter on Youth Orchestras a few words are necessary about the "young violinist of 8 years old" whom I mentioned earlier, who joined the Croydon Youth Orchestra in its very early days. He played with the 2nd violins and eventually led them. He was small, quiet but obviously keen. I used to call him "Schubert" as he wore steel-rimmed glasses. He would come regularly after, probably, quiet a long day at school and often would fall asleep during our rehearsal. His name was Alan Traverse. I watched his career develop with keen interest.

At various periods of our thirty-three years existence, we tended to mark a number of anniversaries when past members were invited to come back and join the C.Y.O. for a combined concert. The first was at the 15th year, when the numbers had gone up from about 30 to 80 which, of course, gave us scope for quite ambitious programmes. We repeated this idea for our 21st anniversary, our 25th, and finally in 1977 our 33rd and last. On this occasion I had invited Alan Traverse to be our soloist in Max Bruch's very well-known *Violin Concerto in G minor.* By this time Alan's career had blossomed with considerable distinction. He was already established as leader of the Royal Liverpool Philharmonic Orchestra under the conductorship of Sir Charles Groves - a post he held for quite a number of years. He went from there to become leader of the Houston Symphony Orchestra in Texas - where, as far as I know, he still is. After he had played the Bruch impeccably there was inevitably much applause at Coloma School, Croydon, where we gave the concert, but instead of accepting the applause, going off and returning to take another bow in the usual way, he practically "killed" the applause in order to address the audience. He then paid tribute to his early days in the C.Y.O. and to me. He recalled how he used to come along to the rehearsals every Thursday evening at 8 p.m. on a No. 16 train from Thornton Heath to Croydon and was amazed how, although a member of the L.S.O., I managed to be there practically every Thursday. He then thanked me for setting him on the road to the musical profession by getting him into the Covent Garden Orchestra - something I had quite forgotten about! His charming and sincere tribute to me touched me considerably and was, I felt, one of the nicest gestures in public that one professional could make to another.

After the final concert at Croydon, the Croydon Advertiser in the person of their long-standing music critic, David Squibb wrote on July 21st 1978, under the heading "Sad Celebration":

With the same kind of festive atmosphere - tinged with sadness - that surrounds the paying-off of a venerable old ship before her last journey to the breaker's yard, the Croydon Youth Orchestra gave its final concert on Sat. at Coloma Convent Grammar School.

This atmosphere of celebration marking the life and work of the Orchestra disguised any obvious demonstrations of grief, although there were numerous public and private reminiscences of specific glorious occasions during the last 33 years . . . R.N. received a specially made presentation treble clef and a signed testimonial from past members.

These were the visible signs of the worth of Croydon Youth Orchestra: the real worth of the C.Y.O. lies in the experience it gave to hundreds of young musicians from 1945 to 1978, and that is something that can never be measured.

(Although the reason for the demise of the Orchestra shall not be mentioned here, it did cause a lot of controversy and bitterness - and much support for us - with the response very much in our favour. I found it most heartening with a feeling that 33 years had been well-spent, a feeling apparently shared by many other people.)

I cannot help looking back with a certain amount of pride at the number of "firsts" I was involved in shortly after the end of the War - not to mention during the early part of the war itself, especially the small beginnings of the Arts Council as the C.E.M.A., and earlier still the Boyd Neel String Orchestra which was the first British orchestra to be invited to play at the Salzburg Festival, as well, of course, as the first to play at Glyndebourne, albeit before the first actual Festival there.

There was what I must modestly call a success which even I sometimes forget happened. Practically single-handed I formed the Surrey County Youth Orchestra. This was divided into four "area" orchestras in the County, with three other willing and able conductors helping me to build the four parts into a whole. As usual there were occasional residential courses and combined concerts in various parts of Surrey. I have to admit I was a little over-ambitious too soon and we took on a rather too difficult overture by Gordon Jacob at an early concert at Redhill. This testing work was a bit much for the young players at that time. I had invited the composer to come to the concert and rather wished I hadn't. He was very nice about it and commented, rather delightfully, that "one or two notes had fallen under the stands!"

But the orchestra developed well and gave some good concerts. The players were hard-working, efficient and happy. I continued to conduct them for the first three years of their existence, but I never had the whole-hearted support from the County Council at County Hall, Kingston. I was not sure whether to write the following but have been urged to do so to strike at the vociferous know-alls and busybodies of this world. These talentless people attempt to thwart genuine, sensitive performers by their hidebound committee-type decisions and obstructive behaviour.

I believe the Orchestra has gone ahead well and even appeared at the Royal Albert Hall at a Youth Festival, though not yet at a Prom. I was never invited back to a concert after I left, though I did go to one once - uninvited. At no time has my name ever been mentioned as having had anything to do with the formation of the

Surrey County Youth Orchestra, although they have had their anniversaries. If one was to enquire at County Hall - for whom I used to work - I doubt that anyone could trace any reference to my original enterprise.

Experience told me whether I was "on to a good thing". Here was a perfect example of a little knowledge being a dangerous thing. You have to take the rough with the smooth in my profession and this was just one episode I would like to forget - in fact I nearly had - in a mainly very happy life which I can look back on with just a little pride.

19. ON SOLOISTS

Soloists and conductors rarely go in for tantrums and become all temperamental as they tended to do in the past, so that when they do go off the handle, you remember it more. For example the L.S.O. were once right out at Walthamstow Town Hall (It is odd the number of town halls beginning with "W" we used for recording sessions, Wimbledon, Wembley, Watford etc.), and the famous pianist Richter was due to record a well-known piano concerto with us. He was a fine artist but inclined to take exception to small things which upset him. We had not proceeded far with the concerto when he stopped, saying he was not prepared to continue playing on that piano. He said it was faulty and they would have to change it. The instrument was, I believe, one of the finest - a Steinway. Apparently one of the notes was causing a string to develop a small "twang", but no-one else had noticed anything wrong! The firm from whom it was hired were informed that they would have to supply a replacement instrument. This entailed loading up another piano from their show-rooms in Central London and driving with it to Walthamstow which is quite a distance out. They always sent one of their representatives out with their pianos just to oversee the arrangements and make sure everything was in order.

The chap in charge on this occasion was a very pleasant fellow, and I had a chance later on to have a quiet chat with him. He told me that there was nothing basically wrong with the original instrument. "They've all got what he complained about and no-one had ever complained before!"

It was another Sunday recording session, this time at Watford Town Hall that I found quite a moving occasion as I witnessed a remarkable example of the affect a much respected "elder statesman" of the musical world had on a number of younger players of very good quality and potential, and also a number of, not exactly upstarts, but individuals inclined to be know-alls.

The recording to be made was what you might call a repeat of earlier days. I think most of the Orchestra had a tinge of doubt as to the wisdom of trying to rekindle the past with success. The details are these. The work to be recorded was Brahms' *Violin Concerto* and the soloist that fine artist Josef Zigeti. One of my earliest records of "78" days was of Zigeti playing this Concerto, and it became a famous recording - an example for other soloists to follow. But now he had become quite an elderly man. Anyway, we started off and things went quite well, but small moments of uncertainty crept in. It was eventually decided to record quite short passages of the concerto at a time and the recording experts could pick on the best sections and then join them up into the complete work. It became obvious that this was going to be a "synthetic" performance, but I began to feel that the end of his long recording days was approaching. I longed to do a whole movement of a concerto or symphony, without stopping, just as in a concert performance.

As the recording proceeded there were a number of delightful moments, reminding one of the Zigeti of old, and one realised that the recording engineers would have quite a job on their hands to produce a finished performance. But there were some less attractive moments and one could observe some of the younger players becoming sceptical, critical, and probably prepared to ridicule as well. Usually at the end of an evening session at 9 p.m., especially on a Sunday, there would be a rush to get out, either to catch a tube-train or dash home in one's car. But on that evening Zigeti had obviously woven a sort of spell over some of the younger players in particular. There was no rush for the doors. Some of the old maestro had, through some of his old mastery and noted skill and musicianship, caused these younger folk to be affected in quite a remarkable way. Josef sat on a chair, just where he had been standing to record the concerto, almost cradling his lovely violin under his arm while fingering imaginary notes from the finger-board and we gathered round as he talked about some of his experiences and occasional problems. Everyone was enthralled by his very presence and it became quite a touching, in fact moving experience, and I felt that we were in the presence of a great man, even if his best playing days were passed.

Another great soloist - and again a fiddler - was due to record the Vieuxtemps *Concerto No. 2* with the L.S.O. - this time at the Abbey Road studios. The Orchestra had already had a pretty full day at the Royal Albert Hall; it was a Sunday after a morning rehearsal and afternoon concert with Sargent. The recording session was booked, also with Sargent, from 6 to 9 p.m. and the soloist was Jascha Heifetz, and it would be difficult to name another violinist who possessed such an outstanding technique as his. One interesting - and also surprising - little incident occurred at the beginning of this session. A number of well-known leaders of other London Orchestras had got wind of the recording and turned up at the studio to listen to and watch the great man in action. Heifetz noticed their presence before the session began and requested that, if they wanted to listen to the recording they should stay out of sight, so they were asked to remain behind a screen. This was rather strange from a man with his fabulous technique and ability, to be put off by a few professionals listening to him. It was, of course, a tribute to his great reputation that he did not see it quite this way. The recording itself was, not surprisingly, outstanding. Heifetz himself was quite imperturbable and un-fussy. He had to record the cadenza three times just for safety. Each time it was perfect!

Emanuel Feuermann

Feuermann was without doubt one of the finest cellists I have ever heard. Very many years ago, when I was a student at the Royal College, I was sent down to Bromley to augment their Symphony Orchestra for a concert in which Feuermann was the soloist in Haydn's *D major Cello Concerto*. I've hardly ever heard such cello playing and, quite recently, I read or heard it said that he was one of the finest ever. His playing of the Haydn was something quite unforgettable, most especially his performance of the cadenza in which the 3rds and 6ths were quite superb with absolutely impeccable intonation. I think he must have died young - like too many fine musicians - for one never heard of him very often after that.

The Bromley Orchestra had a rather special character. There were three - if not four - sisters who were all excellent string players who led the various string sections of the Orchestra. They were one of the five amateur orchestras which W.H. ("Willie") Reed - the leader of the L.S.O. - used to conduct every week.

Albert Sammons

Sammons, a great English violinist, though self-taught, was also a fine teacher. Our own contemporary fiddler, Hugh Bean, studied with him for nearly twenty years. Sammons probably made his reputation by his many performances of Elgar's *Violin Concerto*. Although dedicated to Kreisler, it was Sammons who really championed this work. He once told me he had given over one hundred and eighty performances of it, but he never played it from memory, which I find interesting.

On a Sunday afternoon, soon after the war, Heifetz had just played the Beethoven *Violin Concerto*. At the Royal Albert Hall it is possible to walk round in a circle in the passage above and behind the stalls and if you keep going long enough you will keep passing the same people going the other way. This is exactly what happened to me, and the second time round Sammons spotted me and as we passed he said, in his most modest way, referring to Heifetz's performance, "Can't half play!", to which I felt like saying, "What about you, mate!". Years ago he led the London String Quartet.

Rubinstein

Rubinstein was another "lovely man", with his flowing white hair - rather like Stokowski. He obviously enjoyed every note he played and he exuded charm. Once, at a rehearsal at the Royal Festival Hall, he played a wrong note and his own reaction was to say: "Oh, I play so badly!" I'd love to have played so badly! Whenever he spotted Eileen Grainger in the violas he used to go over and give her a smashing kiss. She was (then) the only female in the Orchestra apart from Marie Goossens (harp).

Gary Kerr

Gary Kerr, the American double-bass player was another with endless talent who treated his instrument as though it was a toy instead of being the largest stringed instrument in the Orchestra. What he couldn't do with that monster wouldn't be worth knowing. After an impeccable rehearsal, with no problems, of a concerto for double-bass, Sargent, who was conducting, said, "Would you like to run through it once more?", to which he replied, "Okay maestro, if you insist. It's quite okay by me" - but we still went through it again, for no obvious reason.

Kerr played on an instrument that had belonged to the virtuoso double-bass player and famous conductor Sergei Koussevitsky who died in 1951. It was given to Kerr by his widow who was in the audience when he gave a recital in New York.

The Goossens family

This remarkable quintet of brothers and sisters - sadly reduced to four through the horrors of the Great War - were a unique group who for very many years graced the English musical scene - each one holding distinguished positions in the profession. Adolph was already developing into an outstanding horn player when he was conscripted into the Army, but he did not survive long at the front, being killed while only in his teens. Léon would have gone the same way had it not been for the fact that, by the greatest piece of good fortune, his life was saved by a metal cigarette case, given to him by Dame Ethel Smyth, the "Suffragette" composer, which prevented a bullet from reaching his heart causing only a minor wound. Eugene started his career as a violinist but was more attracted to the "conductor's desk", and eventually emigrated to Australia where he became conductor of the Sydney Symphony Orchestra. I played under him once in London and remember he had a very long baton and therefore a large beat.

Léon was the supreme oboist, not only of this Country, but all over the world. Students were anxious to become his pupil and he produced some top players at the R.C.M. of the quality of Evelyn Barbirolli and Natalie James. He was reputed, in his early days, to have a distinctive vibrato in his tone and the story goes that, when Beecham asked him for an "A" from which the orchestra could tune, he said: "Take your choice, gentlemen - take your choice!"

Léon told me, one day, of an amusing occasion when he had been playing a concerto in Leeds. He was returning to London on the night train. He had plenty of time to change from full evening dress into something more suitable and comfortable for travelling in, including a pullover. There was a large crowd on the platform as there had been an important football match involving a London side earlier in the day. He went into the station bar for a drink and the barmaid said to him: " 'Ave yer bin playin' luv?" by way of conversation, and Léon answered: "Yes, I have actually", to which she said: "Did yer win?"

The sisters, Marie and Sidonie, were both harpists, and they and Léon all reached their 90s, and Sidonie, the youngest must be spoken of in the present tense as she has just passed her triumphant century, for which we all congratulate her! Marie was for many years a member of the London Symphony Orchestra and Sidonie, even more remarkable, was the principal harpist of the B.B.C. Orchestra for over 50 years. Her long service has been duly acknowledged by the B.B.C.

What a wonderful record from one family - unlikely ever to be repeated. Their pedigree goes back at least three generations - with well-known conductors in earlier years, the family originating from Belgium. For three generations, the head of the family - mostly conductors - has been named Eugene.

20. ON COMPOSERS

I have already written fairly fully of my acquaintance and friendship with Ralph Vaughan Williams, his strong and long association with the Leith Hill Festival at Dorking, and his conducting, especially of his own compositions. I have known quite a few other composers personally, and with two, also famous ones, I have had mixed success with regard to possible performances from them. I had been conductor of the Guildford Symphony Orchestra for only just over two years in 1960 when I had a sudden whim. I had always liked the music of the famous French composer, Francis Poulenc, and I thought it would be fun to invite him to come to Guildford to play one of his works with the G.S.O. - I knew he was also a good pianist - or even to compose a short work for us to play and he to conduct.

I did not know how to contact him as I had not got his address and decided to write to my friend, the well-known musicologist - recently appointed President of the Delius Society in succession to the late Eric Fenby - Felix Aprahamian. I asked him, quite optimistically, whether he happened to know Francis Poulenc's address. Sure enough he immediately sent me his private address in Paris.

It was actually an awful cheek on my part but I wrote to him straightaway in English, not expecting any success. To my delight and surprise he wrote back personally in his own hand, in French, and regretted he was unable to undertake any more public work. He died about six months later and must have been a sick man at the time he wrote to me. He was only 64.

After my fair success with Poulenc, I had another what you might call "near-miss" - a silly expression adopted during the war to describe a near-hit. The L.S.O. had played a few weeks before at an Albert Hall Prom in which one of the soloists was the well-known Australian composer and friend of Delius, Percy Grainger. He played one of the pianos in an arrangementof his of a Bach Concerto for four pianos and grand organ. It was a splendid occasion and an exciting sound, and the four pianos, all lined up together were rather like buses waiting at Victoria Station!

Not many weeks after this Prom, I found myself travelling on the District Line of the Underground in Central London, and sitting opposite me was Percy Grainger! I suppose I do become rather impetuous sometimes or perhaps "have an eye for the main chance". Anyway, the moment I saw him I immediately started thinking things up. He's "a bit of a lad" and might welcome a challenge, thought I to myself. I felt sure he "never stood on ceremony" especially after reading some of his exploits. I know - I'll ask him if he'd accept an invitation to come to Guildford and play the piano part of his *Handel in the Strand* or anything else. There was an empty seat next to him and I was just about to pluck up my courage to go and speak to him - and you have to act quickly when you travel by Underground - when the train stopped at Piccadilly Circus and he left the train and I never set eyes on him again! Ah well!

Another composer of very agreeable music whom I knew, was Armstrong

Gibbs, who lived at Danbury near Chelmsford in Essex. He and my Aunt Nancy, who lived in Little Baddow, a very small village, and was killed by a "doodle-bug" when it destroyed her house, used to collaborate in the summer when a local fête was held and my aunt wrote the words and Gibbs wrote the music for performances on the village green.

He was the adjudicator for the week and had been invited to present the cups to the various winning choirs at the Dorking Halls in the interval of the Leith Hill Festival's final concert one year. When the interval arrived Armstrong Gibbs came on to the platform and to most people's surprise, he was wearing a light brown suit which he'd been wearing when he carried out the adjudications in the morning, rather than the conventional dinner jacket.

Armstrong, who had a nice sense of humour, was a big man and pretty tall. He explained: "When my son came to stay with us a month or two ago, he asked me if he could leave his dinner jacket behind as he was going to stay with friends for a few days and would pick it up on his way home. I said that of course he could, and it was duly hung up in our wardrobe next to mine. I left home in a bit of a hurry this morning. My son is very much shorter than I am . . . . !"

I have already written about a number of other eminent composers whom I knew and those whose music appealed to me. They include, of course, Gordon Jacob, R.V.W., Sir Arthur Bliss, Herbert Sumsion, Sir George Dyson, Constant Lambert, Michael Tippett and Harold Darke. I always felt that Dyson's music came from his head rather than his heart. That is to say, he perhaps lacked emotion but he was a good craftsman, with plenty to say worth hearing. Interestingly, during the First War, Dyson - who became Director of the Royal College - wrote a treatise on "Hand Grenade Fighting" which was officially adopted by the War Office.

Tippett, unlike Britten, stayed the full course at the R.C.M., his last term of studying Conducting with Boult being the term before I entered the College, where I was soon to be studying under Sargent myself. I once led the Festival Orchestra at Tunbridge Wells under Tippett for a performance of *A Child of our Time.*

Herbert Sumsion, for many years one of the "Three Choirs" conductors - he was organist of Gloucester Cathedral - was a charming and modest man whose music is quite often broadcast especially when it is Gloucester's turn to be responsible for one of Radio 3's Wednesday afternoon relays of "Choral Evensong". His music always has class and instant appeal, but he never received a knighthood like his colleagues at the other cathedrals. He is one of the un-sung heroes of our profession and I believe has left us with much church music of real quality

There is one composer who is a good example of writing a "hit" long ago and could sit at home and wait for the royalties to pour in (or ought to). His name was Dr. Harold Darke, who was the organist at St. Michael's, Cornhill, in the City of London. I used to lead the orchestra for his Christmas concerts. He wrote the carol "In the bleak mid-winter", which is still a best-seller. Not many years ago it was one of the items in a Christmas Carol Concert at the Royal Albert Hall with the Bach

Choir under David Willcocks. Darke told me at that occasion that it was over 60 years since he wrote it.

A composer who tends to be forgotten these days is John Ireland. I remember conducting his splendid *London Overture* at a Patron's Fund concert with the L.S.O. at the College, and I went to see him for some first hand advice at his flat in Chelsea. He was very intense in going through the Overture at the piano and, admitting it was difficult technically, he said with considerable confidence: "It all comes off Nicholson". The front-door bell rang while I was there with him. He excused himself and was away nearly half an hour. He explained that Fred Grinke had called to see him about one of his works for violin and piano. I doubt the absolute truth of this statement. There was a pub very near his flat and he smelt strongly of whisky on his return. For a man who wrote such attractive and effective music, this side of him was a great pity. He married a fellow student of mine who was much younger than he. It didn't last long! Ireland is another composer who is probably best known for one work, that delightful song *Sea Fever* with Masefield's words. He wrote some other attractive works including some for solo piano such as *Chelsea Reach* and *Amberley wild brooks*. He used to live in West Sussex near the South Downs, and another example of his pessimistic disposition was illustrated by his taking exception to the sound of sand being excavated from pits not far from where he lived. He sent his objections to the local council but they fell on deaf ears! He spent the early part of the War in the Channel Islands but got the wind-up when he thought the Germans were about to invade Jersey and couldn't wait to get out, which he did just in time.

Paul Hindenith was another composer of fine music and a most friendly conductor. Probably his best known works were for full orchestra but he was also a prolific writer of chamber music and works for solo instruments. Two of his finest compositions were the *Symphonic Metamorphoses of Themes by Weber* and his opera *Mathis der Maler,* but I would add possibly his ballet *Nobilissima Visione* - which, considering its popular appeal receives surprisingly few performances these days.

He was turned out of Germany during the Nazi regime and his music was banned there. But this only encouraged him, becoming an American citizen and eventually Professor of Music of Yale University. In such a full life, covering so many aspects of music it was sad that he should reach the end his life not having realised the limit of his aspirations as a performer. In his younger days (it was said that he ran away from home at the age of 11), he earned his living as a violinist by playing in cafés and with dance bands. But in his more mature days he became a distinguished leader of the Frankfurt Opera Orchestra and then viola player of a String Quartet.

But it had already become obvious to the listener that his viola playing had deteriorated. Even when he played his own *Viola Concerto* at Queen's Hall just before the War, it had been beginning to show - a work, incidentally, popular with fiddlers as he had not written any violin parts!

The crux of this failing - or fading - in his playing, came at a recording session for Decca with the L.S.O. in London, the soloists being the great Russian violinist, David Oistrakh, and Hindemith, as the first work was Mozart's *Sinfonia Concertante for Violin and Viola*. It was one of the most embarrassing moments of my career. Hindemith's intonation was quite appalling. The recording went ahead, and at the end of each movement all those concerned dutifully went into the control room to listen to each "take". We could see them through the glass standing round listening. Oistrakh was the soul of tact with a ready smile. But they could not possibly issue the recording. Luckily the other work was the *Violin Concerto* by Hindemith himself, which he conducted and Oistrakh played finely, and I believe was a success and sold separately. But it is strange Hindemith never realised his shortcomings. (I'd love to hear what the non-issued Mozart work really sounded like.)

21. ON CONDUCTORS

At the beginning of one's career as an orchestral player one quickly realises why certain conductors have gained their eminence and also, if their appointment is not of a permanent nature, one can console oneself that if you take a dislike to the "man on the box" on, say, Monday, there's always the chance of someone more amenable on Friday. As I have indicated in my final chapter, there's nothing like a bit of variety in one's life!

When I set forth on my life in music - from an orchestral point of view - speaking generally, conductors tended to be elderly and foreign. There were very few young ones as there are these days. Some names have even faded into oblivion but recur in one's memory bank when looking through old volumes of recordings. I am mentioning one or two where a certain characteristic of theirs has perhaps "stuck", otherwise I have written a sort of "pen-picture" of quite a few of the 60 or so conductors I have played under in my career.

I have obviously devoted more time to those I knew best and personally, and Malcolm Sargent easily "heads the stakes" - after all, I was lucky to be at the Royal College at the right time. I stick by what I have said - that Malcolm had the best conducting technique of anyone I've known or seen. It may seem strange that I also say that I would rather lead an orchestra for Beecham than for Sargent!

Josef Krips
Krips was a fine musician and conductor and was appointed Principal Conductor of the L.S.O. in the early 50s. We did quite a lot of recording with him. But he had another side to his nature and could behave in a very childish manner and when taking umbrage at quite small incidents which, on two occasions, caused him to act like a spoilt child. The first was the more serious and the sequence of events could - in a somewhat round about way - be traced back to the fact that I bought a shilling raffle ticket for my daughter, then aged about two, in aid of a village hall in Sussex. If this sounds a bit far-fetched I will elucidate. It was at a time when I was conductor of the Withyham Choral Society. They were in the process of doing up the village hall and, in order to raise some money ran a raffle with tickets a shilling a time. I bought three - two for myself and my wife and one for Diana.

Some weeks later I had a phone call from Withyham - "When are you coming to collect your daughter's prize?". "What prize?", I asked. "She has won first prize in the raffle!" We made a nice week-end of it, staying with friends, and collected her prize, which turned out to be a "Pye Portable" radio set. It was quite small - perhaps twice the size of a woman's hand bag. You raised the lid and it played!

In 1954 the L.S.O. celebrated its 50th anniversary. The special birthday concert was due on a Sunday, with Krips as conductor. The B.B.C. used to have Sunday morning programmes on the Home Service called "Music Magazine", and they had invited the L.S.O. to send a representative to give a resumé of the Orchestra's first half century. I think it was about 20 minutes long - perhaps less. Before the Sunday we were asked if anyone happened to have a portable wireless set so that we could time our Sunday morning rehearsal coffee break at the Festival Hall to coincide with the broadcast and then we could listen to it. Although this was only just over 40 years ago, nobody had one - except me! I was asked to bring it with me to rehearsal and at the relevant moment we all trouped off to the coffee bar, half way back from the front stalls. We grouped round this modest little set - including Josef Krips - and I opened the lid. Harry Dugarde, our Chairman, had been deputed to go to the B.B.C. to make the broadcast, and off he went, first mentioning the various early distinguished conductors like Hans Richter and Nikisch, and others of that era, and of course saying something of the history of the L.S.O. In such a short talk it is not possible to mention every conductor who had been in charge. He mentioned Beecham, of course, Sargent, Boult and various other wavers of the magic wand, but, to everyone's horror there was no mention of Krips! Of course it was a monumental faux pas not to refer to him at all, but it was an unintentional error and in no way deliberate.

One of the nicest members of the Orchestra at that time was John Cruft - oboe. His father and grandfather were both professional string players, his father having been principal double-bass in the B.B.C. Symphony Orchestra. John himself had done noble service for quite a considerable time playing 1st oboe when the Principal had been ill. He is the last person who would ever do anything underhand or hurtful. After we had listened to Harry's broadcast, Krips was in a towering rage and sought out John Cruft who was having a quiet cup of coffee with a colleague at the refreshment bar. Krips came up from behind and without any provocation or warning slapped John in the face, saying: "You and Harry are in league together against me!" and stormed out saying he would not be conducting the concert. It was, of course, absolute nonsense and a figment of Krips' imagination. No such animosity existed between the two, or anyone else. But we had a crisis on our hands, with Her Majesty the Queen Mother due to come to the evening concert to join and honour the celebrations. Who would be conducting that evening?

It is here that there seems to be some confusion about what did really happen. One thing is certain and that was that an announcement was made which said that Prof. Krips had been taken ill - which was untrue - and that : who would conduct?

This is where the facts are not clear. According to some newspaper reports which a friend has come across, it was said that four different conductors - all friends of the Orchestra - were conducting one work each out of a total of five. If that were so, there was no serious crisis, with four conductors - one of them Malcolm Sargent himself - and only one work needed to be allocated to each one of them. If my memory is to be relied on, this was quite untrue and there was a crisis to be resolved fast, and I am almost certain that - not for the first time - the ever-reliable George

Stratton (the leader) was called upon to conduct the whole concert. (I really envied him!) I am almost certain that my interpretation of events is the correct one. If I am wrong, then why did we need a 3-hour rehearsal in the morning, with only one work for the conductor - Krips - to be concerned about, and no sign of any of the other four conductors in the morning? It was most unlikely to have been the case. At any rate the L.S.O. got away with it, with no thanks to their Conductor-in-Chief!

The other example of Krips' uncontrolled petulance occurred also at the Royal Festival Hall. He was again taking a rehearsal of the L.S.O. for an evening concert. Hugh Maguire was the leader on this occasion. Hugh was a very pleasant person with his gentle Irish manner, quiet touch of calm and nice sense of humour. He also said what he thought without hesitation, with no malice aforethought at all.

Krips was rehearsing a Beethoven Overture when a question of bowing arose. Apparently Maguire had queried it, as he had a perfect right to. Krips was immediately cross at being criticised and snapped at Hugh saying: "What is wrong with the bowing?" Hugh, in his quiet Irish brogue said exactly what he thought, and answered: "I think it's bad bowing". "Bad bowing? What do you mean bad bowing." Again he took umbrage and stormed out of the building. Not quite - he hoped to go down in the lift and leave the Festival Hall with as much speed as possible - but this little scheme was thwarted. The lift had other ideas! It was a dual-purpose lift which, after conveying orchestras etc to the concert hall, had other duties to perform. There were various functions to be provided for, and large crates of beer and other beverages had to be taken down to the basement to be dispensed to the various bars, so that frequently during the day the lift was not immediately available and individuals often had to wait quite a while. This rather spoilt the drama of Krips' sudden exit.

Meanwhile the L.S.O. had to hang about aimlessly until about mid-day when someone said: "Go on Max. You know how to deal with him. Take your car down to the de Vere Hotel". This was a very nice hotel half way between the Albert Hall and Kensington High Street. "Max" was a viola player who had parked conveniently and was just the person to deal with such a crisis. He found Krips sitting on his bed in the hotel, in tears! He and Max duly appeared back at the Hall and the rest of the rehearsal continued without any comments.

This childish side of Krips' nature was a pity and rather silly, and it did not really endear him to the Orchestra - and it was quite unnecessary as he was a fine musician who produced some memorable concerts and recordings. And he had quite a sense of humour when he relaxed. He often said to me' "Ah - Sir Thomas!" I think he had been to a little party given by the Directors when, apparently, I'd had the cheek to do my impersonation of Beecham.

One of Krips' favourite soloists, and obviously someone he became quite fond of, admiring not only her playing but also her charming personality, was Rutu Lady Fermoy who was the grandmother of the late Diana, Princess of Wales. She played a number of times with the L.S.O., and an occasion I remember particularly well was a concert at the King's Lynn Festival where she played a Mozart Piano Concerto.

Nicolai Malko

One of the earliest occasions when I was really aware of the humour stemming from within a professional orchestra, occurred before I was a full member of the L.S.O. and was still playing as an "extra". I was about No.11 2nd violin so I was quite a long way from the conductor's desk at the Queen's Hall. (Malko was one of those who liked to have the 1st violins on his left and the 2nds on his right. Generally these days all the violins sit together on the left of the conductor.) Malko was rehearsing the well-known Fantasy Overture *Romeo and Juliet* by Tchaikovsky. Towards the end there is a solo bar for the timpani played *forte* followed by a diminuendo, after which the whole orchestra joins in with the cellos playing what I call the "tear jerker" theme. But Malko did not want the timpanist to play his solo bar in the "conventional" or usual way, with the player employing a 'roll' with the sticks going at "full speed" right from the start of the bar. "No, no. Please not ze vay you usually play it but start viz de sticks going slowly, then go quicker right devay in de distance - you understand?" "Right you are, Maestro", the timps player said, "It's not the way I usually play it but I'll do it your way if you insist, so long as you stop" (i.e. the rehearsal) "by 1 o'clock." (A typical union pro.!) So off he goes again with the sticks starting very slowly and deliberately until a proper roll is reached in the normal way. Malko stopped again. Meanwhile, a bit of a wag sitting near me, said to his companions: "Anyone ordered any coal round here?", to which his partner quickly responded with: "Yes, mate. 'alf a ton of kitchen nuts". I was listening to all this and quickly twigged what they were getting at. When the coalman delivers a sack of coal, he leans over the bin and a few nuts come out from the top until he can get the sack off his shoulder and holding it vertically the whole lot goes "whoosh" into the coal bin.

What a marvellous imagination and quick reaction. It did sound quite like that. By this time Malko was again addressing the player: "Zat is good. You 'ave ze right speed, but it is too loud. I vant it to sound further avay. Play it softer. This he does. There comes a voice from the back: "Next door's 'avin some now!"

Albert Coates

Coates was another fine pre-war conductor. He was born in Russia, but he must have been naturalised as he was as English as the next man, and he had a very nice daughter who studied oboe at the Royal College at the same time, I believe, as my daughter Diana. Coates was a big man - both in stature and in his performances, especially when he conducted large-scale works, particularly the Symphonies of Tchaikovsky. I first came across him in my early days in the L.S.O. before the war. They were the days when audiences were small and there seemed to be some lack of enthusiasm. But Coates had a way of stirring people up by his exciting performances which, literally brought people to their feet. I well remember a performance of a Tchaikovsky Symphony which so roused a man sitting in the stalls - not very far from the stage - that he actually stood up at the end, waving his hat in the air and cheering.

None of my three "appearances" at Covent Garden concerned playing an instrument - but all had connections with an opera. The opera was a Russian one by Mussorgsky, *Boris Godunov*. The conductor was Albert Coates and the Royal College was called upon to supply some extra voices for the chorus, and I was one of them. We had a certain amount of singing to learn but during an earlier scene we had to behave like rioting peasants, making as much noise as possible. The fact that we, when singing normally, were doing so in Italian, and Chaliapin - the big star of the opera as Boris - was singing in Russian did not seem to worry anyone. There were three nights of this opera at the Garden, but on the third there was an opera performance at the R.C.M., which left only three of us who were not involved in singing at the College, Natalie Caine (oboe) - who later married the bassoonist, Cecil James - myself and one other. The rest of the other replacements had to be enlisted from students at Birkbeck College. I was put in charge of them and gave them a short "pep talk" - as, of course, none of them knew anything about the music. Not many of them were needed for singing, but all were for their number to make the riot scene more effective. I warned them about one thing and said it was most important that they all remembered what it was. I told them to watch the conductor assiduously from the beginning as there is one moment when there is a bar's silence. "Coates, the conductor", I said "will cut everything off with a big sweep of his baton and then keep absolutely still as the music dies away." After that moment I told them they could do anything they liked, making as much noise as possible just as they would do in a riot. "So", I said, "be prepared by facing forwards to stop dead for that moment when everything is silent and still."

Did they observe this warning? As we approached this dramatic moment, I could feel things were getting out of hand and I was sure they had forgotten. It was not really surprising when you come to think about it - a whole lot of enthusiastic students finding themselves on the great stage of Covent Garden for the first time. They were out to enjoy themselves by "letting their hair down" for this heaven-sent chance of a life-time. I was getting more and more apprehensive as this motley crowd had lost any control, most of them with their backs to the conductor as the dreaded moment approached. Then it arrived. Silence was an unused commodity. They were shouting all sorts of threatening noises - and I can remember one - "Down with Baldwin!" (that *dates* it), and other irrelevancies. I gave up. It was no good saying anything in such circumstances!

As for the rest of the evening, most of the choir, especially the aforementioned students, were free to go, but a few men were required for the final scene when, dressed as monks, we had to go on the stage while Boris dies. This was, literally, hours later! We had an opportunity of seeing what goes on behind the scenes. One abiding memory is of the very long straight iron staircase leading down to the changing rooms. Believe it or not, there was just one cold water tap for washing!

Other memories include a tendency for some of those off stage to try to distract those on stage by doing naughty things. There was a woman in distress and seemingly in tears, sitting by an open window, while some of those watching - but of course out of sight of the audience - were trying to make her smile.

About three hours later, eight or ten of us were on stage again as monks. One - a huge man with a fine tenor voice, called Howard Hemming, had got fed up with hanging around and had decided to leave his trousers on to save changing , and had merely rolled them up out of sight. As the scene proceeded, I noticed his trousers - which had not been rolled up too securely - began to unroll and appear under his garb. I wondered how many observed what was happening. Luckily he got away with it.

Howard himself was a great asset at the Royal College both in opera and oratorio. I remember his delightful fooling in my pantomime "Cinderella", when he tried to part the railings - when he was supposed to be in Hyde Park - to get at someone, and managed to bend the "iron" railings to get through, and they closed to the upright position again! And he made a splendid figure in "Lowatha" with his huge head-dress of feathers.

What times we had in those days with so much talent. I don't regret any of it - it did not interfere with anyone's career - and there seemed more time to relax and have fun. Things obviously have had to move on with the times and one has to recognise the tremendous change these days, with challenges all the time, especially from abroad.

Constant Lambert

Here was a brilliant man both as composer and conductor. I suppose his *Rio Grande* is his best known composition and most often performed. I got to know him partly as he took the conductors' class at the College for a time. There was no doubt about his talent and it is no exaggeration to say he was a genius. He wrote a book called "Music Ho! A Study of Music in Decline"(1934). I read it many years ago and I had to admit it was rather beyond me As I have a copy I might even get round to reading it again.

Lambert became Musical Director at the Old Vic Ballet at Sadler's Wells. He trained at the Royal College of Music, later becoming a Professor of Conducting there. He was a very unusual person in many ways. He liked collecting names of firms appropriate to their calling. There are quite a number and I wish I had collected them myself. Lambert asked me to let him have any I came across. I always remember a butcher near Victoria Station named De'ath! There was a shop in Dorking called "Swaddling & Co" which sold baby-carriages! The shop disappeared years ago and the site was bought up by Waitrose. One of the Swaddling boys once played for me at Guildford - I believe in the trumpet section. Another shop, which I believe still exists, was rather appropriate to Lambert and I think he enjoyed it. It was in Bath, and is a wine-merchant called rather delightfully, "Fuller and Hick"!

An "ambition" Lambert had was to conduct one symphony he considered had been sadly neglected. He felt that the public did not understand it and he wanted to put it on the map - so to speak. It was the *4th Symphony* by Sibelius which is obviously less appealing to the general public than *2nd Symphony in D*. At last his great chance came. He was booked for a Prom at the Royal Albert Hall and the main work was the Sibelius No 4. He was obviously delighted and he said he had planned the best way of putting it across and helping to popularise it. It went down quite well but he had decided he would not go right off the platform at the end, but half-way down the slope to the artists' room he would reverse and return to the platform so as to keep the applause continuing. This scheme started well, but just as he was approaching the platform again his world went flat. His progress was halted by the booming voice of a certain Mr Hammond - a nice enough man - whose job was to announce any special messages over the public address system. It always started - "Ladies and Gentlemen" - which always achieved immediate silence. "Ladies and Gentlemen", he repeated, "Is there a doctor in the Hall? If there is, would he proceed to the St.John Ambulance room by the main entrance". Poor Constant Lambert - he had to return to his room "with his tail down" - "All the best laid plans . . !" Being of an enquiring mind he decided to find out what was the cause of the announcement. He was told that a poor girl among the "prommers" had fainted through the stifling atmosphere. About twenty-seven doctors turned up - and all she wanted was some fresh air!

There was a very sad side to Constant's life - and I think was the main cause of his early death. Just as cancer is a dreaded word, so can another word indicate matters sinister - if taken to excess - that is alcohol. And that really was Lambert's failing and became the cause the world of music's great loss. It was sad to witness his failing taking charge of his life. The L.S.O. had a rehearsal planned at St. Pancras Town Hall for a concert elsewhere. Lambert was to be conductor. In the morning the rehearsal was due from 10 a.m. to 1 p.m. He did not turn up till 10.30 and had obviously been on a "gin session" most of the night. He had a large jug of water by his rostrum, all of which he consumed pretty quickly.

Another time was at the Royal Festival Hall, even later than the concert just mentioned, where the chief work was his own composition *Summer's last Will and Testament*. We were all fearing the worst, and this time we couldn't imagine how he could possibly deal with such an extremely complicated work. It is a very fine work and most enjoyable to listen to and play, changing time signature nearly every other bar. In other words, it could not be much more tricky even for a conductor "cold sober" .

The moment arrived and we were "keeping our fingers crossed" - which does not help one's technique! - and Constant shuffled on, perspiring from every pore. Fortunately the rostrum was at its lowest and he did not have to step up far for the conductor's stand. The anticipated "great disaster" never happened - much to everyone's relief. He never put a foot wrong - or rather, beat - wrong. His conducting was clear and never ambiguous, with everything disciplined and assured. Every time change and variation of tempo was exemplary. It underlined once more the sadness that a man of such talent and integrity, should throw away his life so regardlessly when he was probably at the height of his career, with so much still to give.

Constant Lambert, who was married for a while to a small but quite exotic girl from some distant American State, never reached the age of 50. He died aged 46 in 1951. It is amazing the number of great composers in the past who never even reached the age of 40, which included Mozart, Chopin, Mendelssohn, Purcell and many more. Of course we also lost a number of very promising young composers during the Great War, among whom was George Butterworth, some of whose quite small but delightful output can often be heard on the radio.

Reginald Goodall
Goodall was in the same conducting class of Sargent's as I, so I was able to watch his development with interest. He used to keep himself very much to himself and seemed to take part very reluctantly in the activities of the class. From the start it was obvious that he and Sargent were not going to see eye to eye. It seems an odd thing to say at such an early stage of a student's career but there was a very slight feeling that Sargent felt a tinge of jealousy towards him! Goodall would never think of asking any questions and gave the impression, in a way, that he already knew it all and did not want any help - not in a conceited way - but perhaps he wanted to work everything out for himself.

He was in fact a very unusual person - not unpleasant or aggressive - and could be quite friendly. He and I seemed to get on quite well together. I also think I was beginning to see something - not obviously discernible - that he was going to surprise quite a lot of people. He was an obvious loner who was going to plan his future in his own way.

It wasn't long before I was able to see clear signs of him becoming something of a genius. He was at the time organist of a well-known Church in High Holborn, known as the "Musician's Church", - and I am sure there was some connection with Sir Henry Wood, as he is buried in the churchyard..

Goodall was going to conduct a concert there of three choral works. He had invited a very small orchestra for the accompaniments - and there must have been organ as well for the wind parts. The strings consisted of four first violins, two seconds, two violas, two cellos, and one double-bass, a dozen in all - plus timpani, which I played, so I had a close-up view of all that went on. He certainly aimed high for he had invited the principal string players of the L.S.O. led by Willie Reed, and other well-known players including Anthony Collins, principal viola - later to become a conductor - Cedric Sharpe, cello - a delightful man and fine player - and Adolph Lotter, double-bass - the last surviving pupil of Dvorak, a Czech who became a very good friend to me. Goodall couldn't have chosen better than this select few, so it was likely to become a worthy performance. I was witness to two eye-openers at that one 3-hour rehearsal which I have never forgotten.

The programme consisted of works which I doubt anyone there had heard, let alone played before - except perhaps for one, a little-known Mass by Haydn. The other two were by composers whose names were practically unknown, and not one of the Orchestra had ever set eyes on them and they were extremely difficult. Goodall dealt with the whole rehearsal with great efficiency. But when he started to rehearse each part separately, I anticipated trouble. I said to myself: "Watch it mate, you're dealing with the top experienced orchestral players and they are not used to this sort of treatment from a music student". But I was to be proved quite wrong in my assessment of the situation. I was quite surprised to find this sensible as well as experienced group of players were only too glad of the opportunity to learn their parts quickly, reading them, of course, for the first time, and they wanted to give of their best.

The concert itself - though long ago - I remember as being most successful and enjoyable and to the complete satisfaction of the conductor. To cap it all, Reggie Goodall conducted the whole concert from memory. What a pity Sargent could not be there!

As time went on, Goodall devoted his life to opera, especially some of the greatest works of Wagner at Covent Garden. He eventually received a well-deserved knighthood. In watching him in action not so many years ago, on T.V., I was surprised to notice, first his non-use of a baton, and secondly his somewhat strange way of conducting but somehow achieving good results. Perhaps it was another of those occasions where personality supercedes technique.

Another disappointment to add to others in my life happened during a tea party at the R.C.M. after a Fellowship presentation by the Queen Mother, who was present at the party. I saw Reg Goodall sitting against a radiator at the back of the room with no-one talking to him. I always regretted not having done so myself.

Dr. Cyril Rootham

Rootham was another disappointed man who felt he had never received his dues in relation to his talent - and probably with good reason. He was organist and choirmaster at St. John's College, Cambridge. My brother was there for five years during his "reign". Clive always spoke well of him though he also recognised his faults. He had a hyper-active ear for intonation and pitch generally whether with a choir or orchestra.

Rootham was always disappointed at never receiving a knighthood. There was a story of him waiting for a train at Cambridge Station and being overheard saying to himself: "Sir Cyril, Sir Cyril", - just to see how it sounded.

One way and another I found myself occasionally involved in Cambridge music, though I was never a member of the University. One such time was when that fine player, Alan Richards, had to be away from leading the C.U.M.S. Orchestra.(Cambridge University Music Society), and I was invited to take his place. The old town hall - before it was rebuilt - had rather a strange set-up with regard to the stage. The organ was immediately behind the stage - in fact at a slightly lower level in relation to the platform - and with an orchestra in place, the leader, conductor, and any soloists would come on, not from the side of the platform, level with the first violins, but straight up on to the rostrum. Normally, walking on parallel with the first violins, one would have plenty of chance to watch the conductor's progress to his desk, usually accompanied by welcoming applause, but in the old days at Cambridge, it would be possible not to notice him immediately. As Rootham passed in front of my desk in complete silence, he said: "I've come on unperceived!".

Rootham's wife was a remarkable lady, who was a great source of strength and inspiration for "the Dr." in his moments of doubt. She used to give a tea party every Sunday afternoon, and my brother told me she could carry on an intelligent conversation with one person after another, say four or five people, and then return to the first one and carry on at the point where she had left off.

There was a story of a C.U.M.S. orchestral rehearsal at which a student wanted to query some point in his part, addressing Rootham as, "Sir". There was no reply. "Dr. Rootham", he called out, but again - no response. Getting a bit fed up with this he said: "Oh my God!", to which quickly came the reply: "Yes, yes. What is it?". On another occasion, someone addressed him as Dr. "Ruth"ham. "No! No! *Root*-ham - like Beethoven!".

Cyril Rootham was no mean composer. He wrote a work for full orchestra and choir called *Brown Earth*, which, of course, received performances in Cambridge itself. It eventually found its way to the Royal Albert Hall. My father and I bought tickets for the concert which went down quite well after a good performance. As the applause tended to wane we kept it up as loudly as possible - we had seats just below the organ, level with the choir - and we achieved another "curtain call" as the composer came on once more to take a bow. I wonder if this work has been performed since - or is ever likely to be heard again? That is the depressing side to music-making and performing, after all the "tears and sweat" that goes into its inception.

On another occasion at Cambridge, when I was playing but not leading, there was a rather curious concert, almost exclusively of music by an Italian composer with the forgettable name of Ildebrando Pizzetti - born in 1880 - who conducted his own music - pretty badly - and could not speak a word of English, so his instructions were interpreted by his young son. There were about four of his works - all very curious - and I remember the relief when we reached the final - familiar - work! He will probably never be heard of again.

Richard Tauber

I am sure most people will think there has been some mistake in finding Tauber among "Conductors" - and would probably also be quite surprised if he was to be found under "Composers", but he actually qualifies for both. It has been done quite deliberately, although I only came across him once and he was involved in both guises. I was equally surprised when this event took place. Many people will think of him - rightly - as a famous tenor from Vienna who made his name with his singing in a show called *Land of Smiles*, based on Lehar's music, and especially with the song in which he sings "You are my heart's delight" with great fervour.

I played in the Orchestra at the Coliseum in the West End in a concert given to raise funds for a Jewish Charity and I remembeer the well-known concert agent, Harold Holt, was in the audience. Tauber conducted - in a blue "boiler suit"! - and was most impressive with a clear, well-controlled beat. What was really memorable was his own four-movement Suite for full Orchestra. Why is it never played now? As far as I know it has never been played since, and had not been played before this concert. It was a most attractive and well-written work which conductors wanting new ideas for their programmes could do worse than consider.

Rudolf Schwarz

Schwarz was an experienced, hard-working and quite pleasant conductor to work with. There was just one oddity about him. He suffered an injury to his right arm during the last war - though it is more likely that he was tortured by the Germans as a prisoner of war - and this affected his conducting. His down-beat was done with the right elbow, with the baton facing upwards, and reversed the action for the 2nd beat. It could be quite confusing and one tried hard not to follow the beat too literally.

W.H.Reed

Generally known as "Willie" or "Willy", Reed was a great character - a friend, R.C.M. Professor, composer, examiner, conductor, orchestral leader, and much else besides. One of his quite extraordinary achievements was to conduct - on five evenings each week - the orchestras of Redhill, Croydon, Bromley, the Great Western Railway as well as the Strolling Players. At the same time, apart from teaching the fiddle at the R.C.M. and conducting the Third Orchestra, and taking its conducting class, he led the London Symphony Orchestra. If he happened to be talking to someone in the entrance hall of the R.C.M. as you passed, he was such a friendly man that he would have time to shake your hand as you went by. He was one of whom it could be said - "He could walk with Kings and Princes nor lose the common touch". Willie was a friend of Elgar and advised him in the composition of the Cadenza of his *Violin Concerto*.

My first connection of any kind with him must have been in 1917 when I took the "Higher" grade in an exam of the Associated Board. Reed was the examiner and I still have the Certificate signed by him. Not surprisingly he was not always available for conducting because of a professional engagement, and quite often he asked me to deputise for him at rehearsals - especially at Croydon or Redhill. Later on it transpired that two first cousins of mine, both unmarried, found themselves living opposite the Reeds in Chatsworth Road, Croydon, and when he saw them going to the post with some letters, he used to call to them, asking if they would mind taking his dog for a walk!

I was always grateful to Willie - although I had a proper audition, at which I played in front of the Directors quite a testing programme of Bach's great *Chaconne*, Beethoven's *Kreutzer* Sonata, and part of a Mozart Concerto - for a lot of his influence came to bear in my being accepted as a member of the L.S.O. in 1937. One of Willie's little quips was - if a student turned up late for a rehearsal - "Fog down the line this morning?".

Sir Arthur Bliss

Bliss was a fine example of the finest type of Englishman and never really lost his military bearing, having been an Army Captain in the Great War. His only brother was killed in action in France and he wrote a fine and moving work in his memory called *Morning Heroes*. His compositions were always impressive and original and he made a splendid "Master of the Queen's Musick", often being called upon to write suitably patriotic music for state occasions which always seemed more natural and suitable than music specially written by others holding this office. He was, of course, not paid as this was an honorary appointment, with just the honour of holding the Office (though I believe he did receive something like £25 a year!).

Bliss eventually became President of the L.S.O. His conducting was in the same high class as his compositions. There was one particularly memorable concert which we took part in under his direction. It was given in memory of the fallen in two World Wars at Ypres in Belgium, and took place in the "Cloth Hall", an impressive building which gave the feeling of having stood there for years. Actually it hadn't as the Germans had flattened it during a Great War bombardment. Through the great skill of men who have the ability and desire to overcome apparent irreparable disaster, the building was rebuilt with all the original bricks and everything else so that the fine Cloth Hall rose again from the ashes, and no-one - such as ourselves - could have any idea it had ever been any different. It is such achievements as this that make one feel very humble, especially compared with any small efforts of one's own which may have given satisfaction at the time.

I don't think we were paid for this concert. The audience - with free entrance - packed the Hall and were even sitting on the window sills. The music was suitable for the occasion, but the timing was of considerable importance as I shall describe. At the end of the concert there were two speeches - one from the local Burgomaster, in Flemish, so we could only guess at what he was saying, and the other from Sir Arthur, "couched" in most appropriate terms that made one proud of being British. I am sure we all felt how lucky we were in having a President who could rise to a special event like this in the most natural and moving way.

The time was rapidly approaching 9 p.m. and we all "downed instruments" and walked up the road to the Menin Gate - which was quite near -and at exactly 9 o'clock two trumpeters in uniform stood in the centre of the main road into the town, under the concrete archway, and blew the Last Post. This was a most moving moment. The Menin Gate was erected after the First World War, and this ceremony - which naturally halts all traffic - is held every single night of the year and is a constant reminder of the horrors of war. The "Gate" itself is an impressive edifice of an archway, I suppose about 20-25 yards long with solid walls each side, and going up to a gallery above, where are the names of all the men known to have lost their lives, especially in the 1914 -18 conflict, and the fact that it took me the best part of 20 minutes to find inscribed on the walls among the many thousands there, the names of my wife's mother's two brothers who were both killed when in their teens, gives some idea of the scale of the undertaking and of the wars themselves.

The fact that the covering over the road is built of concrete, and so amplified the sound produced by just two trumpeters, made the effect even more stunning. I wonder how many people actually know of this impressive ritual. After the ceremony we wandered down the road and were confronted by a cemetery of the graves of thousands upon thousands of men lost in war, which made one realise what an indictment this was of man's bestiality at its worst - and still it goes on around the world!

I got to know Sir Arthur quite well when he was President of the L.S.O., and he also came down to Guildford while I was conductor of the Symphony Orchestra there, to conduct his own *Piano Concerto* with Frank Wibaut as soloist. It was about this time that he suggested to me a short work of his he thought would be a suitable addition to our repertoire. I followed up his suggestion, but never having heard of it - and I haven't heard it since, nor do I remember its title - beginning with "A". Bliss thought I might like to hear a recording of this piece which he had and invited me to his house in Maida Vale one day. He had a most delightful and attractive small house, "off the beaten track" but surprisingly near areas of great activity, including Lords cricket ground. The short road was a cul-de-sac, so no traffic passed by. But for those on foot there was a pub - reached through a gate at the end of his small garden, where - after listening to the record - Sir Arthur took me for a snack lunch consisting of sandwiches and a pint of beer. No-one appeared to recognise him - there were only a few in the bar - and it was a pleasure and privilege to be in the company of such a distinguished man in the most natural and relaxed environment.

Jascha Horenstein

Horenstein was a conductor of distinction and integrity as well as being a pleasure to work with. I remember well one of his biggest undertakings with the L.S.O. which was to conduct Mahler's huge *"Symphony of a Thousand"* at the Royal Albert Hall. His control of such large forces spread around the Hall was indeed impressive.

I was once most unexpectedly involved in a very unusual activity and for a most unusual reason. The L.S.O. played in a "Provincial" concert in Leicester and after the afternoon rehearsal, I hurried to get to my car which was parked in a nearby street. I was keen to hear the broadcast, on my car radio, of the Ryder Cup Golf match (England v. the U.S.A.), so I foolishly started to run. Not for the first time, I tripped up, and in trying to save myself I broke the little finger of my right hand. This naturally put me out of action for some time, but had it been my left hand it would have been much more serious. After I reached home - which was then Esher, Surrey - I went to see our local surgeon, who set my finger in what he called "the functional position", i.e. to enable me to hold "a violin bow, a tennis racquet - or a pint of beer!". As I was out of action for a week or so, the L.S.O. had pity on me and were able, at least, to offer me one engagement which did not require me to play an instrument.

Horenstein was again due to conduct a concert with us but this time at the Royal Festival hall. The main work to be performed was Mahler's *3rd Symphony.* In this work there are two places in the 2nd movement where a rather unusual instrument - with quite a distinctive sound - is required to play two short passages "off" - that's to say, out of sight but within the hearing of the audience. The particular instrument goes by the name of the Flügelhorn - a rather misleading name, for it is a form of trumpet, a bit "bulkier" than a normal trumpet but played in the same manner. Now the Festival Hall was not the ideal place for this arrangement, there being only one spot where it would be practical, high up and in a passage about level with the tops of the organ pipes. There is also the smallest "balcony" imaginable where one person can just stand. I was given the job of conducting - or passing on the beat - to the player, who in this case was Denis Egan who had often played 1st trumpet for me at Guildford.

I did not know the work at all and I was merely given a full score to follow, placing it on a small ledge in front of me. The player cannot be expected to hear the orchestra and then come in correctly, and had to rely entirely on me, and anyway, once he had started playing he could not hear anything else.

As I have mentioned elsewhere, doing very little in or with an orchestra is much more difficult than playing all the time, and this was probably the most nervy and tricky of all the "bit parts" I had been landed with during my career. And apart from anything else, my right arm was still in a sling and I had not only did I have to conduct but also turn the pages of the score at the same time!

Anyway, we were off and the two flügel passages were a few minutes apart. It is amazing what one can achieve with a bit of ingenuity. But there was no obvious landmark leading up to the first entry as the orchestra had been playing almost up to the critical moment. One just had to concentrate on the score like mad. The moment came and went in almost a flash at the rehearsal, and though I felt quite relieved when it was over, I still couldn't be sure of the reaction from "down below". Eventually the Orchestra reached the end of the movement. I then heard the voice of the conductor: "Mr Nicholson!", he called up. (What had I done wrong? Had it not synchronised properly?) I came to the edge of my "box" and looked down at Jascha Horenstein and he repeated: "Mr Nicholson - very good!" Was I relieved! All went well at the concert and Denis and I had to do this again on other occasions. We jokingly suggested going into partnership. And once again Malcolm Sargent was right when he suggested to members of the R.C.M. conductor's class: "Go up and sit among the percussion players and count a few bars' rest!"

Sir Landon Ronald

Landon Ronald was another of the "old school" under whom I played in my earlier days. His reputation was probably established when the pre-electric gramophone records were becoming available in the 1920s, when his name appeared frequently on labels in association with the Royal Albert Hall Orchestra - later named the New Symphony Orchestra. As often as not these would be excerpts from the Wagner operas, many selections fitting nicely on to one side of the original 78s which lasted approximately four and a quarter minutes before you had to get up from your chair to wind up the gramophone and turn the record over!

I remember Ronald as a well-dressed and unexcitable man of kindly disposition, as well as having a high standard of excellence. It was said (rather unkindly) of him, that he only conducted about half a dozen works, but nevertheless he did them all extremely well. This was, of course, an exaggeration, but it does suggest that his repertoire was somewhat limited, and perhaps not too adventurous. He seemed to excel when directing a "broad canvas" of musical forces in a number of large-scale works - rather in the way Adrian Boult did. Many of Ronald's concerts were held at the Albert Hall - often on a Sunday afternoon - but not exclusively there. He had a clear beat; he did not waste time, and the Orchestra and Ronald had a mutual respect for each other. He was not wanting in humour. I remember one afternoon rehearsal at the Queen's Hall, when the pubs opened at 5.30 and he wanted to rehearse a passage again, he appealed to the Orchestra for patience: "Just once more, gentlemen, please", and looking at his watch which he produced from his waistcoat pocket at about 5.30, he said: "They're not open yet, you know!"

He would probably have had a much fuller life as a conductor had he not been appointed Principal of the Guildhall School of Music in the City of London. He began his career in the days of songs of popular appeal and more often than not tending in the direction of sentimentality, and ballet music concerts were very much the order of the day. The very name of the famous Irish tenor, John McCormack, or Dame Clara Butt, the Australian singer would result in an immediate sell-out.

There have been many composers who have made a name for themselves - and possibly a small fortune as well - with just one work. But probably most of them lived before composition was a "money spinner". One can think of scores of examples - from Sinding's *Rustle of Spring* (what else did he write?), Järnefelt's *Praeludium*, Walford Davies' *Solemn Melody*, Raff's *Cavatina*, and even Handel's *Largo,* Elgar's *Salut d'amour* and Parry's *Jerusalem*. Sir Landon Ronald will probably be best remembered for his song *Down in the forest something stirred.* Whether he *did* make a fortune at 1/6d a time is another matter!

Felix Weingartner

Weingartner was another conductor of the "old school" - in fact one of the first I played under when I was still a newcomer on the orchestral scene. He was a man of few words, economical gestures, and did not waste time. If some well-known Symphony or other familiar work was due for rehearsal he would leave it alone if nothing needed special attention. I shall never forget his "rehearsal" of Schubert's *8th Symphony*, the "Unfinished". He went straight through the whole work without stopping, nor did he say anything at the end - there was no need to. The tempo seemed absolutely "right", his intentions were clear - and when it was performed at the evening concert, there was no variation whatever. It was as though the conductor was saying to the audience: "There you are - Take it or leave it". I am not saying it was in any sense dull or boring - more a feeling that that was exactly what Schubert had in mind and how delighted he would have been with the performance.

There was a fairly familiar occurrence later on concerning Weingartner. We were due to record Brahms' *1st Symphony* for H.M.V. at Abbey Road studios one Monday morning. The previous night we had performed the Symphony at the Queen's Hall. So we settled down and tuned up in the studio. Mr Geisberg, the producer, came up to Weingartner who was already standing on the rostrum and said to him: "Would you like to rehearse, Mr Weingartner?". "Rehearse? Vy do we have to rehearse? The Orchestra know dis verk and I think I do. Ve vill make a record". And by about 10.20 we had already recorded the first side!

Weingartner - thought of as one of the greatest conductors of his age - showed his sense of diplomacy on one particular occasion when we were recording again with the L.S.O. One of the nervy things that can occur in the profession is when a tricky passage, or just one note - especially in a recording session - can upset one's equilibrium and cause a bout of nerves. The more you think about it the worse it gets, like sweating of the hands and the quickening of the pulse - something that in the ordinary way you would not think twice about and take in one's stride. We were recording the *2nd Symphony* of Beethoven. Towards the end of the 2nd movement there is quite a nasty and exposed passage for the horns - a sort of quite slow arpeggio. Our principal horn player - who shall, of course, remain anonymous - must have had "a thing" about this short passage and "fluffed" it the first time round. The trouble is, it is repeated a few bars later. We had to re-record the whole movement. The fact that it was towards the end made it all the worse for the unfortunate player. We did it again with the same result. The recording engineers had a brainwave - something that is routine nowadays - which was to record a few bars before the offending bars and a few bars beyond - obviating any anxieties of the player having to wait so long. Meanwhile Weingartner did his best to calm his nerves. He said: "I vill not look to you. I vill look somevere else". Several takes were made and one of the "perfect" bits was inserted satisfactorily. Weingartner's calming attitude obviously did the trick.

It was reported that Weingartner was once taking a class of hopeful students and one was "holding forth", much to his displeasure. He went up to the stage and tugged at this young man's trouser leg saying: "Please - no talk - do it vith de stick!"

Many years ago there was a semi-amateur orchestra on the south coast at Brighton, named the "Southern Philharmonic" and Weingartner was due to conduct a concert with them. I was given the responsible job of taking all the preliminary rehearsals, the Maestro only turning up on the day itself. It must be a nice feeling to reach such eminence - though, of course, Weingartner would not have thought of it this way.

Istvan Kertesz

Kertesz did a few concerts with the L.S.O. and also quite a number of records. He was another conductor who purchased about two dozen batons through me. Tragically he was to drown whilst bathing when on holiday in the Middle East.

Charles Mackerras

Mackerras was born in Australia and when he came to this Country joined the Sadlers Wells Orchestra as one of their oboists. He conducted a few concerts with us. He was fairly friendly but I did not take to him too enthusiastically. Since those days he seems to have gone right ahead and he is now one of our busiest conductors. My opinion of him rose considerably when I heard he had been conducting Delius' *Mass of Life*. I had to get him two dozen batons, most of them within a few weeks. What *did* he *do* with them?!

Nadia Boulanger

Boulanger was a women who was held in high esteem everywhere, but especially in her native France. Her home - and birthplace too - was Paris. She was not just a conductor but a great scholar and administrator. When she directed a concert with the L.S.O. at the Queen's Hall, I was lucky enough to be playing the viola. Viola players always seem to be in the centre of activity by virtue of their location in the orchestra and one tends to feel more in touch with the conductor.

Boulanger composed a number of works for orchestra and many songs, but she was best known as a teacher of composition, her pupils coming from many parts of the world. She was born into a family steeped in music, her grandfather winning a prize for cello playing as long ago as 1797, and her father taught singing at the Paris Conservatoire for 27 years. She had a sister, Lili, who if not quite so distinguished, was nevertheless well thought of as a composer. Nadia Boulanger came to lunch one day in the Professor's dining room at the R.C.M.. I spoke to her as I was leaving the room, saying I had played for her at the Queen's Hall and she said - rather delightfully: "Do not say the year!". She died on November 13th, 1979, aged 92.

Antal Dorati

Dorati seems to have been on the go for a long time if the number of times one hears his name on the radio is anything to go by, but, of course, many broadcast programmes are recorded. One of his "scoops" - if it was due to his own enterprise - must have been one of the best any conductor could have thought of. Haydn wrote far more full Symphonies than any other composer - 104 in all. What an achievement to have recorded all of them - and a windfall for him if someone else had suggested the idea!

Dorati did a certain amount of recording with the L.S.O. and a number of concerts. Unfortunately he, like Krips, blotted his copybook with us with some childish behaviour. We were doing some recording at Wembley Town Hall when something quite trivial upset him and he walked off and behind the stage threatening to pack up and leave us to it. I wonder if these spoilt conductors, who behave in this fashion, do their image with the orchestra any good. One merely derides such behaviour. Once again, our leader, Hugh Maguire had to go behind the scenes to persuade him to return and there was no more trouble.

Ernest Ansermet

It seems odd but we only worked with Ansermet on one occasion. It was a recording session - and a very pleasant one too - of *La Boutique Fantasque* by Rossini. I never heard the finished product but presumed it was good. Ansermet must have had a remarkable career for he was conductor of the Swiss Romande Orchestra for over 50 years. One can imagine one member of the Orchestra asking a fellow member one morning: "Who's on the box today?" He hardly needed to ask! I don't feel it is the ideal plan to work with the same conductor for over half a century; one's playing must tend to get in a kind of groove, but there must be compensations. Their reputation remained high and they obviously continued to make life enjoyable and I've no doubt their conductor had the ability to make it so.

Anthony Collins

Collins was another who had "been through the mill", - that's to say - he had been principal viola of the L.S.O. at one time. But this does not always imply that the players are sympathetic to every conductor who was originally a player himself. In the case of Collins, he had some strange prejudices. One thing you could be pretty certain about was, if there happened to be a large-scale work requiring percussion players, he would "cross swords" with that department within 10 minutes of the start of the piece - I can't think why! But he did achieve some good results with the L.S.O., including recording all the Symphonies of Sibelius.

Leopold Stokowski

Stokowski and I had something in common. We had both been students at the Royal College. It seemed he had not conducted the L.S.O. before - or, at any rate, not for a long time - when he was booked for some concerts and recordings, as a list of "rules of behaviour" had been sent ahead of his visit and stuck up on the notice board. It was quite an unusual and strange "document" of about half a dozen items which included :- Every player must arrive punctually and be seated on the platform at least 10 minutes before the commencement of the rehearsal /There should be no talking and all instruments tuned to the Oboe's "A" /No-one must be in the hall just to listen to the rehearsal - and a number of similar "rules" - all very odd and we all began to wonder who this "ogre" was from America. Naturally there were mixed feelings before his arrival. The day arrived and we more or less complied with the advance "commands". The first thing that occurred was that Gervase de Peyer, our principal clarinettist, arrived about 10 minutes late - all smiles and a mumbled apology. Not a word was said, with (apparently) no reaction from the "Maestro"!

Stokowski had an unusual method of rehearsing, which tended to be consistent. If there were three rehearsals scheduled, he would, at the first one, usually go through each work, stopping if or when necessary. The second would be thorough and detailed - remembering anything which needed attention from the first rehearsal. The final rehearsal would be a complete run through, stopping only if really necessary, otherwise it was exactly what he aimed at for the concert itself.

There was no controversy or unpleasantness at any of the rehearsals, and at the end of the first one, he addressed the Orchestra in these terms: "Now the next rehearsal is on Sunday afternoon. I should like to invite your wives - preferably only one - at the break and to the rehearsal itself". What a difference from what we had been led to expect!

When we were doing a recording session he would be sitting on his stool by the conducting stand watching the large clock above the window leading to the recording studio, and at exactly 2.30 - or whenever - he would say: "Start recording" - so he was very punctilious about timing.

Once again I found myself involved in small errands, this time for Stokowski, and I do recollect how it all started. There was at that time, an orchestra named the British Women's Symphony Orchestra of which there were over 100 members. They had decided that there ought to be an audition for string players, especially with regard to sight reading, and they were arranged to be held at the Royal College. The Director, Sir Hugh Allen, and I, had been asked to carry out this task and, of course, I found myself meeting a number of the "high-ups" of the Orchestra. I always remember one candidate with bright red hair coming in for an audition, and not only was her playing somewhat brash she had put so much resin on the hair of her bow that when she played it was like looking through sea mist. I mentioned this, in as kindly a manner as possible in my report, and later was slightly embarrassed when I found she was Secretary of the Orchestra. Someone else I was to meet was the President of the whole concern - Baroness Ravensdale. I don't know how Stokowski learned that I knew her but I found I had to take little messages from him to this lady who lived in Eaton Square. What things I became involved in!

George Hurst

Hurst was a busy conductor - starting his career in the North of England. I did not feel he left any lasting impression but he was efficient and pleasant enough. I did not think he would be the ideal person to be our permanent conductor - not that the post was ever offered to him or that it was "on the cards".

There was a scheme at that time - and for all I know it still exists - which was of mutual benefit to professional and amateur societies alike - regarding orchestral parts, especially with the various B.B.C. Orchestras where the condition of some material had become substandard - and even between professional orchestras - where second-hand parts can be obtained at a lower cost and money is saved all round.

Orchestral players are not slow at "taking the mickey" out of conductors when the chance occurs. Some of the remarks players have scribbled on their parts are little gems of wit. There was one - probably 2nd flute part, possibly of a Haydn Symphony, and he had very little to play and was getting really bored. He wrote in his part - "George Hurst stopped here at rehearsal 57 times on March 10th 1972".

Bruno Walter

Walter was a much revered man - a fine musician and conductor - who had a tragic-looking face, with deep-set eyes, as though he had really been through it - perhaps at the hands of the Nazis. He was a great admirer of the singing of Kathleen Ferrier whom he enjoyed accompanying on the piano. I was looking forward to playing under him at a concert for the first time, but fate intervened, and ironically I played for merely an Overture - *The Magic Flute* by Mozart. There were two connected happenings. The programme, with the L.S.O. under Walter was a "conventional" one - Overture, Concerto and Symphony. We performed the Overture but for the Concerto (piano) he decided to cut down the number of string players and I was a desk "surplus to requirements", so that my services would not be required until after the interval, which would be followed by Brahms' *4th Symphony*, when all the Orchestra would, of course, be required.

I had a letter in my pocket I wanted to post and now I had adequate time to walk round the corner to the nearest pillar box and wander back again. I was still a bit naive and instead of doing it calmly I felt I ought to hurry and started to run. In those days, on pavements, there used to be sky-lights for the benefit of flats and offices below ground level and nasty little metal knobs set into the glass to protect them from damage. In my hurry I caught my toe on one of these small protrusions and went flying, catching me left hand on the ground as I fell. So, instead of enjoying the Brahms Symphony, I had to go to the Middlesex Hospital (quite near) to have my bleeding hand stitched!

It was such an unnecessary mishap and a great disappointment to me. Luckily it wasn't my only experience of playing under the Maestro for, not many weeks later the L.S.O. recorded the Brahms No.4 under Walter and I did play on that occasion. He was one of those conductors who knew how to reach the heart of the music he was performing.

Charles Groves

Another case where I was present at the start of another more-than-promising career is that of Charles Groves. From time to time there were requests made to the R.C.M. for players to strengthen amateur orchestras, schools, etc at their concerts. One such was made by Sutton Valence School in Kent, where the Director of Music, Leslie Russell, who was originally a fellow student with me, and Groves was still a schoolboy. The programme for their concert included a work which was still comparatively new - Constant Lambert's *Rio Grande*, with its brilliant piano part. Groves was the piano soloist and not only did he play it in the first half but again in the second. This was an excellent idea for it helps people, unfamiliar with a work, to get to know it better by hearing it twice over. This idea might, with advantage, be adopted elsewhere. (I have only come across it on one other occasion, when I was playing for Reginald Jacques when he was Professor of Music at New College, Oxford, and we performed Vaughan Williams' *Benedicite* twice.)

One moment which remains with me - apart from Groves' fine playing - was when Russell, who never minded what he said to anyone - told the Headmaster, who was sitting in the gallery, to stand up with everyone else when they were singing a carol or something. Leslie finished up as Music Adviser at County Hall, Winchester - but not as a result of this incident! Groves - as is universally known - after training at the Royal College, became conductor of the Liverpool Philharmonic Orchestra and was eventually knighted. He remained there for many years and died "in his prime" and was a great loss to English music.

Clarence Raybould

Raybould was what you might call one of the B.B.C's "house conductors" - that's to say, he conducted any of the various studio orchestras, and was reliable and efficient. He was pleasant to work with but could be quite sarcastic if he wanted. The L.S.O. had a broadcast from Broadcasting House itself one Sunday afternoon with a rehearsal in the morning, the soloist being the noted viola player, Lionel Tertis, who had once been the viola of the London String Quartet of which Albert Sammons was leader. Tertis did a great deal to popularise the viola, which should not just be an adjunct to the orchestra - or speaking in choral terms, varying from "alto" to "tenor" - but an instrument in its own right. It is more often now being considered a solo instrument - so much so that composers in fairly recent years have actually written concertos for it, the most notable in our Country being that of William Walton. Tertis was so determined to further the cause of his devoted instrument that he actually designed a viola larger than any current use.

On this occasion at the B.B.C., the concerto was to be Elgar's *Cello Concerto*, arranged by Tertis for the viola. His playing was not to everyone's taste, especially in the way he had adopted the rather out-of-fashion form of expression by overdoing the "portamento" - i.e. change of position which taken too slowly becomes more of a slide and can be slightly nauseating. I often found his playing rather sickly.

Anyway, on that Sunday morning, Clarence Raybould also took a dislike to his playing, not only for his tendency to overdo the "slide" but more particularly for his freedom with the tempo. Eventually Raybould got exasperated and stopped the rehearsal and said: "I'm sorry Mr Tertis, but the Orchestra just can't keep with you if you play in such an "ad lib" fashion. The ensemble is already showing lack of cohesion and the whole set-up is getting out of hand". Tertis was furious. He appealed to the Orchestra saying: "My musicianship is being called into question I appeal to you Gentlemen". Unfortunately there was little support from the L.S.O.. He then took complete umbrage, walked off the stage, went straight to his viola case, did everything up, collected his coat and made for the door of the concert hall. Just before he reached the exit, Raybould called out, rather sarcastically: "Don't forget the broadcast is at 2.30 Mr Tertis!"

Naturally we all wondered whether we had a real crisis on our hands. But about 20 minutes before the transmission, Tertis reappeared and the concerto - when the moment arrived - went without incident, and at the end there were handshakes all round. It just shows that these very occasional moments of loss of control and temperamental outbursts don't pay or go down well with orchestras.

Incidentally, years ago Tertis lived a mile or so from my home at Sutton in Surrey and near Carshalton, and I often saw him doing some shopping, usually with a tray of lunch he was taking home to his wife who was an invalid. The excellent organist of Christ Church, Sutton - which was my grandfather's church next door to him - was a very good friend of mine, and even gave me a few singing lessons, the first in my life! His name was Derrick Ashley and he knew Tertis quite well. It got to the ears of the latter that I possessed the music of Nicholas Medtner's "Three Nocturnes" for violin and piano, and I was asked if I would lend them to him as he wanted to ask the composer if he could be allowed to arrange them for viola. Medtner refused and they were eventually returned to me.

Pierino Gamba

Gamba was a "one-off" conductor - in fact an infant prodigy who never really made it. We were booked for a series of concerts at Harringay (when it was spelt like that) Town Hall in East London. Gamba was a small boy of 8 who came from Italy. He must have been less than 5 feet high and when he went actually into the orchestra to check someone's part - as he did once or twice - we could not see him at all - he was so small!

He had obviously learnt everything by heart and used some quite "grown-up" words to describe what he was aiming at. Someone was obviously exploiting him and it should not have been allowed. His interpretations were clearly not his own - he had been taught everything and had a good memory. He produced quite good results and, as it was a straightforward and well-known programme, the Orchestra helped him along. But he grew up and, although he did quite a bit of conducting until he was quite a tall boy, at 17 he seemed to have more or less disappeared from the public eye and was never heard of again. It was a sad little story really.

Sir Dan Godfrey

Sir Dan Godfrey was sometimes unkindly referred to by orchestral players as "the toothbrush conductor" because of his little moustache and his way of passing his baton rather close to his mouth when he was conducting. Apart from that he did a great deal of good for the music of Bournemouth. He was the third generation of that name and most of his work took place in that popular seaside resort on the South Coast, though I did play under him once when he was invited to conduct a concert at the Royal College.

The Bournemouth Symphony Orchestra has had its ups and downs and several times has nearly had to close down. The local Council must have seen that they had a priceless asset on their hands which must have attracted visitors to their town, for at the present moment the Orchestra is riding high and is reputed to be one of the best provincial orchestras in the Country. They have had a number of excellent conductors, including Sir Charles Groves who was their Principal Conductor for a number of years.

There were quite a number of stories about Sir Dan Godfrey which tended to earn him a bit of mild ridicule. One such was while he was conducting an afternoon concert and he felt that "afternoon tea" was approaching - anyway, he was ready for his! He was in the middle of Tchaikovsky's *Pathétique* Symphony - No.6 - and had reached the famous march tune, when he decided to look at his watch - they always seemed to have large "chronometers" in their waistcoat pockets in those days - and decided to quicken the pace, marching on (to tea!) in a definitely quicker tempo!

On another occasion the Orchestra was giving one of its popular end-of-pier concerts. It was high tide and the sea was pretty rough, so Godfrey indicated a stronger tone from the Orchestra to drown the waves!

Basil Cameron

Cameron was another who had "been through the mill" - that's to say - he had learnt his trade the ideal way for anyone with an ambition to become a conductor, by first being an orchestral player. In his younger days he played in the Torquay Symphony Orchestra and later became its conductor. He was a most proficient and, of course, experienced musician who could always be relied on but who never pushed himself or seemed at all anxious to reach the heights of fame. If he had not been of such modest disposition he might have achieved more and gained more popularity. I sometimes thought some other conductors took advantage of his rather quiet manner. Most notable was one occasion which was a final night of the Henry Wood Proms at the Albert Hall when there were three conductors, and I think two orchestras - the B.B.C and the L.S.O. combined - with Boult, Sargent and Cameron. I'm sorry to say that Sargent quite obviously was ensuring that Cameron should remain in the background - that is to say - there was a feeling of an unsaid "you know your place", i.e. a 2nd fiddle, which he once was. How unnecessary that such a feeling should exist. Perhaps one should blame Cameron for some lack of "push". I found him a most friendly and amenable man.

It is a pity the expression "2nd fiddle" has tended to represent something derogatory, meaning a "bit below par". An orchestra without 2nd fiddles would not be an orchestra, just as altos are an essential part of a choir. Yet the number of times one is asked whether you are a 1st or 2nd and you happen to say "2nd", they change the subject!

Colin Davis and Edward Downes

I have included these two together - not that I have ever played under either - but it is perhaps another case where I have seen the beginnings of very successful and officially recognised careers. Both are products of the R.C.M. It was while they were both students that I was able to put in their way a little early experience of orchestral conducting, for which I expect they were grateful at the time, but no doubt have long since completely forgotten that it ever happened, as they have risen to the pinnacles of their careers. I remember I paid the "large" fee of one guinea to Colin for taking a rehearsal of the Pearl Assurance Orchestra for me. I paid rather more to Downes - something like three guineas - as he must have done a bit more than Davis. It matters little but it is interesting to look back on earlier days. Both Colin Davis and Edward Downes have - since those days - been awarded knighthoods.

George Stratton

Stratton was a professional to his finger tips and - with no previous warning - he would be willing and able to take over conducting an orchestra, in place of actually leading it, and very well did he accomplish this responsibility on any occasion, great or small, in an emergency.

Willy Boskovsky

Boskovsky did only one concert with us at the Royal Albert Hall, and he was certainly "different". Although he was billed as "conductor", he rather surprisingly came on with a violin and bow. These he placed on the conductor's stand. The reason for this was that he was used to giving concerts in Vienna of less serious music - such as Strauss waltzes and other items of lighter music, and every now and then, while conducting, he would pick up his fiddle and join in with the orchestra. If he needed a motto, it could be "Life is there for enjoyment". He certainly showed this to be true in his case.

Samuel Barber

The American composer, Barber, seems to be famous chiefly for his *Adagio* for Strings, judging by the frequent performances of this piece, which he also arranged for four part choir. He was due to visit the Three Choirs Festival in Gloucester one year to conduct the inevitable *Adagio*. Neville Marriner, who led the 2nd violins of the L.S.O at the time, had taken a lot of trouble to get all the bowing organised to ensure unanimity, making sure we all changed together. The awaited moment arrived when the composer reached the rostrum. One of the first things he said - in his U.S.A. drawl - was: "Don't worry about the bowing. Change the bow when you reach the end. All I want is a continuous sound". After all that wasted effort! (Stokowski also sometimes referred to "free bowing".)

Fritz Busch

Busch, who lived in Switzerland, was one of the family of string players of that name who formed the Busch String Quartet. His brother, Adolph, who was leader, was possibly best known as a fine solo fiddler. Fritz, the cellist, excelled as a conductor of Opera. I enjoyed playing under him at Glyndebourne in Verdi's dramatic opera *Macbeth*. He not only gave fine performances but conducted from memory. One example of this was when the principal cellist - always most reliable (and was, in fact, Jimmy Whitehead himself) came in a bar early during the first performance. Busch remembered this and, at the next performance, just before this bar, he looked towards Jimmy to make sure all was well.

It was strange that Busch, who gave such masterly performances of opera never really came to terms with the slightly different medium of Symphony Concerts. He was neither the draw nor so well known at the Queen's Hall as he was at Glyndebourne. As an individual he was obviously well liked.

Anatole Fistoulari

Compared with Fritz Busch, Fistoulari was a strange personality. He seemed to have a permanent look of worry - in fact sadness. He was a perfectly safe and reliable conductor but he had some strange and tiresome habits. One was, when we were doing a recording session, just a few seconds before the red light came on he would start to empty his pockets of anything he imagined would "chink" while he was conducting, like loose change, which he placed on the conductor's stand. He was once married to Mahler's daughter, but I don't think it lasted long.

Zoltan Kodaly

Kodaly was a collector of Hungarian folk tunes who was much admired as a composer, particularly by Bartok, though he did not write a great deal for orchestra. However, there were a number of works which are well known, such as the *Harry Janos* Suite and *Psalmus Hungaricus*. He conducted the L.S.O. in a concert at the Royal Festival Hall which featured one of these works. Both he and the music were well-liked, but as he had a bit of a squint, it could sometimes be confusing!

André Kostelanetz

Kostelanetz was a conductor from America whose wife was the famous soprano, Lily

Pons. He himself was known mostly for his connection with light music and films. We had one concert under his baton, during our series of concerts at the Harringay Festival. I happened to be one of the last to leave the hall and he came round the back hoping to see someone to thank for what he considered an outstanding concert. He saw me and came up saying how delighted he was, and shook me by the hand on behalf of the Orchestra!

Pierre Monteux

Monteux was a most loveable conductor. You could not help giving him one hundred per cent at all times. He had in his broken English/French accent, a nice sense of humour. He was appointed as Principal Conductor of the L.S.O when he was approaching his mid-80s, and at the very first rehearsal after his appointment he addressed the Orchestra with the words: "Good morning gentlemen. I understand you have been expecting a young man. Well, here I am", pointing to himself! His very long experience helped to make everything he did authoritative and clear. All his performances were memorable and thoroughly enjoyable. He was a landmark in the Orchestra's history. He first came into prominence in Paris where he gave first performances of some of Stravinsky's ballets, and he had a long and fruitful collaboration with that composer in the 1920s.

He did not always use a score, conducting a lot of music from memory. On one occasion - either at a rehearsal for a concert or at a recording session - one of the percussion players was having some trouble seeing the beat and hitting the bell at the right moment in the finale of the *Symphonie Fantastique* by Berlioz. He explained his difficulties to Monteux, - "I'm sorry, Maestro, but I can't see everything at once". He was quite a short man and he had to strike a tubular bell at the exact spot and it was high above his head. The bell has to be hit approximately 23 times in the course of not many minutes. Monteux, who was conducting from memory, had, surely, enough to attend to in the orchestra without helping a percussionist to come in at the right moment. "Don't worry", said the maestro, "I will give it to you", and, true to his word, when it came to the performance, he gave a lead to the player for every strike of the bell until he had finished.

We made some quite memorable records with him - probably the most notable being of Ravel's *Daphnis and Chloe* suites. I could never understand why so much recording took place at Kingsway Hall in London, the "home" of Donald Soper, the Methodist minister and political speaker at places like Tower Hill and Speaker's Corner in Hyde Park. As a recording studio it never seemed to lend itself to such activities. The main hazard was that the seating was tiered, sloping down from the higher level at the back of the hall to the lower stage. The stage itself was level but some of it at different elevations. The trouble was that, with a large orchestra, quite a number of the players were seated in the auditorium. One of the main snags was the proximity of the London Underground Railway. The Kingsway Hall was situated just above the end of the District Line, a branch line going up to one station, Aldwych, which was a terminus. For this reason trains weren't running every few minutes, but when there was a recording session, it seemed to be often enough! The orchestra would be all poised with the red light on indicating "action stations", and silence in the hall, when the ominous rumbling of an approaching train could be heard and the recording was held up and everyone relaxed once more until another start could be made. I often wonder if anyone has a record with the sound of an underground train which managed to escape detection. I suppose it could be a collector's item! But it must often have caused irritation to the recording studio.

When the actual recording of Ravel's *Daphnis and Chloe* was made, there was another problem. Towards the end of the work there is a wordless chorus of women's voices joining the orchestra for a grand climax. The trouble with the Kingsway Hall was that the voices had to be situated some way away - in fact, at the back of the gallery - and there was always a danger that the singers would begin to lose pitch once they had started singing. It is very easy for singers - especially a fairly large group - to go flat through their own sound partly clouding the exact pitch of the orchestra when it is some way away.

Monteux had thought up a wise ruse. He arranged for a string quartet to provide a harmonic background for the choir to help maintain the pitch. The quartet sat up in the gallery quite near the choir. I don't think anyone has ever heard this unintentional intrusion on the actual record! This "trick" reminds me of a similar occasion concerning myself at a performance of *The Planets* at the Queen's Hall but details of that will appear in the section devoted to Malcolm Sargent.

Someone once asked maestro Monteux: "Excuse me asking, Monsieur Monteux, but I am intrigued by the fact that your hair is black but your moustache is grey", to which he replied: "P'raps it eez zat my mouse-tache eez more ex-per-i-enced than my 'air!"

On another occasion Monteux was taken ill while conducting in Sweden and it was thought he had had a heart attack He vehemently denied it was any such thing. He just said: "When you eat smoked salmon you must remember to drink ze Schnapps!". I remember him having to go off during a concert with the L.S.O. at the Festival Hall, and we feared the worst. Happily he was back before long, and in full control.

A final word on Kingsway Hall - I am, of course, not affected by it personally, but I cannot but feel interested in at least three things: i) Was there a shortage of suitable halls in London? (It was perhaps fairly central for most people to get to.) ii) Were the acoustics of the hall very special and vastly superior to any other in London? and iii) Is the Kingsway Hall still being used for recording? It must have been a gold mine for the Methodist Church in those days, in terms of hiring fees.

Sir Malcolm Sargent

Sargent was a man of immense talent - a brilliant performer with a near-perfect technique as a conductor and yet he tended to spoil it all by being too concerned with his own image and what people thought about him. In short - though it is sad to say so - he was a snob. If you were to ask an orchestral player if he liked him, he would probably answer "NO!" Equally, ask him if he'd ever "let the side down", he would also answer emphatically "NO!" Ask any member of a Choral Society the same questions and you would get an enthusiastic "YES" to the first question and, of course, "NO" to the second. Why was this I wonder? He was so well equipped with natural ability and skill; he need never have been anything other than a man who sailed through life on the crest of a wave and remained there for the whole of his career. There must have been something in early life to have caused a very large "chip" which governed his whole being and never really left him. It is true that he began life in humble circumstances. He was born in Leicestershire to quite impecunious parents. When his father died it was reported in the press that he left something like £94 in his will, though what that has to do with anything I don't know!

Malcolm Sargent showed at an early age that he had a brilliant career ahead of him. He gained his Doctorate at the University of Durham, where for a time he became Cathedral organist, later to be articled to the organist of Lincoln Cathedral. While living in the Midlands he gained his early orchestral experience by becoming conductor of the Leicestershire Symphony Orchestra.

He first came into prominence in London when Sir Henry Wood included a short work of his - his only work as far as I know - at a Prom. It was called *Impressions on a windy day*. Sargent himself often said that people frequently got the title wrong by changing one letter, changing "on" to "of". He said it was not meant to be a pen-picture of a windy day but impressions gained on a windy day - a subtle difference!

One of Sargent's specialities - and something he did with consummate skill - was children's concerts, notably those given on Saturday mornings at the Royal Festival Hall under the banner of the Robert Mayer Children's Concerts. His great asset, of course, was being a natural and brilliant pianist. He knew exactly how to gain the immediate interest of young people, and an example of this was when he would show them a way of remembering a tune by adding words to it. Take, for example, the well-known opening of the sixth and last movement of Handel's *Water Music*. He sat at the piano and sang the main theme adding the words - "I'm most important, I'm most important, I'm most important. I think a lot of myself, I think a lot of myself . . ." etc. I'm sure it made it easier to remember the theme.

From then on the musical world was - so to speak - laid before him, and he never let the chances go. Although I have always seen his weaknesses in his personal life, I have gained so much - I suppose from a selfish point of view - to my own advantage, that I have tended to overlook the less attractive side of his life. It has been - as quite often happened - a case of being in the right place at the right time. The "right time" in my case happened to be when I was studying at the Royal College and was a member of the Conducting Class who attended the 2nd Orchestra rehearsals on Tuesday afternoons from 2 p.m till 5 o'clock in the concert hall.

162

Sargent - who managed to be there practically every week in spite of his busy life, a lot being outside London - was in charge. There were about half a dozen of us in what was known as the Senior Conducting Class, and I think I was the only actual orchestral player in it. To the others "Dr" Sargent used to say, if they were not immediately involved in conducting but just watching the score: "Go and sit among the percussionists and count a few bars' rest" - very sound advice, for counting bars in orchestras is a very important item, especially if you are a percussion player, and can be a very nervy occupation as I know only too well from practical experience!

Sargent himself, as I never tire of repeating, had one of the clearest beats I have ever known or watched. As a teacher of young students he was the ideal example. He may have been conventional and beating - say a 4/4 passage - in the precise direction, with the third beat going towards the cellos if they sat on the right of the conductor. How sorry I have often felt for them, never to have a beat coming towards them. Too many conductors stop in the middle. Some even seem to be wanting to send the beat over their heads as if conducting an orchestra behind their backs! There was a story of a very incompetent conductor being warned by the leader of the orchestra: "If you go on conducting like that we'll follow you!" In a very general statement, apart from Sargent, I can think of only two conductors who had a real 3rd beat (or 2nd in 3/4 time) that couldn't be faulted. They are Sir Henry Wood and Warwick Braithwaite. Too much "knitting" goes on - the more vague and mysterious a budding conductor is, the more important he feels. There is much more to conducting than some people realise and they think that - in past coinage - all they need is "five bob" to buy a baton and they've arrived!

Sargent was very particular about batons. No-one had, it seemed, ever bothered about the weight and balance of a baton, which are all-important. Any average music shop would sell you a piece of wood - much too thick and possibly with a cork handle - with no scientific thought having gone into its manufacture. "Flash Harry" - one of Sargent's nick-names - told me the name of the man who made his batons for him. He was a certain Col. Porteous who lived in Putney and used to produce batons of perfect balance from the branches of the trees lining the tow-path of the Thames at Putney! I took advantage of this information for my own use. This underlined the need for a proper manufacturer of this very necessary commodity in a conductor's "armoury" and it is really surprising that for so many years up till then nobody had given any thought to this matter. I achieved quite a reputation among visiting conductors to the L.S.O., and I often received "orders"! I later learnt of a man who lived in Wellington in Somerset, who used to make excellent batons - I think in his own home - and I was probably one of his best customers. I think he must have died "without issue" with no-one to carry on the trade. Wellington, a mere 6 miles from where I now live, was once famous among string players for "Tom's Strings of Wellington". When I went to the town not long ago I could find no trace of the shop.

Returning to the "Tuesday Orchestra", those really were luxury days at the

College, for at 5 p.m. - when the Orchestra dispersed - that was by no means the end of Sargent's "class" for we all then "repaired" to a teaching room upstairs with him and it was here that we learnt a great deal from his many years' experience. It was very much a "question and answer" session, and he was very willing to answer any questions we put to him. He would also criticise some of our faults made at the afternoon's rehearsal. And a further "luxury" - we had another session with Sargent in a teaching room on the Wednesday morning after the choral class in the concert hall, and if we didn't take advantage of all these opportunities to learn the art and the pitfalls of conducting, we only had ourselves to blame. One student asked him, during one of his classes, how you put things right when they start to go wrong during a performance. He said: "There's no precise answer to that as they never go wrong in the same way. You have to keep calm and not panic or lose your head while thinking quickly". It's not everyone who can deal with a crisis the way he could.

One of his assets - since he was a first class pianist - was that he could put a full score of a very complicated work in front of him and would give a fair impression of the sound of the work, as though - in spite of all its various transposing instruments in different keys - it was written for the piano! Those who wanted to learn from him had every chance to do so at these classes - and I was happy, and privileged to be one of them. This was not the case, as I have already mentioned elsewhere, for one Reginald Goodall, who was also a member of the conducting class - but he was someone rather unusual and somewhat different from the usual run of students.

I would like to mention at this point something which underlines the tremendous advances made over the years, and one such change will cause a few raised eyebrows. I was not in the full swing of things in the first few years at the College but I had an opportunity to observe how things were as an ex-schoolboy, and I realised that the influence of the First World War was still being felt. If I went to listen on a Tuesday afternoon to a Second Orchestra rehearsal, I would view quite a block at the back of the string players in khaki uniforms. It was only eight years since the end of the Great War and it is difficult to believe that without this contingent from Kneller Hall Military School of Music, the Second Orchestra would have been reduced to string players only. There were not enough wind students at the R.C.M. to provide even a nucleus of players beyond the First Orchestra, which met on Fridays. There was just one wind player available on a Tuesday and he was a moderate lone horn player named Christopher Mason. I always remember him as he went on to Cambridge University where he met my brother Clive and they both took part in a rare performance of Handel's Oratorio *Semele*. The wind situation at the College soon improved, and by the time I was in the conducting class there was no-one other than students in the Orchestras, though occasionally we had a professional double-bass.

As time went on I found myself quite often being called upon to play in the percussion department by Sargent, even though I had done most of the rehearsal playing in the first fiddles. It seemed he had more faith in me after a particular student had proved unreliable at rehearsal. On two occasions at the College I had no rehearsal whatever. I hardly knew what was coming to me having never set eyes on the parts before. These two occasions involved playing the cymbals and the triangle, the first being the more important of the two. Anyone who imagines playing a few notes just occasionally is easier than playing practically all the time couldn't be further off the mark. It is infinitely more difficult, in most cases, and can become quite a nervy occupation and often a very important and prominent one. You cannot get away with a wrong entry whereas an occasional slip by a string player can often occur and pass unnoticed.

The first of these occasions was when Sir Edward Elgar made a personal visit to the College and sat in the centre of the balcony to hear a concert of his own music, including his *Cello Concerto*, which was played most beautifully by a lovely girl and super cellist called Gladys Corlett, of whom I became very fond. She had a natural talent for everything musical. She hailed from Liverpool and sadly was to die at an early age leaving a gap in many people's lives. Her talent was like that of Jacqueline du Pré.

The other main work in the same programme was Elgar's *Enigma Variations*. One instrument which does not have much to do - but when it does its presence is very much apparent - is the cymbal. There are at the most six, or possibly seven, "clashes" throughout the work. Each one has to be precisely timed; there is no "cover-up" by blaming someone else; there's no going back or pretending it didn't happen. One of the troubles is that the entries are not all exactly on the beat but what we call "um-chas", so precision has to be exact. I must say I concentrated like mad, especially on such a very special occasion.

The second time was when I was taken out of the 1st violins in the Second Orchestra, where I was sub-principal, to play triangle on the day of a concert. It was for a performance of Liszt's *2nd Piano Concerto in E*. It's sometimes called "The Triangle Concerto". It certainly has a prominent - and isolated - part! Sargent could not rely on the student who had played it at the afternoon rehearsal, being a bit tentative and obviously not very assured. Sargent said to me: "You'll have to play tonight, Nicholson!". Always full of practical ideas himself - and certainly self-assured - he said to me - as it was a very important moment - that to prevent the triangle spinning round in my hand after I had struck it (as it easily could have done), "you must attach it to the music stand at two corners and find two long nails and play it with two hands". He was absolutely right in all respects, including about the unlikely event that I would find two identical "beaters" usually used with a triangle.

When it came to the performance, I did not know what I was in for. My normal position would naturally have been playing with the strings. One would of course have been aware of a triangle solo at this point, but one's only occupation was to be ready to play again after a stipulated number of bars' rest. It wasn't when I reached my position in the Orchestra - I had arrived early to make sure I was prepared for the worst - but when the actual performance of the Piano Concerto had started, that the full "horror" of what was ahead of me hit me - with literally only a few seconds' notice. This concerto is not designed in the more "conventional" three movement format with a full stop between each one. It is in three sections but with only a momentary pause between each. To make absolutely sure - and not being at all familiar with the work I started counting bars' rests right from the very beginning. Had I known in advance, this was quite unnecessary as I did not have anything to play in the first part and it was very obvious that the middle section - normally the slow movement - had been reached, when I was immediately concerned. The time signature, which from the beginning had been 4/4 - i.e. four crotchets to the bar - now changed to 3/4. Sargent looked towards me to see if I was ready, and we were off straightaway, starting with: "one, two, three, one, two" . . . In that short time of five beats, there wasn't a sound from anyone else. I thought: "Is no-one going to play?" Then it was entirely up to me - "ti-ting, ti-ting", followed immediately by the solo piano - "tum, tiddley tum", and again the triangle "ti-ting, ti-ting", and then the piano again. "Easy!" you may say. "Try it!" I would reply.

It is one of the hardest things, to do very little at precisely the right moment and do it correctly, without fuss. There are few other moments for the triangle to join in the general sound, and none so important and prominent as that solo effort. Did I feel relieved when the moment had passed! I didn't even have a secret "flask" in a convenient inside pocket! At the end of the performance, while the soloist, Dorothea Aspinall was acknowledging the enthusiastic acclaim, Sargent gave me a signal to stand up and share the applause - with a wink, as he did it as a joke - but it was also satisfying to me that he was well pleased with my performance.

With reference to Dorothea, she was the sort of person who would join in anything with enthusiasm and joy - she exuded happiness, humour and charm. While I was at the College, I was invited down to Dorothea's very nice house in Berkshire with a large garden, to play tennis. It was a lovely day and we played late, when it was quite difficult to see the ball, and there was the most brilliant sunset I had ever seen. The whole sky was a vivid red. I remember saying: "I'll never see one like that in my whole life, I'm sure". And up to now I never have! Sadly Dorothea, who was a super character, was another who died far too young, before she could enjoy the full fruits of maturity.

There were a number of other occasions when Malcolm engaged me for small percussion parts - but outside the college - in fact with professional orchestras. The first was quite a small affair and not vitally important, but nevertheless the part would have been missed had it been omitted. The work was Brahms' well-known and popular *Variations on a theme of Haydn*, and one of the last variations has a part for triangle. This did not cause any anxiety, and lasted no longer than two minutes. I presume Sargent was saving money for the Society that organised the concert . I know I was not paid, but being a student I was glad of the experience. The concert

166

took place in the London Museum which was (is still?) situated off St James' Park, a short way from Buckingham Palace.

A more important concert took place at the Royal Albert Hall, again conducted by Sargent. This concert was given by the London Philharmonic Orchestra, and the main work was Walton's *Belshazzar's Feast* with the Royal Choral Society. There is quite an important place where tubular bells are required - actually only one note of the range has to be struck - I have an idea the note was E flat. Sargent called on me to undertake this "task". There were two rehearsals called for this concert, on two days before it. I approached "the Dr" just before the rehearsal began and said that there did not appear to be any bells in the hall. "Don't worry", he said, "they will be here on Saturday" - the day of the concert - "Just follow the part and see where you have to play", (which I did). When the Saturday came, the Orchestra were all settling down in their places, tuning and warming up, with various wind players practising some of the tricky bits in the forthcoming programme - and there was I, young and inexperienced, faced with a set of tubular bells. No-one said anything to me or even particularly noticed my presence.

There is quite a knack in striking a bell correctly and getting a ringing note and I wanted to try it to see the sort of effect I could contrive from the bell. The wooden mallet or hammer has to strike the rim at just the right angle to produce the right tone. If I hadn't been so shy (naive?) I would at least have just tried a few practice blows above all the din around me but I didn't want to draw attention to myself (I'm luckily not like that now!). Well, the performance eventually got under way and I started counting carefully. Once again there were - as so often in percussion parts - not many places where my presence was required, but as usual they were important. I believe there were, in all, seven places where the bell was required to make its contribution to the whole, all in fairly close proximity. My first strike was barely audible, the second slipped off the bell entirely and finished up giving the thumb of my left hand a nasty blow. For the third I was still sucking my poor thumb! After that I think I achieved moderate success but I remember saying "I was the man who took the bell out of *Belshazzar's Feast!*" What surprised me was that no-one seemed to have noticed my not over-distinguished contribution to the performance - least of all Malcolm Sargent himself. Perhaps, for once, I had got away with it - and it was appropriate that I wasn't paid! It reminds me of another "quote" from Sir Henry Wood - referring to audience reaction to a less than perfect performance - "they don't say anything, but" - pointing to the side of his forehead - "they think it!"

My connections with Sargent seemed to be endless. Some years later he was due to give a cello and piano recital at Londonderry House, Park Lane, with the well-known Portuguese cellist, Wilhelmina Suggia. He asked me to go along to turn over for him at the piano. This is another musical activity which can also be nervy. There is quite an art in carrying out this task successfully. There are quite a number of "don'ts" to be observed, such as - don't let your hands or arms get in the pianist's way - don't obscure his or her view of the music and turn in good time, not too early. And the worst thing that can happen - especially with very thin or sloppy copies - is that you drop the music onto the pianist's hands! The ideal is to turn the page from the top right hand corner and not the bottom. This will mean you can start to turn a little in advance and in this way you avoid getting in a player's way with your hands or arms and you start revealing what is on the top of the next left hand page without covering anything. One should, if possible, turn the top corner of every other page in advance and be ready to notice the quick nod of the pianist to indicate he or she is ready for the turn. Some pianists have memorised the first bar or so over the page.

At the end of this recital, Suggia came round to the back of the stage where she had been playing, to put the valuable cello away in its case. I, ever helpful, assisted her in doing this but unfortunately managed to close the door of her case on her fingers. She "emitted a piercing shriek". Luckily it was her right hand, which was less serious and all was soon forgiven.

One of the strange things regarding Sargent's performances - for he was involved in so many musical associations and activities - concerned his method of giving concerts with the Royal Choral Society of which he was conductor for many years. At no time can I remember the Choir attending any rehearsal with the full orchestra. Naturally they knew Handel's *Messiah* extremely well, giving regular performances, including two during Easter week-ends and one just before Christmas, but at other times, with other works, the actual performance would be the first time they had heard the orchestral accompaniment. It was all very well relying on the skill of Malcolm Sargent to "bring it off" but I never thought it was the ideal way of performing. If I had been a member of the choir I would want to know the sound of the orchestra before the actual day of the concert. This does not compare well with the practice of the Bach Choir who might even have rehearsed on a Tuesday morning and about two thirds of the choir would turn up. On the day of a performance I once saw three members of the Royal Choral Society sitting in their places, just following the score.

During the 30s - when I was still a student - Sargent fell to the then fairly prevalent disease TB and he was recuperating in the Treloar Homes for TB patients in Hampshire, near where Jane Austen had lived. I drove down to see him one day; it was in summer-time and a very hot and sunny day. I found him lying outside on a balcony, just wearing his pants and looking very brown. I remember him saying to me: "If I die tomorrow, I've had a wonderful life", - and he was still quite a young man!

He did recover, of course, with his doctors prescribing a considerable reduction in his workload. This did not suit Sargent, and before very long he was back on the rostrum, rushing hither and thither, working twice as hard as before. That was how he lived. My wife once sat next to his son, listening to a recording session with the L.S.O. in the Kingsway Hall, and he told her his father never relaxed, always needing to be on the go. If he happened to have no engagements he would be listening to gramophone records - which in those days was hardly a relaxation as you needed to get up every few minutes to turn the record over!

The Treloar of Treloar Homes was once Lord Mayor of London and his firm made and sold carpets. There used to be a coloured advertisement which showed a picture of Ludgate Hill covered with a huge carpet with the caption "In the Shadow of St Paul's". They were obviously also concerned in the care of the sick.

During my days when I conducted the Withyam choir for the Tunbridge Wells Festival I used to stay the night at a charming small house, called Buckhurst Cottage, where lived two sisters - maiden ladies named (Dr) Ef and Hil Wharton. This became my spiritual home, shared later by my wife Gill, and then our daughters, Diana and Elizabeth. Ef, and later Hil, became successively Di's godmother. During the winter months nothing was more pleasant than to repair to Buckhurst Cottage after a choir rehearsal for a bowl of home-made soup in front of a roaring log fire. The cottage was rented from Lord de la Ware, Postmaster General in the Labour Government, who had a house in the same village, at the other side of the estate. Their position must have had one of the finest, most unspoilt views in the whole of England. They were on the fringe of the Ashdown Forest with not an eyesore in any direction - just an occasional cottage or farm, and mostly open country or woods. We loved going to stay there at holiday times. The Whartons were great characters. To give them their correct names, Dr Effie and Miss Hilda were most loveable people from a splendid family, their three brothers all distinguishing themselves in, or in connection with, the Royal Navy and, during the last war, one of them, Eric, was naval attaché to the French (non-Vichy!) Government of Paul Renaud. He got out of France before the Germans took over. Sadly all five members of the Wharton family died within ten years after the end of that war.

In 1909 - four years after Ralph Vaughan Williams and his family had started the Leith Hill Festival in Dorking - Mrs Wharton, their mother, had instigated a similar choral festival in Tunbridge Wells, known as the "West Kent and East Sussex", where the same sort of excitement and healthy rivalry was engendered between five or so village choirs during the day with a combined concert in the evening, with professional soloists and conductors such as Boult or Sargent. One year, when I was leading the orchestra, the main work was by Tippett's *A Child of Our Time* and the composer conducted. He and I nearly overlapped at the R.C.M. as he had just left the term I arrived. He was in Boult's class and I was in Sargent's.

Fairly early on in my "stint" as village conductor, the Whartons and I walked over the fields to Lord de la Ware's house where Malcolm Sargent was staying, and we went in and met everyone, including Sargent's only daughter who was in a wheelchair. She was suffering, and eventually died, from polio which was a great tragedy for Malcolm who doted on her. She had been a splendid horsewoman destined for great things in the jumping and "eventing" world.

One of the attractions of conducting a real village choir was the personnel you had to mould into a unified unit, and it was most enjoyable. For instance I had at Withyam, not only the Wharton sisters, who were also members of the London

Bach Choir, but another two sisters who were the daughters of Field Marshall Earl Haigh, as well as two brothers called Nelson, who both sang tenor, and I believe could not really read music, yet I cannot remember them ever singing a wrong note! They were both local gardeners and very quiet men who kept very much to themselves.

After the final concert of one of the Tunbridge Wells Festivals, the Whartons' cottage was a "full house" with a formal dinner served by a village helper. Everyone was still in evening dress and one of the guests was Malcolm Sargent himself. He was in a very expansive mood, full of goodwill and he was most entertaining and amusing, especially describing a story he had been told by Sir Hamilton Harty about himself following an incident which occurred during a concert which had taken place some time before at Llandudno. Sargent had conducted a concert as part of a morning series of popular music. He had - not too seriously - objected to ladies in the front row knitting while he was conducting. This was taken up by the Press who made quite a lot of it. It was even reported in PUNCH, and they immediately jumped on it saying: "It must be very distracting for a conductor to have ladies dropping stitches in the front row!" This was not the end of something said quite lightheartedly, for Harty told Sargent he had read in the French press the report of (apparently) the same incident which came out thus: "The well-known Roman Catholic priest Dr Malcolm Sargent objected that when people came to Westminster Cathedral to take communion, they not only talked but ate sandwiches!"

On Ash Wednesday, heralding the start of Lent, there was an annual performance, maintained for several years, at the Royal Albert Hall of Elgar's *The Dream of Gerontius* with the Royal Choral Society, which was regularly conducted by Sir Malcolm. One year it took place not long after we had recorded a very good orchestral suite in F sharp minor by Dohnanyi - played by the L.S.O. under Sargent and, with all due modesty, he said it was the finest recording of the work. He said to the Orchestra at about 12 o'clock (the rehearsal was timed to end at 1 p.m.): "We've played this work many times together before, gentlemen, I think I can leave it in your good hands until 7.30 this evening!" And that was the (popular!) end of the rehearsal of "Gerontius".

He then invited about half a dozen of us to join him at his flat, just across from the Albert hall, to listen to this "outstanding recording" we had made together. His flat was in the Albert Hall mansions - a stone's throw from the Hall - on about the 6th floor. We all crowded into the lift and up we went to his flat. We were all made most welcome and sat listening to the recording. Recordings by now were electrical, so that the sound was more "acceptable", but it was still pre long-play which meant that his manservant had to come in - noiselessly - every three minutes or so to turn the record over, or produce the following one and to rewind the gramophone. What a revolution has taken place since those days!

Meanwhile our host had provided a bottle of sherry for us to imbibe freely. I always remember making a note of the name; it was "Manzanilla" supplied by the

C.S.S.A. in the Strand. During our stay in his very nice and spacious room we noticed other things to do with another aspect of his life - already well-known - being his obsession with Royalty and his determination to feel associated with them and with any other high-ups around. On his mantelpiece, for instance, were four photographs - signed from "George and Marina, with love" - i.e. the Duke and Duchess of Kent, and there were similar sentiments from "Dicky and Edwina" - Lord and Lady Louis Mountbatten.

As 1 o'clock approached and passed, we were well into the second bottle of sherry. I began to feel we had outlasted our welcome when, suddenly, the phone rang. The manservant answered and said to him: "It's from Princess Marina, Sir Malcolm. She wonders why you haven't arrived for lunch". The call came from Coppins, their home at Iver, not far from Denham film studios near Uxbridge. Sir Malcolm immediately dealt with the situation and said: "I'm sure there is nothing in the diary. There must be some mistake". I am sure too that Sargent would not forget an engagement with Princess Marina of all people!

I think it was just a trick, in collaboration with his manservant, to "show us the door". Anyway, we quickly took the hint and made a swift departure. It was an interesting episode in our modest lives - and thoroughly enjoyable - and perhaps came under the heading "How the other half live!"

Of Sir Malcolm's technical control of any situation while conducting, he once told us he had never had to stop for anything at a performance, and I can well believe it. Whereas Sir Adrian Boult, to my knowledge, stopped at least three times at concerts - mentioned later on - I have known Sargent overcome a crisis in a flash. I was present at the time and the concert was at the Royal College. A girl student was playing a Mozart piano concerto from memory. Suddenly she jumped eight bars. Malcolm immediately realised what had happened. The lid of the piano was open and he leant beyond it and got the attention of the orchestra by pointing to himself indicating something was amiss - i.e. "Watch me!". He then tapped eight strokes of his baton on the lid of the piano - the girl could not see him - which meant "cut eight bars". From then on the performance continued to the end without further incident. I doubt whether the soloist realised what had happened even to this day. What fun if she ever reads this narrative!

While I was in Sargent's conducting class a new student joined, Sidney Beer by name. He was reported to have "bust the bank in Monte Carlo". Whether that was true I know not, but Sargent had obviously befriended this man. He introduced him to me saying: "Look after this chap, will you?" He didn't need too much "looking after". He had already shown ambitions re conducting, forming the "National" Orchestra which he conducted himself. He actually learnt music in two terms - that was how long he was at the College!

He was a very friendly individual with a strange nervous little laugh. He gave a concert in the Queen's Hall with his Orchestra and started with the *Figaro* Overture by Mozart. It is a very short overture, especially if it is taken very fast - the average time being something like 4 mins 24.5 seconds - but Sidney Beer must have beaten all records, his time being a little over 3 minutes. Ernest Newman, that great music critic of the Sunday Times happened to write this concert up - wondering perhaps whether a new genius among conductors had arrived on the scene. Judging by the way he dismissed the opening work in a very few words you would not have thought he thought so. Writing in the style of a sports writer and in the way horse racing is reported, he merely said - with reference to the great speed of the performance - "Winner trained M. Sargent"!

Beer was always very friendly to me, so much so that he invited me to his box for the performance, at Covent Garden, of Wagner's *Götterdämerung*. I - still a student - felt a little like a manservant who had pleased his master and had been invited to mix - briefly - with the fringe of the "high-ups", but I can't remember who they were exactly. I know we were in Box No. 1 - I am not sure whether a second box was used by our party or not, which of course included Sargent, but we were level with the orchestra pit and practically over the timpani, and of course very near the stage itself. When the timpani were playing at "full throttle" (which was frequently) we felt the full blast through the position we were in. Melchior was the principal bass.

This opera of Wagner's is very long - over 5 hours - and there is an interval of an hour and a half before the final two Acts, so for those living in London there was time to go home, change into evening dress and have a meal. That meant - on this occasion - me. Everything had been organised in advance and it had been arranged for me to be taken to Sidney Beer's house in Eaton Square where I would be able to change and have something to eat. I was not invited to join the grandees of the main party who were due to go off somewhere for a dinner party. So off I went alone to Eaton Square where I was greeted by a footman who took me up to a bedroom to change. I always remember that my dinner consisted of hot egg sandwiches and a glass of beer!

We eventually foregathered again at "The Garden" for the second part of the opera. I remember also one female member of the party - she was a Lady somebody-or-other - whom I did not take to. She had a loud tiresome voice and tended to hold forth with her opinions, making sure everyone heard her!

When the opera finished, I think the others went on to a party and I quietly returned home. It was an experience and certainly a chance to hear Wagner without having to pay. I had been to others of the Ring Cycle as my father was mad on them and tried to make me read the story in advance. I was always a bit bored with reading all about the Ring - I preferred to listen to the music itself, and still do. I remember my father had seats in the "the Slips" at Covent Garden. This was right high up at each side of the balcony where there was just a form to sit on and it cost "five bob". You could only see the stage if you stood up. I would stand for a minute or so while Brunhilde was sitting on a rock, singing away, with the general action practically nil, and then resume my seat for, say, another 20 minutes before I stood up again. When

I did so, Brunhilde would still be singing, sitting on this rock!

It was a great pity Sargent laid so much store on self adulation - which he definitely encouraged - instead of accepting applause or praise modestly, but it was not in his nature to do so. For instance, when the Royal Choral Society was performing at the Albert Hall, the choir had instructions to keep the applause going at the end when they thought it was beginning to wane, and he would come on to take another bow. There was quite a ritual in the order in which the performers left the platform. He would come off first, followed by the soloists, and eventually the leader, and then he would return again, walking through the returning soloists in a kind of counter-marching military operation. As he left the Albert hall - where young supporters would be crowding round the artists' entrance to see the great man leave - he would sometimes get into his car and drive twice round the block before going into his flat which was only a few yards from the hall. There was a rather unkind story circulated by some wag that after a concert in Leicester, the attendant looking after him said: "Are you signing any autographs tonight Sir Malcolm?" "No", he said, "I'm too tired today - oh well, send in the first twenty", to which the attendant replied: "There are only six, Sir"! All of this was rather unnecessary - in fact, rather sad - and it underlined how he went through life with a very large "chip on his shoulder". Sometimes it seemed he couldn't live up to his obviously quite outstanding talent.

He had some funny ideas too. When conducting one of the many Easter-tide performances of Bach's *St Matthew Passion* in Liverpool, he arranged for all the windows - and any pictures on the walls - to be draped in purple covering - a strange, almost theatrical effect, and he "allocated" the timing and applause each of the wind players was to receive. "Mr Goossens, you will come on with your No. 2 and take your applause, followed by . . ." and so on. This was really carrying things too far.

I have said so often - he didn't need to be like that, and it was a pity he wouldn't have as his motto "By your deeds they will know you". But he had a very warm and friendly side if you only knew how to find it. My very last communication with him was, I suppose, due to my tendency to remember some people's birthdays. I happened to know his, which was the same as that of Sir Thomas Beecham, Rudolf Schwarz - another conductor - and my distinguished aunt, the broadcast actress, Gladys Young - the date being April 29th.

Whilst Sargent was conductor of the Royal Choral Society (which was for many years), each year for a fortnight in mid-summer they put on at the Albert Hall performances of *Hiawatha* - The Wedding Feast, Death of Minnehaha, and Hiawatha's Departure - by Coleridge-Taylor. It was quite a "spectacular" with all the effects - wigwams etc, and in the middle movement, the lights down and there appeared to be snow falling all over the Albert Hall, with weeping and moaning women - so effective was it that a lot of the audience were in tears too! Right at the end, when Hiawatha departs in his boat as it sails out of sight at the far corner of the hall, the music soars upwards with the orchestra playing a rising octave passage, and it had such an effect on the players that they wanted to stand up with the music. And in fact they did - I must say, it was "contagious". The conductor at that point was always fully occupied giving a huge beat to the principals and choir with his back to the orchestra and was unaware of what was going on. Sargent never "caught us in the act", but it must have looked funny to any of the audience who saw it, especially any sitting behind the orchestra in direct line with the action - suddenly finding their view temporarily obscured.

But this was before Sargent had to give up all work to recover, down in Hampshire, from what was suspected TB, and the conducting of *Hiawatha* was taken over by Muir Mathieson, a contemporary of mine at the College. He must have known of our little joke for he - for the first time - saw what we were up to. He said to the leader, Sammy Kutcher (who was very much on our side) that he wanted to see every player in the band who had stood up, but Sammy soon "scotched" that, saying: "Oh you can't stop that, Muir, it's an old Spanish custom!" The main singer in most of the performances was that fine Australian baritone, Harold Williams.

When Sargent was on tour on what turned out to be his last visit to Australia, I found out roughly where he was likely to be on April 29th and sent him a card, hoping the timing would be right. With a bit of luck he received my greetings card on the very day and he was obviously very touched by it. I had a card back from him, full of enthusiasm. He had been giving successful concerts including symphonies by Walton and Vaughan Williams, which were going down well, and he spoke of looking forward once more to the forthcoming Prom season at home. Sadly this was not to happen in spite of his optimism. His adoring audience had to face up to a sad farewell as Sir Malcolm lived for only another fortnight. Without doubt he was a great loss to British music.

Abendroth and Weisbach

Among the Conductors I first played under with the L.S.O. were Hans Weisbach and the better-known German, Herman Abendroth, with whom we recorded some well-known classical symphonies - on the old "78s" of course. There were comparatively few first rate Conductors in those days. Weisbach was the one who for several years running conducted Bach's *Art of Fugue*. He brought his own parts - and it is quite a long work when it is played complete - and he had put his bowing in, but each year he had apparently rubbed them all out again. Unlike the scores of Delius's *A Village Romeo and Juliet,* mentioned in the section on Beecham, this was Weisbach's own material, so that it was a considerable waste of time to have ever touched the parts again since everything that had been rubbed out had to be restored!

Sir Adrian Boult

Boult was quite a different type of English Conductor but, nonetheless, a most distinguished and well-thought-of musician. He was sarcastically called - by the orchestral players - the "gentleman conductor". He did behave in a dignified and gentlemanly manner, but he also had quite a hot temper and didn't suffer fools gladly.

But his flashes of irritation caused by a slovenly or thoughtless act did not last long and did no harm - just the reverse. He was an upright conductor with a large baton which blended well with his considerable height and bearing.

They all say he was easy to follow but I didn't agree. I found his beat too vague, with none of the absolute precision of Sargent. Boult once wrote a text book on the art of conducting, with diagrams of the direction a baton should be following at any given moment, which, frankly, I found quite difficult to follow. In fact one illustration seemed like a plan to help you find your way out of Hampton Court maze!

He sometimes resorted to bitter sarcasm when something particularly irritated him, as, when he was rehearsing the First Orchestra one day in the concert hall at the Royal College. Some girl students were sitting in the centre of the hall chatting and joking rather noisily, and he turned round and said, "Is the common room closed upstairs?"

Sir Adrian was a great supporter of "home-grown" music and was noted as a fine interpreter of works with a "broad canvas", such as Symphonies by Elgar, Vaughan Williams or Brahms. I had one of my numerous small disappointments in my life when I was leader of the First Orchestra and Boult was conducting. I remember the programme included Walton's *Portsmouth Point* Overture and Brahms' *1st Symphony*. In the slow movement of the Symphony, at the end, there is a solo violin part which is both grateful to play and a lovely moment in the work. I was really looking forward to playing this solo but, unfortunately for me, this was not to be. The concert was due the very next day but though I nearly survived to the end of the rehearsal, I had to leave urgently for home. Instead of being at the concert I was having my appendix out at a nursing home in Sutton. My father - soon after this happened - looked up his insurance policy just to make sure I was covered. There were a number of exceptions listed at the end which he glanced through again, thinking all was well until, to his horror, although non-covered eventualities were in alphabetical order, for some unknown reason it did not mention appendicitis until the very end! This operation these days means a couple of days in hospital before returning home, but my operation was due to retain me "in custody" for a fortnight, and I persuaded my father to let me have an extra week - there was an attractive nurse looking after me. My scar is a rather untidy affair, at least two inches long - possibly longer. Nowadays I believe there is just a small incision and you are left with little to show for it and are soon in action again.

It is strange how my family seemed - in those days - to be afflicted with this phenomenon - the necessary removal of this (apparently) useless little part of the human body. My mother had quite a bad do in her case, and one of her many sisters had her appendix removed, and all four of her daughters (my first cousins) were also afflicted, two within ten days of each other. One would think it was contagious!

Returning to Sir Adrian, - who lived to a considerable age and was never, as far as I know, ill - he was a bachelor till quite late in life when, to many people's surprise he married the ex-wife of the well-known tenor, Steuart (later to be Sir

Steuart) Wilson. It was surprising - not only that he would also have "taken on" Wilson's four children, but the fact Sir Adrian was, at the time, Director of Music at the B.B.C who had themselves just lost a case in which Steuart Wilson had claimed defamation of character by a B.B.C. critic who wrote that in a performance of Bach's great *St Matthew Passion* he had introduced the "intrusive H" into his performance as the Evangelist. He won £2000 from the B.B.C.!

I have already mentioned that Sargent never stopped for anything at a performance, determined to put most things right, if at all possible, on the spot. Boult was rather different and gave way if something went wrong. Of the three or four occasions I know where he stopped, the first occurred when I was still quite a junior student at the R.C.M. and was playing in the 2nd Violins of the First Orchestra. Oddly enough it was during another performance of Brahms' *1st Symphony* (he must have had a particular affection for this work). It was quite an occasion for it was the finale of the last work in the programme of his final appearance as Chief Conductor of the College's First Orchestra before he returned a few years later. The hall was packed, all the performers in full evening dress, and the performance was building up to a thrilling climax. I think most of us were surprised when he stopped, and probably had not noticed the principal oboe had come in wrong. I shall never forget that sudden stoppage. It seemed like minutes before Sir Adrian was able to re-start but it was probably only a matter of seconds. He had quite a lot to do before the performance could continue. For one thing he was conducting from memory, so the first thing he had to do - he had his full score on the desk with, as usual a spare baton placed between the pages but, of course, not necessarily in the last movement - was to find where we had reached and the nearest letter on the score to where we had got to, before we could re-start. It was an awful moment and (I thought) completely spoiled the performance. The principal oboist - a fine player named Sylvia Spencer ran into Dr. Boult (as he was then) some while afterwards and tackled him about the incident. "I would have come in correctly at the next entry", to which Boult replied, "I wanted to hear it right" - quite a good reason but hardly needing to spoil the performance!

The reason I remember was because I was playing 2nd Violin on that occasion and I was on the Conductor's right. Most orchestras these days have all the violins sitting on the left of the rostrum, next to each other with their instruments sloping towards the audience - quite often 1st and 2nd Violins have passages together forming their own ensemble, with violas in the centre and cellos on the right. It doesn't really matter where they are situated as long as they are near the front.

I once had the opportunity of speaking to Sir Adrian while standing in the Festival Hall during a rehearsal and I tackled him on the subject, and he insisted that his seating of the 1st Violins on the left and 2nds on the right was the most effective one. I always wished I had brought up the example of the beginning of the finale of Tchaikovsky's *6th Symphony*, "the Pathétique". In this, the tune is shared between the 1st and 2nd Violins, with each playing alternate notes - the 1sts playing the first, third and fifth notes of the theme, and the 2nds playing the second, fourth and sixth notes. I've never discovered why Tchaikovsky did this, for the theme is repeated a few bars later, this time with the 1sts playing the whole theme themselves. I could imagine, right at the beginning of the movement, that for anyone sitting in the front row of the audience there could be a case of one's head turning from left to right as the theme leapt from one side to the other! Boult remained stubbornly assured that his seating was right, and I must say that when I started playing in professional orchestras his seating was indeed "the norm".

Some claim that Adrian Boult had no sense of humour. I can prove that this was incorrect and can give two examples to show that he certainly did have one. At one rehearsal on a Friday afternoon, I tackled him at the tea break, saying: "Do you think I could be excused the second part of the rehearsal, Dr. Boult, it is my 21st birthday and my parents are taking me out for a meal and then to the theatre?", to which he replied, "I think this could be arranged. After all, it is not likely to happen very often, is it?" The other occasion was much later when I happened to be in a room at the R.C.M. when Sir Adrian and I were on our own with no-one else within earshot. As most people know, Sir Adrian was completely bald on top with the only growing hair at the sides and back. "I went into my barber's" he told me, "and said, I wonder if you would mind, since it's rather a cold day, if I kept my overcoat on", to which he replied, "Not at all, Sir. You can leave yer 'at on as well if you like!"

He often used to say to me: "How's your brother?" He never forgot that Clive looked in on him when he was a patient at the Homoeopathic Hospital and my brother, who also switched to this form of medicine, was studying under Lord Horder there.

It was during Adrian Boult's period as Conductor of the R.C.M's First Orchestra and my early days as a student there that I saw the famous French composer Maurice Ravel for the first and only time. Boult was rehearsing the Orchestra for a concert that evening. Among the works being rehearsed was Ravel's *Daphnis and Chloe*, and during the course of it he came up to the Conductor's rostrum to discuss some point in the score. He had another engagement in the evening and so could not come to the concert itself. I remember he was a very small man - especially standing next to the tall Dr. Boult - and, one of those little things that you tend to remember particularly, he wore a bright pink shirt!

Sir Henry Wood

Here was a character if ever there was one. Sir Henry Wood was a pioneer in so many different ways, forming his first orchestra in about 1895. He had a great aversion to what became known as the "deputy system" whereby a player would do the rehearsal(s) and someone else the actual concert. And this was the main cause of the formation of the London Symphony Orchestra in 1904, with its Board of Directors made up of actual players from the Orchestra.

Sir Henry was a most methodical man, working out everything in advance to the smallest detail and precise timing. Had he not been so well organised he could not have carried out seasons of Promenade Concerts single-handed, starting, of course, in the old Queen's Hall, Langham Place - sadly destroyed by one fire-bomb in the 1940s.

It is worth recalling, and should never be allowed to be forgotten (and I feel it will open a few eyes) that, right up to a number of years after the war, he would undertake to conduct the Proms night after night, except Sundays, for eight and sometimes nine weeks, entirely on his own. The exception would be when a new work had been accepted for a first performance, and if the composer was also a competent conductor "Henry J" would allow him a stipulated time for rehearsal - usually about 15 minutes, sometimes slightly more, often less - and woe-betide a composer who erred to the extent of daring to go a minute beyond his time. Henry would be sitting in the stalls with his large "chronometer" and a bell, and would call out: "Time's up!" and that would be that. It was the only way he could carry out his enormous job successfully. This was remarkable when you consider how many conductors and orchestras are involved in the Proms nowadays - which in the 1996 season amounted to 60 and 47 respectively - as Sir Henry managed all the concerts in the 30s single-handedly with only one orchestra, the B.B.C. Symphony Orchestra. (Three cheers for Sir Henry Wood.) One of his hobbies was painting watercolours. How he ever had the time for such diversions in such a busy life is remarkable.

Many stories abound about "Henry J", as he was generally called. Even if tinged with ridicule they are also a sign of affection. His voice tended to be somewhat rasping - perhaps rather surprising for a man who had written a book on voice production! The most famous of his sayings comes probably from the occasion when he was somewhat displeased with the playing of the cello section and said to them, "Cellos, what do you think you're doing of, sitting there sawing away regardless!" On another occasion he addressed a player saying, "What d'you think you're doing?", and a voice came from the double-basses, "OF, Sir Henry, OF". They would pull his leg sometimes. He was very punctilious about exact intonation and occasionally, it was said, he lined up all the violinists to pass in front of him, each one playing his open strings to test the tuning: "Sharp . . . Flat . . . That's all right", and one would quickly be passed towards the back without adjusting the pegs in any way, and when the "sharp" offending instrument came up again, having been declared sharp, it would this time be called "flat"!

When I first played under Sir Henry, I knew little about him and was going to hear for myself an example of the many sayings which he trotted out time after time whenever certain works were played. Malcolm Sargent told us that Wood wrote his stories (in note form, as reminders in his scores) so that he could bring them out at the next rehearsal. He said that he had seen some of his full scores, all covered in "blue pencil" which he used freely in marking parts. Sargent said that in the slow movement of some work he was looking through, he found on one page "weeping women". He had no idea what this referred to but probably it was a reminder to himself to tell a certain story. My own experience of these repeated sayings came with a rehearsal of Wagner's *Meistersingers* Overture. There is a passage quite near the beginning where the violins shoot up to a high A and run down the scale on their own, and Sir Henry knew the danger when a lot of violins run down the top E string of accidentally touching the lower open A string and producing an unintentional "drone" effect with the bow. Every time he got to this point he stopped the rehearsal and I immediately heard whispered "Scotch effects, Scotch effects" and, of course, I wondered what was coming. Sure enough, out it came - "Now, now, violins, be careful you don't touch the A string coming down the E. We don't want any Scotch effects in this Orchestra." It is quite possible to do a kind of bagpipe or drone effect on a violin by bowing on two strings together, with an open string below the higher one which is used for fingering.

Something occurred which underlined Henry J's meticulous timing when he and the L.S.O. travelled to Scotland to play in what was called the Glasgow Exhibition of 1938. We had a morning rehearsal for our own concert, and at about 12.45, with a quarter of an hour left, it was found while playing a new work there was something amiss with the harp part (which, I presume was in manuscript) for he said - very much put out - "I was up till 2 o'clock this morning checking the part and it's queered my pitch for the Symphony", whatever that was - obviously one we all knew. He was left with exactly 10 minutes to rehearse it - after correcting the error in the harp part!

One of Henry J's little foibles when he was conducting and wanted a really effective *pp* would be to get his face down almost level with the conducting score, bringing everything as low as possible. One player in the Orchestra - the principal double-bass, Claud Hobday, seeing the conductor nearly disappear from view, was said to have climbed up his instrument and called out: "I see you, Henry!"

Sir Henry was a very practical man who must have devoted quite a lot of time and thought to some of his unusual ideas, one of which was put to the test in Wagner's *Tannhauser* Overture, where it builds up, over quite a lengthy period, to a great climax. This concerns the violins who are busy playing a continuous passage of slurred semi-quavers while the brass, particularly, play the main theme.

In passages containing hundreds of semi-quavers, they naturally use up a lot of space on the printed page. "Timber" (one of his nicknames) knew that when the violins reached the bottom of the page, the "inside" player would have to have stopped playing in order to turn the page and so the tone produced by the violins would momentarily become halved in volume. To overcome this he had bought a 2nd set of violin parts sticking one page below the existing one producing what looked like a lot of over-sized chess boards which would have something like 32 staves instead of the usual 16 or so. Those sitting at the rear of the violin sections must have felt like half standing up in order to read the upper lines. It must have looked somewhat strange to audiences, but Henry J. wasn't concerned about that! Some wag had once written at the bottom of the page, "I've enjoyed my stay here!"

Sir Henry had quite a number of special sayings which he doled out when he thought appropriate. One, when he felt either the intonation or ensemble weren't quite up to standard, was: "They're listening to you with their miniature scores" (referring to an imaginary audience). "They don't *say* anything" - then, pointing to his own head - "but they *think* it!"

It is interesting that Sir Henry never really commanded the same popular following in concerts throughout the rest of the year, away from the atmosphere of the Proms - rather like the great Opera conductor, Fritz Busch, who seemed slightly less inspired and effective on the concert platform. But just as Sargent brought so much of his influence in the years when he taught at the Royal College, so past students at the Royal Academy of Music, who were in the First Orchestra there, must have cherished the invaluable experience they gained under the persuasive guidance of that father figure known all over the world by the rather American way of referring to a person - Henry J. Wood.

Meredith Davies

Meredith Davies was organist of Hereford Cathedral, assuming the mantle of Sir Percy Hull, and naturally conducted at Three Choirs Festivals for a number of years. He was quite approachable and friendly. As a conductor he was efficient, though he did not leave any particularly lasting impressions. In later years his name became associated with the music of Frederick Delius, especially with some of his less known compositions such as the *Mass of Life*. The trouble with some large-scale works is the excessive cost of the forces required to stage them, which, of course, is a pity. The opera by Delius, *A Village Romeo and Juliet*, is rarely put on and is a case in point. The only excerpt from the opera that is well known is the *Walk to the Paradise Garden*. This is taken out of context and it is sometimes a bit tiresome to listen to by itself, but I suppose it is some consolation to know that the name of Delius is kept before the public. And for that alone one is grateful to Meredith Davies for, when possible, giving performances of these fine works.

There was one occasion at a "Three Choirs" when he gave a performance of Handel's *Messiah* - very unusually with no interval at all - which I remember only too well. At the end, Meredith was easily the first to vacate his rostrum and disappear from view - and others of us were not too long in following him. I suppose one could warn people not to drink tea before a long session! But it was a bit thoughtless of the "authorities" to test us in this unreasonable way.

Sir Hamilton Harty

Harty was a very fine all round musician and a very likeable Irishman. His wife, Agnes Nicholls, was a distinguished contralto who was the first singer to take the part of the Angel in Elgar's *Dream of Gerontius*, and gave the first performance under the direction of the composer. Harty himself was not only a fine and popular conductor but a first-rate pianist and would accompany his wife at recitals. He himself composed some memorable music including An *Irish Symphony*. It was sad that he suffered a stroke in later life, causing him to use only his right hand, and his speech was a little affected. This did not deter him from conducting any more than it did Sir Henry Wood who had two strokes.

There were two delightful stories concerning Harty, one hearsay, but it was more than likely to have happened - it is difficult to think that anyone could have made it up. The other is absolutely true for, as the Welsh comedian used to say - "I knor because I was there!" The first was told to me by another character, Bertie Lewis. He himself was in the first fiddles of the L.S.O. and was previously the leader of the Bournemouth Symphony Orchestra. He was a very talented man and a great wit. He used to make his own furniture and painted quite attractive pictures, one of which I still have. His story concerned a concert in Leeds Town Hall. Harty was at that time conductor of the Hallé Orchestra, and with the choir, the famous Huddersfield Choral Society, the work to be performed was Handel's oratorio *Israel in Egypt*. There was a crisis before the rehearsal ever began. The Hallé's 2nd trombone was taken ill and a replacement had to be found, quickly - not an easy job. Eventually a player was located, one not that acquainted with a full symphony orchestra but normally a member of a quintet whose usual occupation was playing in a down-town theatre pit.

The player found his way to the Town Hall and took his place with the Hallé. Very unusually for Handel, he had included trombones in one of the quick choruses, where there were fast-moving semi-quaver bars. They were probably difficult enough for an experienced pro but for a local "gig" player were rather more of a problem. Harty was a calm reasonable man, but this man's playing, to say the least, was not up to it, and he stopped the rehearsal and, though fairly sympathetic, showed considerable displeasure at his efforts, to which the North-Countryman upped and said, " 'Appen Sir 'Arty yer dorn't play trombone. Well if yer did, yer'd know that if there were as many bulrooshes in Egypt as there are black notes on this page, they'd never 'ave found Moses!" There's no answer to that!

The other story concerning Sir Hamilton, when I was present, occurred during a rehearsal with the L.S.O. for a later broadcast at B.B.C. Studio One at Maida Vale. It was about mid-day when Harty was rehearsing *Pictures at an Exhibition* by Mussorgsky in the orchestration by Ravel. He must have conducted this work dozens of times before but something in the full score, for some reason, puzzled him. Being Ravel's orchestration I presume all the instructions must have been printed in French. I have never set eyes on the score myself but presumably it was published in Paris. Harty decided to put the point to the Orchestra itself and said to us: "Any of you boys" (his favourite term for us) "have any idea what this means?", and he proceeded to read it out to us. Our second flute - named Gilbert Barton, once a fellow Director with me - had a delightful, quiet sense of humour and he replied at once. It wasn't what he said - which was absolutely non-sensical - but the speed of his reply, which was: "Well I don't know, Sir Hamilton. Perhaps it means take your teeth out and rattle 'em on the stand!" Collapse of Orchestra! Sir Hamilton couldn't speak for two minutes, he was laughing so much. It was one of those moments when your stomach goes in and takes a little time to recover. The time of this "event" was about mid-day, but five minutes later it was 1 o'clock - that is to say, time flies when this sort of thing happens. Everyone is put in a good mood and is immediately relaxed.

We were naturally sad to learn that a man who had given so much to the world of music should have had a stroke, but he carried on conducting with distinction even though his left arm was pretty badly affected. When he eventually died he left behind memories of a man of great distinction who was always thought of with affection.

Otto Klemperer

Klemperer had gained quite a reputation - especially with the public - and in his latter days was considered a great interpreter of the music of Beethoven. I was not playing under him at that time but heard some of his performances. I was not so enamoured as some people - in fact I was decidedly "anti" some of his performances. Some became so slow that I once said, flippantly, if they went much slower they would start going backwards! No, I did not think I was listening to authentic readings of certain works given by a man of vast experience. I just felt that age was beginning to catch up on him! His actual conducting seemed to lack anything dynamic. When, say, the brass had a strong *fortissimo* entry he would tend just to point rather gently in their direction unlike a more dramatic conductor whose gestures at big moments would cause that unmistakable thrill down the back-bone. And players themselves like to be encouraged to play with confidence by reacting to a strong beat. And his general demeanour was far from friendly, and his rather cross-sounding speech seemed to indicate a sort of speech impediment. Yet he was quite a one for the girls, not that he lacked female company, having a most attractive daughter who often stationed herself not far from his desk when he was conducting at rehearsals.

Years ago, when he wasn't too conscious of the time - he had gone well beyond 1 p.m. - various players started getting up and leaving the rehearsal - some of them had afternoon matinees to play at - and he called after them saying: "Are you artists or workmen?", and with one voice they replied "Workmen!"

There is one rather nice story about Klemperer. He had been away from this country for quite a long time, having previously just recorded Beethoven's *5th Symphony* with the Philharmonia Orchestra and he wanted to hear it. So he got on to his agent who went by the delightful name of Mr Mendelssohn and, on the telephone told him he had not seen any sign of the record in the shops, to which Mendelssohn replied: "I am sure it is selling well and is very popular, Dr. Klemperer". To prove his point he said he would take him to a large record shop near Oxford Circus. This he did and the assistant said: "Good morning Sir. Can I help you?" "Yes, you can", he replied. "I want a recording of Beethoven's *5th Symphony* conducted by Klemperer." The young man thought for a moment and then said: "No, it doesn't ring a bell. I'm afraid I don't recall that name, but I can recommend some other excellent recordings that are selling well conducted by Kraus, Kempe, Kubelik . . ." "Who are these people?" he interrupted, "I want Klemperer's - nobody else's." By this time Mr Mendelssohn was getting a little worried, so he suggested taking a taxi to Selfridges. "They have practically everything in their record department." So off they set again and went through the same process with the same lack of success but an even larger choice of conductors, none of which, naturally were of interest to Dr.Klemperer, until the shop assistant started to get a little exasperated and eventually said: "Why is it, Sir, when I can offer you such a wide choice of highly acclaimed conductors, that you continue to persist with the name Klemperer?", to which he replied, angrily, "Because I am Klemperer." The assistant beginning now to feel this rather cross customer required a bit of humouring said, "Oh yes, and I presume your companion here is Beethoven?" "No", he snapped back - "Mendelssohn!"

Sir Michael Tippett
Tippett studied conducting with Sir Adrian Boult up to a year before I arrived at the Royal College of Music. I only played under him on one occasion which was when I was leading the orchestra at Tunbridge Wells and the main work the choirs had all been learning in the winter months - and been competing with against each other that morning - was *A Child of our Time*. I found him very direct and business-like and knew exactly what he wanted but, though perfectly amenable, especially if you had a query, he was somewhat lacking as regards a sense of humour. If his music is not to everyone's taste or may even feel beyond them, there is no doubting his scholarship and serious sense of purpose. Much of his music is enjoyable on a first hearing or else "grows on you" with repetition.

Hans Schmidt-Isserstedt
Isserstedt was a very pleasant German conductor who, I believe, conducted the Glasgow Symphony Orchestra for a time, but as far as I can remember only did one concert with the L.S.O. He had a nice sense of humour and told us a very amusing story against himself from when he was in the North, when he said his English was even worse. The story concerned, again, the timpani. Timpanists have quite a selection of drumsticks from those with very big heads, more like a bass drumstick, giving a more mellow tone, to much smaller ones which are harder and which can produce a more assertive and commanding tone when playing *fortissimo* and also often a very clear and effective sound if played *pianissimo*. Hans wanted a softer effect than the timpanist was producing. "When I spoke to him the orchestra laughed. I exclaimed - what have I said? I merely said: Sir, your balls are too small." We laughed too!

Sir John Barbirolli
Barbirolli - for many years Conductor of the Hallé Orchestra, could, in a way, be

described as "one of us", that's to say, he began his career as a very good cellist, and that's a great asset for any conductor. One would perhaps call him a "musician's musician". I first met him at an L.S.O. concert at Queen's Hall, and by a remarkable series of coincidences I was to meet him three more times in the same week which included once at Glyndebourne. I think the intensity and deeply-felt readings of his performances was the result of his Italian roots. I was very pleased at one rehearsal, when he admitted that as a cellist, when he was conducting an orchestra and gave them an up-beat in a passage starting "down-bow" he wanted to beat in sympathy with the bowing. I couldn't resist going up to him to say I felt the same way.

Sir Thomas Beecham
Of the 60 or more conductors I have played under, I come now to the one who stood above them all. Apart from saying he was larger than life, if I had to pick a single word to describe him, it would have to be "genius". He was a law unto himself and to fully sum him up would really require a whole chapter. He is, of course, Sir Thomas Beecham, Bart. - popularly referred to as "Tommy". What a man - what a life! I cannot think of a world of music without him. He did, of course, do some outrageous things in his career, but they are all the more fun in retrospect. Financially he often ran into trouble and his father, Sir Joseph Beecham, who knew of his son's weakness in this direction, had a cunning clause in his will which would prevent his large fortune going to the State should Thomas ever be declared bankrupt.

Beecham's name must have been well known in our house from his early days as a conductor as I have found some programmes of the L.S.O. going back to about the first decade of the last century, which were adorned with Beecham's name and photograph as being the conductor of quite a number of the monthly Monday night concerts at the Queen's Hall. The programmes were well put up with the covers being wider than the inside pages. There were copious programme notes and musical examples from the various works to be played, and the pages were all stuck together - not stapled - so that there was no danger of loose pages falling on the floor.

My very first experience of performing under Beecham's inspiring direction was in 1929. This special occasion was one of the concerts of the Delius Festival and was given special significance by the presence in Queen's Hall of Delius himself, whose music had already appealed greatly to me. The work I was involved in was his *Appalachia* which has a wordless chorus towards the end. Beecham felt he needed more singers to augment the "London Select Choir" and he sent an urgent request to the R.C.M. for a dozen or so to swell the numbers. Little did I ever dream of singing in such a distinguished sounding choir. Any way I was chosen and went. I well remember this adventure for several reasons. The first was that as a young and not very experienced performer, I was still a bit naive when I was told the dress was "evening dress". If they had said "D.J.", I should have known what that meant - but I was the only one in the choir not wearing a "white tie". I hoped it was not too obvious - nobody said anything to me like "incorrectly dressed". What made it equally disappointing for me was that I had recently acquired a new tail-coat and trousers (made-to-measure - 6 guineas!) and this would have been a "first time". Secondly I learnt that sitting in *front* of instruments such as the timpani or three trombones is almost unbearable, but naturally the players behind them get no such discomfort, as I was soon to discover when I took up the timpani.

The programme consisted of - I think - one of the two *Dance Rhapsodies*, the *Piano Concerto* with Evelyn Howard Jones as soloist, and one other work before *Appalachia*. Delius himself, who was already blind and paralysed, had been wheeled over from the Langham Hotel where he was staying, opposite Broadcasting House, and of course there was tremendous applause at the end. All he could do was raise an arm in acknowledgement. It was, naturally, a momentous occasion. The choir's contribution to the evening's music was a small but very important and beautiful one in four parts.

There was another occasion when "Tommy" requested reinforcements from the College - this time violins. He had a strong affinity for the music of that doughty woman composer Dame Ethel Smyth, and he readily agreed to take on conducting a programme devoted entirely to her music. She was a formidable lady in whose life politics played an important part. She was a supporter of the Suffragette movement and wrote music for her fellow creatures, including her *March for the Women.*

The concert, given by the London Philharmonic Orchestra, originally formed by Sir Thomas in 1931, took place in the Royal Albert Hall on a Saturday afternoon. In Ethel Smyth's programme was a major work which is rarely heard (but deserves to be) - her *Mass in D* (no connection with Beethoven!). Beecham, in spite of his large orchestra, felt he needed more violins to augment his own and I was one of quite a number selected from the R.C.M. We were only needed for the *Mass*, which was quite a substantial piece. The concert was due to start at 2.30 in the afternoon and we had a rehearsal in the morning with the Royal Choral Society.

Beecham was obviously worried about the programme, especially the *Mass*, and I was to witness at first hand his unreliability regarding the time and not planning the rehearsal with the methodical exactness of, say, Sir Henry Wood. We had had a thorough and long rehearsal of the *Mass* but he still had to rehearse at least three other works, including the Overture to Smyth's opera *The Wreckers* and her *March of the Women*. Quite a lot of people were worried about the time, for it was a special event, not just because it was Ethel Smyth's music, but also it was to be a "Royal Occasion" with none other than Her Majesty, Queen Mary, due to appear in the Royal Box at 2.30. The rehearsal with the L.P.O. did not end till 2.20! Meanwhile, we fiddlers from the R.C.M. started wandering back soon afterwards. At 2.30 we were due to play two verses of Elgar's special orchestration of the National Anthem, with the Royal Choral Society. Most of the L.P.O. had gone off - some for a quick smoke - when, to everyone's horror, at about 2.29 Her Majesty suddenly appeared in the Royal Box! Panic - no sign of Beecham and only a nucleus of the Orchestra on stage! There was no chance of singing the Elgar version of the Anthem. Paul Beard, the

185

leader of the L.P.O. at that time, rushed on with his fiddle under his arm and conducted one verse in the conventional key of G - *not* in Elgar's B flat. From then on everything seemed to return to normal, after the eventual appearance of Sir Thomas. It was an embarrassing moment.

At the end of the concert there was an edict from Beecham to the effect that he wanted to see everyone in his room who had not been on the platform in time. Of course, the guilty one was Beecham himself. I was actually on the platform but hadn't time to reach my fiddle, which was on a chair a bit further on, so I stood dutifully to attention while those who could make it did the honours.

In the 1950s Beecham showed an admirable side of his concern and understanding for his players at a Sunday afternoon concert, again at the Royal Albert Hall. From about 1912 he had often been conductor - especially in the second decade of the century - of the London Symphony Orchestra at their monthly Monday night Winter series of concerts at the Queen's Hall. After the Second World War he was less often seen with the L.S.O., especially as he had formed, in 1931, the London Philharmonic Orchestra, and later, the new Royal Philharmonic. Wherever he conducted he was welcome both with orchestras and public alike, though he eventually fell out with the old L.P.O.

On this particular Sunday, it was an isolated concert with the L.S.O. and not part of a series. The final work in the programme was another of his favourites, the Suite *The Fair Maid of Perth*, by Bizet. The last movement starts quietly with a solo flute and harp alone. We had not gone very far when "Eddie" Walker (son of the previous principal flautist, Gordon) who was playing the solo, played an F natural instead of F sharp. Oh dear, - we thought - Sunday afternoon, perhaps too heavy a lunch - when, on the return to the tune the same thing happened and Tommy stopped. The two flute players had a quick discussion and Beecham re-started with No. 2 now playing the solo. At the end there was the usual applause, but Tommy did not let it continue too long, for he held up his hand for silence and thus addressed the audience: "Ladies and Gentlemen, lest any of you are under any misapprehension as to what occurred during the performance of the last movement of this Suite by Bizet, Mr Walker, the eminent flautist (he had a curious way of pronouncing it "flotist") had some trouble with a key on his instrument preventing the correct note from emanating, so that the solo was played by the second "flotist".

Now this was a most generous and quickly thought-out gesture. How easily people, unaware of the facts, could have jumped to the wrong conclusion and blamed the player for his "carelessness". Such incidents can adversely affect a player's whole career. In one brief, but perfectly timed moment, Beecham had immediately scotched any such thoughts. Eddie told me later that he had written to the "maestro" to thank him for his concern and his gesture.

By a strange coincidence both Eddie and I, when in the refreshment bar only a few weeks before, had been introduced to a man who said he was going round to every London orchestra to enlist the help of one person who would be responsible for reporting any incident which could be used as an interesting news item concerning each orchestra. He was a retired Army officer who was working for the Daily Express and wondered if one or other of us would be the representative for the L.S.O. Not really thinking much would happen we said "yes" and he gave me his card. After the Bizet incident I said to Eddie: "Now's your chance - ring up the Express!" He suggested I did it on this occasion, so later I rang this man at his office. He thanked me very much for bothering but said he happened to be at the concert himself, so knew what had occurred. The report was eventually published, and thinking this was the end of the matter I was surprised, some weeks later, to receive a cheque from the Daily Express with which was enclosed an invoice in my favour which read - "To assistance to Reporter in Flute story - One guinea."

After the war, having spent most of it in Australia and latterly in the U.S.A., Beecham returned to this country with the comment: "The emergency appears to be over so I decided to emerge". He never really courted unpopularity, or even anger, and there was a sort of feeling generally of - Come back, all is forgiven! - whatever people thought of him. As usual wit would always win the day.

There was another unforgettable occasion at the Albert Hall, again involving Beecham, not long after the war. He was the real star at the end of a very long and boring evening. It concerned the Fabian Society for whom Beecham and the L.S.O. provided two shortish periods of popular music. In front of and just below the Albert Hall organ was a long table but out of sight to begin with, being covered by curtains which hung across the top of the platform.

Among the joys of playing under Beecham were his asides to the Orchestra which could not be heard by the audience. When he came on to conduct something like a suite from Bizet's *Carmen*, he looked up from his rostrum towards the organ, and observing the rather unusual set-up, said "I presume that behind these curtains lies the body of the original Fabian!" A rather irreverent thought did occur when the curtains were eventually drawn that there was the setting of a re-enactment of the "Last Supper". From the moment Tommy arrived on the scene we could see he had a naughty look in his eye. He had also noticed that, level with his conductor's rostrum was a microphone on a stand close to him. Pointing to it he said: "I never can resist these things, you know". We could all feel that something was going to occur before the evening was out and sure enough it was - but not until near the end of the concert.

After our introductory music we all traipsed off and left the stage to the politicians. The curtains were drawn aside and five people were sitting behind the long table. They were Clement Attlee - the then Prime Minister, Margaret Bondfield - a very left-wing politician, John Strachey - the Post-Master General, Professor Laski, and one other whose name escapes me. Gill was there in the audience and joined me as we wandered aimlessly round the hall, occasionally looking in from an empty box to listen to a few very boring speeches which were received in complete silence by those in the hall. One might add there "wasn't a wet eye in the house!"

To make matters worse, being a Sunday and moderately early in the evening, there wasn't even a bar open! At last the Orchestra returned to the stage to play the final short programme of music to bring the evening's "entertainment" to a close, but not before Sir Thomas had his bit of fun, much awaited by us, of course. He made his usual dignified progress to the rostrum, making sure before he stepped on to it that the microphone was live. He then produced a quite masterly performance, "stealing the thunder" of everything that had preceded it earlier in the afternoon, waking that audience up from the somnolent state into which they had drifted during the previous hour or two. Eventually the whole place suddenly became alive with cheering, laughter and applause, as Beecham absolutely "flayed them" with his invective, mostly aimed at the politicians who had recently occupied the stage and had returned to the Royal Box from which they were to listen to the rest of the music. I wish I could remember, after all these years, the exact words "Tommy" used, but I do remember his opening "salvo". "I was a Fabian once" he began "but never again", he shouted. "What have you done for music?" he asked, "Built a lot of houses nobody wants. We want a concert hall." (The Festival Hall had not been built by then.) And he continued in this vein for two or three minutes, making this alone an occasion not to have missed. If this was not a "tour de force", I don't know what is!

For some reason, when the Royal Festival Hall was at last built, it was some time before Sir Thomas would agree to conduct there. There was no such reticence on the part of Boult or Sargent - especially the latter! Eventually Beecham did condescend to be seen there. At his first concert, the hall was packed and at the end the applause was tremendous and continuous. Everyone wanted obviously to hear him speak. Eventually he called for silence and said: "I suppose you want me to tell you what a wonderful hall this is, or what a wonderful hall it isn't - bit I'm not going to. If you come to my next concert here on October 28th, I'll tell you all about it." We all went home feeling a bit flat, but it was typical of the man to keep us all guessing - as well as to do a bit of self-advertising for future concerts.

Beecham's command of the English language and use of unusual words really made him the "Churchill" of the musical world. Even when, at an orchestral rehearsal, he might be addressing the 2nd clarinet about, say, a B flat in his part, I often used to feel I'd like to put my instrument down for a moment and write down what he was saying. There is a memorable passage in an article he once wrote for the weekly Saturday music page edited by Ralph Hill in the Daily Telegraph. He had recently returned from a visit to the U.S.A. where he found the political situation just as chaotic as it was over here. He finished his article thus: "I look forward, therefore, to a highly ironical and diverting climax to the current epoch of political myopia". He never used an ordinary expression when he addressed a player in the orchestra and it was always in a most gentlemanly way. It was said that when he was taking a rehearsal of the B.B.C. Orchestra - many years ago - when the leader of the 2nd violins - whose name I forget - asked Sir Thomas a question about something in his part. (I remember he had a very odd style of bowing. He held his right arm very high so that he could almost see the music and the conductor under it!) Beecham wasn't quite sure what the problem was and said: "Play it to me." This chap suddenly got a fit of nerves - I suppose he found himself playing a solo in front of the whole orchestra and did not make a very good "fist" of illustrating his little problem. Tommy glanced at the score and then said: "My dear Sir, I regret I cannot find anything in the score remotely similar to the passage you have just played to me."

It has been said that Beecham never used two words when twelve would do just as well. And his method of addressing a player was nothing if not unique. There was an occasion when, rather unusually, three rehearsals were called for a concert which probably had a new or unfamiliar work in the programme, and which needed more rehearsal than a conventional one, and at the middle of the three - i.e. the 2nd one - Tommy decided to make a pause at one point which was not printed thus, and he asked the Orchestra to mark the parts accordingly. For years Beecham had the same two bassoonists - both in his original L.P.O. and later in his new Royal Philharmonic Orchestra which he founded after the war. They were brothers - George and John Alexander - two quiet but very reliable and excellent players. For the 2nd rehearsal John had asked to be excused as he had another important engagement that day. Unfortunately George had omitted to mark his brother's part as well as his own so that at the final rehearsal everyone stopped at this point except John who "soared on regardless" (as Sir Henry Wood might have said). At this point Beecham addressed George - John's brother: "Mr Alexander - will you kindly inform your relative there is a slight hiatus at this place". It would be difficult to imagine anyone else dealing with a situation of this kind in this original manner.

Regarding another aside or stage whisper during one of Beecham's concerts, they were performing one of Mozart's symphonies, and just before the slow movement Tommy started to have a slight tickle in his throat. He said to the players nearest him: "Has anyone such a thing as a cough lozenge?" The principal viola was sitting opposite him - just below the conductor's stand - and putting his fingers into his evening dress white waistcoat, he produced some sort of sweet. Sir Thomas held up proceedings for a moment or two, very deliberately unwrapped the sweet and popped it into his mouth. At the end of the slow movement, he said to the principal viola player: "That lozenge you handed to me a few moments ago had a rather peculiar flavour", to which the player responded: "I'm not surprised, Sir Thomas, it's been to the laundry three times!"

Beecham had a delightful way of insulting people without actually doing so by his cunning use of words. One such occasion concerned the Triennial Festival at Norwich. The L.P.O. was engaged one year, and a welcoming speech was made at the first concert by the President of the Festival - a certain Lord Albemarle - who made a long and completely humourless speech. After the final concert, Beecham - never slow to take the opportunity of "taking the Mickey" out of someone - always in a subtle manner - made his own speech, starting: "I have no desire to emulate my

Lord Albemarle either in brevity or wit . . !"

One of the secrets of Beecham's orchestras - especially the original L.P.O. - was the quality of sound he persuaded from his woodwind section, who used to be called "The Royal Family"! With the quality of players such as the great oboist Leon Goossens, it was not really surprising.

It was quite common for an orchestral player to be owed quite a lot of money in the earlier days, representing unpaid fees, but Tommy was held in such affectionate regard that they would still play for him, even if the were owed more than £100.

On another occasion at Covent Garden during those critical days, Beecham was conducting Dame Ethel Smyth's opera, *The Wreckers*, and was called away to discuss some problem with the Composer. When he eventually returned, he said: "Let me see, gentlemen, where exactly were we?", and an oboe player, with a stutter, said: "On the, er, on the rocks, Sir Thomas!" A similar occasion at "The Garden" concerned another rehearsal where Beecham had left the orchestra pit rather too long and the orchestra were getting restive - I think it was a Wagner opera. It got round the orchestra that when Sir Thomas returned they would not play any more Wagner but strike up with the famous *Blue Danube* Waltz.

One event which gave me a great deal of pleasure occurred when some years after the last war, the B.B.C. decided to make a film of Beecham, but it was discovered that all film of Sir Thomas's life had been destroyed, though, unbelievably, I think they discovered some of him in America. At this point I became involved when they learned about one of my "party pieces" of taking him off. I am not sure whether word of my exploits at the Queenís Hall Proms at the beginning of the war in 1940 had reached the B.B.C. but in this T.V. film, I was engaged to take the part of Beecham when the short episode was re-enacted when he unwittingly conducted the Blue Danube. It was rather fun as I had to be made up by the professionals in the Lime Grove studios of the B.B.C. at Shepherds Bush and then driven across London by taxi to the artist's entrance of Covent Garden - rather amusing to arrive at the great theatre, not as myself but as Sir Thomas! The Opera House was empty - not even an orchestra in attendance - but lots of Directors and Producers and, of course, cameras and the recording people. I was on the conductor's podium in the orchestra pit and I had to imagine a full orchestra while the actual music was provided by a recording. I remember at one moment they had to shout up to a woman on one of the upper floors of boxes to stop hoovering as the microphone was picking up the sound! I eventually saw the transmission on T.V. I think my appearance lasted 57 seconds. It was a small but somewhat diverting episode in my musical career. And I think I was paid £50 for my effort.

I doubt very much that many - or anybody - remembers the very first concert given by the Philharmonia Orchestra or where it took place. The strings of the Orchestra were mustered by my old friend, the cellist, Jimmy Whitehead, and it took place in the Kingsway Hall - and the conductor was Beecham - on a Saturday afternoon. I always remember the slight embarrassment of the percussion players, who turned up in casual clothes - not surprisingly since this was the venue for much recording and they had not realised it was a public concert, and percussionists tend to be in prominent positions, standing at the rear of the orchestra.

I was one of the string players engaged, and the leader of the Orchestra was another colleague of mine, Leonard Hirsch, who only died a few years ago, aged 93. During a slight hold-up in the morning rehearsal, Leonard stood and spoke to Tommy. Apparently he pointed me out, saying I had quite a name for taking him off, and I heard Tommy say: "He must show it to me". I never did!

Many people have played under Beecham's baton, but I consider myself fortunate to have been in the right place at the right time, as although still only a student, I was able to get to know Sir Thomas more personally than many of my more distinguished colleagues due to the fact that he was guest at the Royal College on a number of occasions during the Summer term of 1936 when I was lucky enough to be the leader of the College orchestra - first in the Opera Theatre and later, in the Concert Hall, at a concert by the First Orchestra - all memorable occasions. But in a previous year, before I had got to know him personally, he was conducting Mozart's *Le Nozze de Figaro*. Tommy had made some last-minute adjustments to the viola part, and after the performance had actually started, parts were handed down to the orchestra pit, with the ink still wet (no biros in those days!).

Beecham was obviously very fond of the College and was a frequent Visiting Conductor for the annual opera performances in the Summer terms. I witnessed a typical example of his being insulting without anyone taking exception, as he had a way of saying outrageous things with his delightful "tongue-in-cheek" manner. One year - after the final performance of an opera - a student came up to the stage to present Sir Thomas with a "thank you" gift. He received it graciously and then unwrapped it deliberately to disclose a fine cigar box made of onyx and gold. Opening the lid, while thanking the College for their kindness, he then said: "I observe there is nothing in it!" The following year a similar little ceremony took place after another opera, but this time a student handed him two large boxes of cigars. Again Sir Thomas expressed his thanks, saying he was very pleased to accept the cigars - adding: ". . . though they have taken a year to materialise!"

At an earlier performance in the R.C.M. Opera theatre - it was possibly Vaughan Williams' *Hugh the Drover* - Beecham had called for an extra rehearsal on the morning of the first performance to clear up one or two points. The whole orchestra had turned up and the large cast and full chorus were on the stage ready to run through any small places where Tommy was not happy that everything was secure and assured, but there was one very small moment when two sopranos have a short passage alone with the orchestra. When they had reached this point, the two sopranos did not sing their short solo. Sir Thomas stopped and enquired where the two girls were. It came to light that they were having lessons upstairs with their singing professors. Sir Thomas called out to the Producer: "Mr Gordon, there's no-one here - I cannot proceed." It was a delightful exaggeration since there was hardly room for even one more on the stage!

I came into the reckoning when Beecham came to conduct three performances of Delius' *A Village Romeo and Juliet*. This fine work in six scenes was a big undertaking for everyone concerned. It is not just the three performances that need mention but also the preliminary rehearsals and some of the hassle which occurred.

The three performances were due to take place on three consecutive days in one week of the Summer term - on the Wednesday, Thursday and Friday. It was the first time I had held such a responsible and important position under the "legendary" Maestro. In this Delius opera there is one place where the leader of the orchestra has to go up on stage and play some solo passages - out of sight of the audience, of course - which are allocated to a character in the cast called The Dark Fiddler. At the first rehearsal, I duly went behind the scene and played the first solo passage. I looked down towards the orchestra pit and saw Tommy speak to the sub-leader who sat next to me, and I heard him ask him the name of the leader. He then called up to me: "Mr Nicholson, we cannot hear you very well from where you are standing. Would you come a little near-ar", in the precise manner in which he spoke, and the passage was played again. "Very good", called out Beecham, who seemed well satisfied. From then on he never asked my name again - he always remembered it - typical of him to have memorised such a comparatively unimportant name.

As *A Village Romeo and Juliet* was obviously completely unknown to the orchestra - not even having heard it before - it was not really surprising that Tommy called for an extra rehearsal on the Sunday afternoon before the performances. He had told me he would be letting me have his full score with all his special marks in blue, which could then be transferred to the orchestral parts. Up to the Sunday he had not done so, always saying: "I'll let you have it on Sunday" (or whenever). The rehearsal was called for 3 p.m., so I waited for him to arrive in the entrance hall of the College. After a while a maroon coloured Daimler drew up below the College steps. It was said that Beecham had bought the car from the Prince of Wales (later to become King Edward VIII). But Beecham did not immediately get out and enter the College. I could see him sitting in the back seat, wearing a straw hat and smoking a large cigar! It was about 3.30 before he condescended to enter the College, and I eventually received the score from him. One of the most absurd things about all this was a directive from the hirers that no marks of any kind were to be made in the parts - and never in ink - and must be erased before they were returned to them. How very silly and ignorant of the employee not to know - or else have been informed - that all the marks (bowing etc) were extremely valuable, since - at that time - Beecham was the only conductor to have ever conducted the work - and they should have been directed to leave all Beecham's marks in the parts. We discovered that his blue pencil marks were still just visible even after being rubbed out! I know the name of the Publisher/Hirer of the orchestral material, and have no wish to be sued for defamation, but they deserved a real "roasting" for this thoughtless act. No doubt

192

they have never learnt that it is often not in anyone's interest to stick to the "letter of the law". In this case Beecham's original personal marks were absolutely invaluable. By the end of the Sunday rehearsal there was little time left before the Tuesday (or Wednesday) to mark the parts. Early on the Monday morning I received an urgent phone call. "Come up immediately to help mark the parts." I arrived to find a state of panic prevailing. Everyone possible had been enlisted to mark as many parts as possible, including the Director himself, Sir Hugh Allen, and one or two professors. The result was that of the six scenes, only one could be completed in time. I suppose we all just reacted to Sir Thomas' expressive direction. This great occasion has remained with me all my life as being something very special.

With an orchestra pit in an opera theatre, the amount of room is naturally restricted. While we were playing that popular section - "The walk to the Paradise Garden" (the name of a public house in the scene) - Beecham did one of his "swoops" accompanied by the usual audible "groan" and knocked my bow completely off the string. He just stroked his "imperial" and smiled contentedly!

A week or so after this great event, Sir Hugh Allen invited Sir Thomas and a number of those of us concerned back to some kind of reception, and then we all repaired to the Royal Albert Hall for some special event of patriotic fervour called, I believe something like "England our England", which was rather embarrassing with a certain amount of flag-waving, and for which we had been allotted a box. Not surprisingly Beecham did not stay very long!

My other memorable event was later that term in the Concert Hall of the Royal College. The end of term - and year - concert was given by the First Orchestra under Beecham again. The programme consisted of the conventional three works - Overture, Concerto and Symphony - which were the *William Tell* Overture, Brahms' *2nd Piano Concerto in B flat* and Beethoven's *Symphony No. 3* the "Eroica". The excellent solo pianist was Norman Tucker, who later emigrated to Australia. In the slow movement the solo cello obbligato was played by Jimmy Whitehead - who also finished up in Australia. It was in fact quite an occasion for cellists. The *William Tell* Overture begins with five solo cellos. It was about this time that Toscanini made a fuss over the quality of his players when he conducted this work with the B.B.C. Orchestra. It seems that Beecham had no complaints!

After the performance of the *William Tell* at the College, something happened which I cannot recall having happened either before or since - people stood and cheered at the end. I must say it was exciting to play the overture under his "electric" conducting. It was during the rehearsal for this concert that I was to become involved in, so to speak, Tommy's delightful choice of words when he was asking quite a simple question. As I have said before he would never use two or three words when a dozen or so would be all that were needed. It was during the afternoon rehearsal of the "Eroica" Symphony that in the course of the slow movement he asked me a question much to my surprise, but luckily I was not "taken" by surprise, and was ready to reply immediately. It was to do with bowing, and particularly the first violins. Any "ordinary" conductor might have asked: "What do you think - up or down bow?", but not Tommy; he never made an ordinary remark like that. He employed a phrase or words which flowed from him like the easy running of Rolls-Royce. He merely said: "Mr Nicholson - what do you consider the most efficacious bowing for this particular passage?" I remember my quick reaction to this query. "Asking me, a mere student", I said to myself. "Does he *really* want to know? Surely he's conducted this Symphony many time before?" But my most immediate reaction was: "Don't panic answer at once - right or wrong." I said: "Well, Sir Thomas, as it is a quiet moment, I think it might be a good idea to play the phrase up-bow at the point to get the smoothest effect." "Very well", he said "we will adopt that. Will you get out your pencils, ladies and gentlemen, and kindly mark the parts accordingly."

I, of course, felt "a thousand dollars" and my ego shot sky-high. But my over all reaction at the time - and has remained unchanged ever since - was that it was a bit of subtle psychology on his part to give me the feeling that I was co-operating with him, and I had become the liaison between him and the Orchestra, prepared to pass on his wishes to the "band". I found this very enlightening. It gave a fascinating insight into the ways in which he produced such great results. I think I am right.

In the early days of his career, when Beecham's Pills were still well known, and Beecham was making a name for himself conducting opera at Covent Garden, there used to be advertisements for these performances under the heading - "Worth a guinea a box". On the cover of one of the volumes of Delius records which Beecham made in the 30s with the L.P.O. I have stuck a delightful cutting from a publication called The Weekend Review. It says the following :-

"SIMPLES"
If they don't think the music of Delius is simply marvelious
They should take a dose of Beecham, that'll teach 'em.

In conclusion, I think it would be appropriate to recall probably one of the last occasions when Beecham made a formal speech. Whether it was his last, I am not certain, but I am glad to say I was present so for me it is an unforgettable memory as it was a "tour de force" and remains with me as a "coda" to his life.

The occasion was a lunch at the Dorchester Hotel given by some musical association, possibly the Orchestra Society of which I know he was a member. Any way it was a tribute to a great English conductor in celebration of his 80th birthday.

The room was full of well-known musicians, and all sorts of people had come to pay respects to one of the most distinguished and unique personalities, the likes of whom are "not likely to come this way again" - not that any-one would wish it otherwise. The occupants of the high table read like a miniature "Who's Who" of high-ups in the world of music. After a number of tributes from a variety of people had been paid, the moment arrived which we had all been waiting for with keen anticipation - Beecham in person. As I have already indicated elsewhere, he would use a lot of words where most of us would find two or three sufficient. But he was also a master of the art of using very few words, so skilfully timed that they would seem to last a comparatively long period of time, and we were soon to witness his skill in this art. He eventually rose to his feet, and after a few preliminaries began talking of his own conducting with everyone hanging on his every word. He started by denying all the praise that had been heaped on him from all quarters and then reached the point when he said: "I have been described - in the Press and elsewhere" - with long gaps between each phrase - " as a great conductor - a great artist - a musician of high standing - a fine interpreter" - and continued in this vein for quite a while until - ". . . I object. It's not true. It's nonsense." Then having denigrated himself still further he suddenly said - "But on the other hand . . .", at which point the whole room burst into laughter. No-one had the slightest idea what he was going to say next. I remember seeing Malcolm Sargent, who was sitting a few seats away from him to his left, toss his head back with laughter. When some sort of order had been restored, Tommy concluded: "But I'm a damned sight better than all those foreigners!" - more laughter all over the room. It was a masterly performance by a master of timing, leading up to just 10 words! At the conclusion of the luncheon, various messages and telegrams were read out by the Chairman, and, true to form, Tommy could not resist a quip by showing mock surprise at the conclusion of the list and saying - "What - nothing from Mozart!" I wouldn't have missed this luncheon for the world! It was as good an epilogue as any.

22. VARIETY IS THE SPICE

I have never been a "9-5" type, going up to Town in the same train every morning and seeing the same "City gents" reading the Stock exchange news in the same carriage and even the same seat. I have enjoyed a life of much variety and a host of incidents from sad to interesting, inspiring and often full of fun.

Among diversionary events concerning the London Symphony Orchestra was a pre-war concert at the Queen's Hall when we were all dressed up in the style of Haydn's day with powdered wigs, knee-breeches and so on, to perform Haydn's *Farewell* Symphony. The story was that his orchestra were unhappy with their conditions, especially with regard to underpayment of fees. Haydn had written this symphony for the full orchestra and towards the end of the performance, the players started to leave their seats, to show their dissatisfaction, blowing out the candles on their music stands as they departed. Only two, the first and second violinists, remained on the platform to attempt to finish the concert. The scene as we re-enacted it, differed in only one respect. Owing to the strict fire regulations in force, we were not allowed real candles. An electric candle-bulb was fitted to each music stand and as we got up to go, we had to "blow the candle out", at the same time discreetly pressing a small switch located lower down the stand !

After the concert, still in full regalia, we repaired by invitation to the splendid residence in London's Eaton Square, of Lord Howard de Walden who was President of the L.S.O at the time. I remember that the staircase had gold and onyx banisters!

We gave two of our concerts in very unusual surroundings. The venues had been in normal use in the morning for agricultural purposes which included cattle markets and rapidly cleared and cleaned up in time for our afternoon rehearsal and evening performance. The first occasion was at Ipswich in Suffolk and there was still a slight aroma of what had gone on earlier but it was by no means unpleasant. Our visit to Carmarthen in South Wales was not so satisfactory. The hall had again been cleaned up after its use for "country purposes" but it was a particularly bitter and windy day. None of the doors closed properly and the hall was extremely cold and draughty. George Stratton, the leader of the orchestra actually resorted to playing in his overcoat!

From time to time I have met up with interesting people like Mrs D'Oisly, friend of Elgar at the Royal College of Music, but have no idea how the association started. I often wonder who made the introduction which began my friendship with a Miss Lilian Griffith who lived in Taunton, Somerset. It was many years before I myself came to live in this pleasant West Country town. I regret that I lost touch with her long ago though we used to correspond from time to time. She was the sister of Troyte Griffith who became "No 7" in Elgar's *Enigma Variations.* Elgar had dedicated this work "to my friends pictured within". Lilian Griffith always seemed interested in my career and gave me a lovely water-colour of a river with boats and a ship in full sail, painted by her brother Troyte. I have it still and it has been much admired.

I had another present from a lady after I had given a talk on music to members of a Women's Institute near Winchester. I must have made quite a point of the fact that I love the music of Delius. This lady came up to me afterwards and said that she had visited Grez-sur-Loire, the village in France where Delius lived for many years and asked me if I would like a picture of the area. I accepted the kind offer with alacrity. True to her word she sent me a framed colour photograph of the lovely countryside surrounding the Delius home. This is another picture that I treasure.

I had many holidays in the Lake district. I knew two sisters who were living in Patterdale at the foot of Lake Ullswater. Though their home was in Newcastle-upon-Tyne where my mother had first met them, they lodged at the end of a row of cottages, high on Place Fell. Beside the cottage was a path which led to the summit of Helvellyn. I had decided to climb the mountain and had reached the steep-sided "striding edge" when a man passed me on his way down. We exchanged a "Good morning!" and as I continued upwards I began to feel certain we had met before. Eventually I was fairly sure he was Clifford Curzon, the well known concert pianist. It transpired that I was right and that he owned the row of cottages just mentioned and the two sisters, (who became my "honorary aunts"), lodged in the best of them all. Clifford had longed to live there but was kind enough to allow the ladies to remain until they reached their "allotted span" before he felt he could move in.

It was some years later that he became Sir Clifford and I had by then got to know him well. I recall a train journey with him and the Boyd Neel orchestra for a concert engagement and of his remarking that he could not imagine anyone not wanting only to play the piano. Some of us did not entirely agree with him when he said that it must be very dull for us fiddlers sometimes only having a single line to play. I did not like to tell him that we did not think just of our own part, but felt involved with the whole ensemble!

My wife and I were later invited to a party to celebrate his acquiring a very attractive home in the Highgate area of North London where, as you stepped out into the garden, you could not see its full extent as the ground rose up into several undulating levels.

One of the pleasures of my career has been to witness the blossoming of talent of many young musicians, not only from Youth Orchestras where I know great strides have been made towards excellence in various areas, but also from individuals who have risen from comparative obscurity to become household names. When I first conducted the Surrey Festival Choir, the opening performance took place in Epsom Parish Church. The work I put on was Brahms' *Requiem*. This requires two soloists, a soprano who has just one solo piece and a bass, who has to sing two fairly demanding arias. Who, at that time had ever heard of Thomas Allen, of course now well-known. One of my disappointments is that due to his global work commitments he was unable to take part in my last concert with the Surrey Festival Choir nineteen years later.

Sir Keith Falkner, another fine singer in his day, was a keen golfer and organised a match on a course at Newbury, between the Royal College of Music, of which he was a Director, and the Royal Academy of Music. The match took place in the morning and after lunch we arranged our own "friendlies" between ourselves and I played against Tom Allen and actually beat him. I always, when recounting this event, like to point out that he gave me a stroke a hole, his handicap being plus two!

I must just mention a few other disappointments. The L.S.O was once recording in Watford Town Hall. The work was Brahms' *1st Symphony in C minor.* The first movement opens in a dignified and impressive manner, the mood being set by the steady playing in 6/8 time of a solo timpanist. The orchestra were playing the second movement (in which there is no timpani part) when the technicians decided to stop the recording and re-do the whole thing from the beginning, not being satisfied with the sound quality. At which point it was discovered that the timpanist, Denis Blyth, had decided to go for a walk as it was a pleasant day and he would not be required for half an hour or so. Crisis! What were they to do? Luckily, or so it seemed, it was known that I could also play the tympani and I was called upon for this short period of deputising. I was already seated all agog behind the drums and the conductors baton was raised, when in walked Denis! Alas my short moment of personal glory had passed, never to return.

Another "near miss" occurred one Saturday morning at the Royal Festival Hall before one of the Robert Mayer children's concerts, given as a rule by the L.S.O and conducted by Trevor Harvey, but on this occasion the conductor was to be that doyen of music making, a delightful man and pride of the Royal Academy of Music, Ernest Read. He saw me waiting in the wings with the orchestra. "You may have to take over from me", he said. "I've got a 'gammy' leg this morning". Unfortunately (again for me!) he was able to take his place on the platform. I should have enjoyed the challenge. It was Ravel's *Piano Concerto in G*, not as complicated as some of Ravel's works but nevertheless very lively and I think I would have managed quite well.

Fate conspired against me again at a recording session at Denham Film Studios in Bucks. I was with the Boyd Neel String orchestra on this occasion and we were due to record the music for a film on the life of that great violinist/composer, Paganini. The soloist was to be Antonio Brosa, that well-known Spanish violinist who also taught at the R.C.M. He was a most delightful and modest man, who became, with his English wife, a very good friend of mine. The conductor, Boyd Neel, had asked me to stand in for him as he knew he might be late arriving at the studios. In the event he did turn up on time and I remained in the violin section instead of on the conductor's rostrum!

During the making of this film I learnt something of the "tricks of the trade". With close-ups one has, of course to be more accurate regarding details and "faking" becomes more difficult. The leading actor was Raymond Massey. They could get away with a distant shot of him "playing" the fiddle but a close-up was a different matter. What they did was most ingenious and successful and even those sitting quite close to the actor could be fooled. Three people were employed for the particular shot, the three being Raymond Massey, with a professional violinist on each side of him. Brosa had to get himself almost under the violin so he could do the fingering with his left hand while another player, Peter Tas, manipulated the bowing from the other side. Meanwhile Massey stood between them with his chin on the instrument and keeping his hands down by his sides! The result was a quite remarkable impression of only one player performing. It was by no means obvious, but when I later saw the film, I detected one very small flaw. The hands of the two "genuine" players differed slightly in that they belonged to two men of different ages, the one of the older man looking a little more gnarled than that of the younger!

Another film that the L.S.O made music for was quite different. It was a Hitchcock thriller called "The man who knew too much" and a different version had been made 30 years before. The orchestral part was recorded in the Royal Albert Hall over one twelve hour day, with Hitchcock sitting in front of the orchestra with his name in large letters on the back of his chair. The background music was by Arthur Benjamin (composer of the well known *Jamaican Rumba*) and was used for both films. The cast, of course was completely different with James Stewart taking one of the principal parts. I remember that we were paid one pound an hour and had arrived at the Albert Hall at around 8 a.m. in full evening dress. (I always wished we had been stopped by an officer of the law assuming us to be making our way home after an all-night party and presumed over-indulgence in liquid refreshment!)

After a great deal of delay while various discussions took place with which we were not involved, the whole orchestra were eventually called and filming started. With all of us playing, the stage resembled a fan which gradually began to close as the cameras concentrated on the central area of the ensemble and those of us on the outer perimeters became more and more redundant and the waiting about began again. We filled in some of that time with two real visits to the nearest hostelry, both times assisting the publican with opening the doors!

Towards the climax of the film one of the characters had to be shot while sitting in the Royal Box and I was deputed to stand up in my seat in the orchestra, showing my shock and horror at this murder. When the film was released later, I recall watching it on T.V at home and of course looking out for my dramatic appearance. But so realistic was the drama of the thriller that I completely missed it!

Remuneration had increased to four pounds per day by the time the orchestra took part in the film "Dreaming Lips", which featured Elizabeth Bergman and was made at Denham Studios. But we went on much later in the evening, to be told that recording was to start again early next morning. We were unprepared for this and had to spend the night in our evening dress, at the nearest hotel. This was the 'Bull' at Gerrards Cross, by coincidence a mere quarter of a mile from the church where I was married. When we came down for breakfast in the morning, the other guests must have thought we were a convention of waiters!

Pinewood Studios, between Denham and Slough, was another venue for the L.S.O when we made a film of Benjamin Britten's *A young person's guide to the Orchestra.* Hopefully the film would enable youngsters to better understand the workings of a full orchestra even though after we had completed it, I think many of us felt we did not want to hear that particular music again for some time! It takes twenty minutes to play from beginning to end but recording took five days.

The conductor was Sir Malcolm Sargent and the director, Muir Matheson. We first recorded the work as a whole and then, which was the reason for Britten's having written it, each section of the orchestra was filmed in turn playing different variations on the theme. The cameras often picked out single instruments, especially the many different ones in the percussion section (which was known by musicians as the "kitchen department"). At the end of the filming there had only been one slight note of discord when Muir Matheson had addressed the conductor by his first name, which Sir Malcolm obviously considered disrespectful!

On the last day of that week the L.S.O, again with Sir Malcolm Sargent, gathered at the Royal Albert Hall for a concert rehearsal. Half the orchestra had prepared a little joke. Whatever the conductor decided to rehearse first, they would play instead, the theme of Purcell used by Britten for his *Young persons guide!* Sir Malcolm entered in an affable mood. "Good morning gentlemen," he said, "I think we have met this week already. We will take the *Freischutz* Overture. Some of the orchestra did, but those in the know dominated the scene with strains of Purcell! At first our conductor was bemused by the strange sounds emerging from the band and then enjoyed the joke with a hearty laugh, shared by all. But it was soon back to business.

Sir Robert Meyer's children's concerts were just getting going between the wars and I recall one in particular. Unusually it was being given by the Boyd Neel String orchestra, Boyd himself conducting and also unusually, it was taking place in the Central Hall, Westminster. When everyone was settled, Boyd introduced himself. "Hands up," he said, "those children who have never been to a children's concert before." Two small girls in the front row put their hands up. They were the Princesses Elizabeth and Margaret Rose. Apart from ourselves of course, most people did not know that they were there. I wonder if Her Majesty still remembers the occasion?

I eventually became more closely involved in those concerts when I was given the opportunity of choosing the programme for one of their Christmas performances. I had previously arranged a number of carols for full orchestra so these were included. The children were asked to sing the full choral accompaniment and they did not need much persuasion. Meanwhile I enjoyed myself, not being under anybody's supervision. Since the children all sang the carols in unison, the matter of harmony did not arise and I was able to put in my own harmonies as I wished as long as the tune was clear. Before another of the concerts I met Richard

200

Baker, about to go on stage to assume the Narrator's part in Prokofiev's *Peter and the Wolf*. I got to know Sir Robert - who lived to 104 - quite well and when I eventually left his orchestra I had a most delightful letter of thanks from him.

No-one has a proprietary right to sound, or notes and harmony and anyone can do what they like with them, but once they are written down in some specific order and shape, that can be claimed as music. Some people just write music for fun and their own private enjoyment, but when the "commercial" side is entered upon things become different.

Sometimes a piece of music which has been much enjoyed can begin to suffer from "over-exposure", by being played too often. Too much repetition can become tiresome to the listener. I feel that some radio programmes are to blame and too much emphasis is put on *tunes*. I do not listen to the 'Hundred best tunes' for that reason but if those who enjoy them become new music lovers, that can only be good. Some works that I think are overplayed are Handel's *Largo*, (originally an aria for soprano), Barber's *Adagio for strings* (which the composer also set for voice), and the *Air on the G string*, accredited of course to Bach, who actually did not write it as such. The tune was one of the movements of his *Suite in D* and it would be difficult to bring off in that key on the G string. In the key of C it becomes quite playable on the lowest string of the fiddle. The German player, Willy Burmester, was the first to do this. Most fiddlers, including myself, have played the *Air on the G string*, wrongly thinking of it as a separate piece that Bach had composed.

Another work which is so often played is "Nimrod" from Elgar's *Enigma Variations* and I must admit it is very impressive when played on Remembrance Day by the massed bands at the Cenotaph, but it was not composed for such a purpose and is not a memorial to anybody. It was written for, and dedicated to, A.J.Jaeger, whom Elgar described as, "a dear friend, valued adviser and stern critic. A record of a long summer evening talk when my friend Jaeger grew nobly eloquent, as only he could, on the grandeur of Beethoven and especially of his slow movements. To be a true record of him however, something more exciting than this Variation would be needed".

The appeal of many fine themes comes from lovely harmony, exciting rhythms and effective orchestration. In one particular work, the *5th Symphony* of Prokofiev, there are just 4 or 5 bars in one movement which are repeated and which I really look forward to hearing. There is something in the harmony which greatly moves me; perhaps it is the entry of the bass clarinet at the end of the phrase. There is a similar passage in a symphony of Arnold Bax. It is difficult to analyse the many different ways in which music affects people.

There are quite a number of amusing stories regarding one of Beethoven's three *Leonora* overtures. At the end of No.3, there are two "trumpet calls", both consisting of the same notes but one is played more quietly than the other, giving the impression of being played further away. The player has to be off stage and out of sight of the audience. Some concert halls are so small that to achieve the right effect, he has actually to be outside. On one such occasion the trumpeter had gone outside and played the first call facing away from the entrance door to give the effect of distance. He then moved closer to the door and facing it, was about to play the louder second call when the inevitable bobby appeared. "Sorry, sir," he said, "you can't play out 'ere, there's a concert going on in the 'all".

Another time, a foreign conductor was becoming upset as he was not getting the effect he wanted at rehearsal. The first call was sounding too near. He shouted at the trumpet player and told him to go somewhere else where it would not sound so loud. They tried again and he was satisfied. That evening, the performance of the *Leonora* No.3 duly began. The first trumpet call was very loud - much to everyone's consternation - and in the interval, the furious conductor sent for the hapless trumpet player. "Zat vos awful. Vot 'appened ?" he stormed, "zis morning it vos good. Tonight -so loud. Vy ?" "I am sorry maestro," said the player, apologetically. "There was some one in there tonight !"

There is a third anecdote concerning this piece. For a number of years the L.S.O were employed during the late summer for a series of open-air concerts at Abbey Wood in North London. It was an ideal place for music-making, being a mile or so north of Hampstead Heath. The setting was lovely. Immediately opposite the stage was a small lake which enhanced the sound of the music and a number of water-fowl would be swimming there. On the further side of the lake the audience was spread out over a grassy slope. *Leonora* No.3 was the first item on this particular night. As usual, the orchestra were in dinner jackets and black bow-ties - except for one player - the trumpeter of the two "calls". On this night it was Sidney Ellison, a friend of mine and a fine player. As we assembled on stage he had driven his sports car to the top of the grass slope and was standing up in it in casual clothes, ready for the blowing of the two calls. He played the first one facing backwards and turned towards everyone for the second. Having accomplished this, he drove off home, leaving us to get on with the concert. Few of the audience had noticed him and the others probably wondered where the sound had come from!

An unusual musical event took place during the 1930s at a village called Rogate, on the borders of Surrey and Hampshire. It was a series of outdoor performances of a work called *Comus in the open air*, and I have done nothing like it since. The music, which was by Haydn, was provided by a string quartet which I led, an oboe played by an old friend from our student days at the R.C.M, Margaret Elliot, and the pianist Guy Warrack (whose son became music critic of the Daily Telegraph). Towards the end of each performance I had to dress up as a "country yokel" in a smock and loose hat and so on and walk up one of the grass footpaths playing the "Dargason" from Holst's *St Paul's Suite for strings.* (Holst had written this having been at one time Director of Music at St Paul's girls school in Hammersmith.) The setting was some woodland belonging to two brothers named Lubbock, one of whom, Mark, was well-known as a radio producer. They had a large house where we stayed for the week, but strangely we never met them! Memories of

202

making music in the woods, playing croquet on the lawn and the extremely generous hospitality we received in this fine house, are still fresh in my mind. There was a decanter of sherry on the table at every meal, even at breakfast. Each evening we wore dinner jackets. The way the manservant set out my evening apparel was a work of art. Every item was laid out separately with, for instance, my dress shirt on one chair with its "tail" folded over to make it easier to put on and the socks on another with a shoe horn ready at the back of one of the shoes! In the mornings when he brought me a cup of tea, he would do a quick assessment of what sort of mood I might be in and select what he considered suitable reading material from a pile of books on a nearby table.

Guy Warrack, who once taught me musical theory at the R.C.M, became a very good friend to my wife and I when he lived in Surrey. He had a delightful sense of fun. Towards the end of the Second World War he was appointed Director of Music for the B.B.C in Edinburgh. He was planning future programmes for them and had decided to do something rather original and certainly unusual. He planned to put on a broadcast using music of composers whose names consisted of only three letters. He had already decided on several, including Bax, Suk, Nin, Cui and Lee but they did not add up to the total time allocated to the broadcast. He was due to go on a fortnightís leave so he asked his secretary to find another composer to complete the programme. She obviously did not realise the need to find one with a three-letter surname. When Guy returned from holiday he asked her if the programme was now complete. She replied that it was and that she had found a suitable short work by the composer Castelnuovo-Tedesco!

My next reminiscences concern the "Hoffnung Festivals". Gerald Hoffnung, (who sadly only lived for about 34 years), was a humorous artist, his subjects almost exclusively devoted to music and musicians. He himself became quite an able bass tuba player, but he also produced some wonderfully amusing books. One of his earliest drawings was of an organist sitting at the console, who looks at himself in the mirror and sees a police car behind him! All his drawings were original and absolutely priceless.

He had planned a programme of absurdities at the Royal Festival Hall, to be produced by Sam Wannamaker and called "The Hoffnung Music Festival". Quite a galaxy of celebrities had been invited to take part, including Yvonne Arnaud, Denis Brain and Malcolm Arnold.

Somehow Hoffnung had got to hear of my Beecham impersonations, and he invited me to do my "take-off" as part of the programme. I was to start the evening off. A full orchestra was assembled and I was told to come on as Sir Thomas. For the very first time I was made-up professionally, including having my hair whitened. I had not at that time turned grey by natural evolution and I must say the make-up artist did a good job. I was perhaps a little too tall for the impersonation but the flowers and plants along the front of the stage helped create the illusion.

I had to walk on very slowly and deliberately while the whole orchestra rose to its feet out of respect! When I had reached the conductors rostrum, I took a bow and invited them to be seated. I opened the score and then slowly walked off again. (I had thought it would have been even more amusing to have gone a little further and have everyone with their instruments at the ready and about to start the music, but the producer did not agree to this.) Next morning I had notices in two newspapers!

After I had removed my make-up and changed into evening dress, I made my way to the back of the Hall and persuaded one of the ushers to allow me to watch the rest of the entertainment from one of the boxes. The rest of the programme continued in the same hilarious fashion. Francis Baines (brother of the well-known bassoon player, Anthony Baines) had written a piece for the occasion. It started with a solo side-drum roll, at first quietly and then growing in sound with a long crescendo. The audience all stood up, thinking it was the start of the National Anthem!

The actress/pianist Yvonne Arnaud played a piano concerto by Malcolm Arnold with the ridiculous title of "A grand concerto to end all concertos" and Yfrah Neaman came up the central gangway of the stalls playing his fiddle, with a little green bag (which belonged to my daughter) hanging on the violin scroll, collecting money for charities. Denis Brain played a hosepipe concerto!

For me, one of the best items was when a small choir came on stage and appeared to be singing a madrigal. They were not actually doing so although their lips were moving. The song had been pre-recorded and was reproduced at tremendous speed and high in pitch. The audience were in fits of laughter. It was an occasion of typical English frivolity. I think there were one or two more Hoffnung "concerts" but somehow one cannot imagine something like that being done nowadays.

Sadly, Hoffnung's sudden death prevented him from carrying out an engagement at Oundle School. He had been invited to judge the brass playing at their annual music festival. As the director of music knew both of us, he asked me if I would take his place. Due to the circumstances and the school's disappointment at not being able to have him as adjudicator, I gave as an additional prize, one of Hoffnung's many humorous books. As it happened it was the second time that year that I had deputised for someone who had died! The other was when the visiting professional, also from the L.S.O, who led the Marlborough College School Orchestra died suddenly and I replaced him.

It is strange how often small, seemingly unimportant happenings stay in one's mind for many, many years. It must be at least 60 years ago that the great pianist, Solomon, was a soloist at a concert in the Queen's Hall and I was asked if I would sit on his left and turn the pages. Although I was slightly nervous, I was very pleased and managed to do this without any mishaps. What has always remained with me was the gentlemanly manner of Solomon himself. He had played, as ever, with great musicianship and immaculate dexterity. At the conclusion there was tumultuous applause, but he did not immediately stand up to acknowledge it, turning instead to me to thank me for assisting him.

I made a third and final "appearance" at Covent Garden due to the making of a film. I cannot recall its title, but the final scene was concerned with the filming of a performance of Wagner's *Meistersingers*, the last part of which, was to be "conducted" by an actor named Alexander Knox. My propensity for "taking-off" Beecham had become known to the producer and I was asked to show Mr Knox as best I could, how to conduct in the manner of Beecham and Sargent. I undertook to coach him at his home in Hampstead.

The actual filming and recording took place on a Sunday morning and I was very interested to watch this from a box near the stage and made one or two suggestions. When they broke for lunch, Alex Knox took me to a downstairs canteen where we collected trays and helped ourselves from a servery. We had not long been seated at our table and general conversation was going on around us when we were disturbed by the somewhat noisy entrance of somebody who eventually plonked a tray down on a table with a bang. It was not long before we realised that it was Harry Secombe.

After lunch we returned upstairs for the continuation of filming. Meanwhile Secombe, a man of irrepressible humour, sat himself down in one of the boxes, put sixpence in the slot and took out a pair of binoculars with which to view the stage. "What's going on here? The Mikado?", he asked. After a while he glanced at his watch and announced that it was time for him to leave as he was half an hour late for a rehearsal of "The Goon Show". I never did discover why he had been there.

I knew a remarkable family of four sisters who lived in Surrey. Their name was Harrison and none had married. They graced the music scene for many years. The youngest, Margaret, died fairly recently. One of them, Beatrice, was acquainted with Frederick Delius, for whom she played her cello at his home at Grez-sur-Loire in France. No doubt she added to her reputation for being slightly eccentric when she played the cello at midnight in the woods near Limpsfield in order to attract the nightingales to join in. I do not know if she succeeded, but the B.B.C made a programme about her endeavours. Her playing of the Elgar Concerto was, for many years considered the definitive version until the emergence of Jacqueline du Pré.

I recall an invitation to one of the parties given by the sisters at their Surrey home. The front door was opened in answer to my knock and I was about to enter when Beatrice came rushing down the stairs calling out that the outside air was very cold and that she feared it might affect the water temperature of the big tanks in the hall. I do not know what sort of aquatic creatures were contained in them.

I was at a friend's house after a chamber recital in which that incomparable accompanist (author of <u>Am I too loud</u>?), Gerald Moore had been playing. He was not only a superb pianist but a most delightful character with a great sense of humour. He kept us all in fits of laughter describing his experiences while travelling with the Harrison sisters and their mother for a concert in Paris. They took a large amount of luggage, which included rugs and hot water bottles. There were also dogs and various other animals. Those were incredible days.

Sometime later I got to know and befriend, May Harrison, who was teaching at the R.C.M. She was a pleasant person and invited me to come with my viola to her flat near Sloane Square for an evening of informal quartet playing. Also included was Jack Steadman, a friend of mine from the L.S.O. May's flat was quite small and I remember trying to be helpful by moving one particularly large plant to make more room for us. To my horror, it came out of the pot and deposited earth all over her carpet. I did my best to clear up the mess and she very graciously accepted my apologies.

May Harrison told me a delightful story against herself. She was at lunch one day in the R.C.M Professors' dining room with the splendid piano professor, Herbert Fryer. He was telling her about a cricket match in which the batsman was on 99. "He was on 99 for 20 minutes", he said again, emphasising the length of time on the brink of a century, by which time her mind had wandered on to something else. "99 for 20 minutes", he repeated, getting a little impatient with the lack of response from May. "Do you know what happened next?" May suddenly came to. "He died?", she asked.

The timing of B.B.C broadcasts is very precise nowadays. Even the difficulty of selecting music to fit the allocated time slot is usually overcome. But it was not always so. I can think of two examples where timing was all awry. The first was during a Queen's Hall Promenade Concert, conducted by Sir Henry Wood. Before the interval, which was timed for 9 p.m. to fit in with the 9 o'clock news, were a considerable number of what were known as the "Plague Choruses" by Handel which occur in his *Israel in Egypt*. It had not been realised how short these are and the B.B.C found itself frantically having to find some music to play for the remaining 40 minutes before the interval! What the atmosphere was like at the Queen's Hall is difficult to imagine!

The other occasion concerned a broadcast by the Boyd Neel orchestra some years later. The transmission was again leading up to the 9 p.m. news. We were playing Schoenberg's *Verklärte Nacht* (Transfigured Night) and when 9 o'clock came, we were still playing the work. The B.B.C. were forced to delay the news for 20 minutes until we had finished!

Looking back over a career of considerable variety, I think conductors, of whom I have written in some detail, have probably had the greatest effect on my musical life. They must themselves feel the great responsibility which rests on them for creating a good or a mediocre performance. All great playing of fine music depends almost entirely on their ability to inspire musicians and singers to give moving performances. I have often felt, and other musicians have agreed, that there are two kinds of conductors, those you perform for in a certain way "because of" their presence and those where you play "in spite of" them. Musicians from different orchestras will always compare notes on their conductors when they meet. A really inspiring and great conductor can produce an effect by the smallest flick of a finger, while others seem to be striving with quite unnecessary energy and showmanship for the same result. I should imagine it could be quite a disturbing and lowering experience to realise you have not gained the confidence and respect of the forces under your direction. Orchestral players are some of the most critical in the world of music.

There was one rather nice story regarding a most respected wind player named Paul Draper. He was the principal bassoon in the L.S.O for a number of years and was one of a number of players of that name - all woodwind players and nearly all related to each other - though the incomparable and delightful, the late George Draper, who for many years taught the clarinet at Charterhouse, never laid claim to any such relationship. Paul Draper was a very quiet individual who would rarely start a conversation but would be a most interesting and friendly man to talk to otherwise. The story was that Malcolm Sargent was rehearsing the prelude to Elgar's *The Kingdom*. "It's too fast", Paul suddenly called out from his seat in the orchestra. Sargent immediately looked round the band to see who had spoken and realising it was Draper, asked him: "Too fast for whom?" "Too fast for Elgar", answered Paul at once. The rehearsal continued without further interruption until the interval when he went round to Sargent's room to apologise for his outburst, explaining that he had actually played in *The Kingdom* under Elgar's own conducting at a Three Choirs Festival. Sargent accepted his apology saying, "That's all right my dear chap. That was how you felt and we'll remain good friends". It was a surprising little episode and if somewhat out of character, it shows how deeply one can feel about music.

Another episode in my musical life occurred when I was asked by the Royal College to provide the music for the Lord Mayor's Banquet at the Mansion House in the City of London. The participants were to be a small string group and a vocal quartet, the latter to sing a grace before the start of the meal and the string group to play the background music from time to time.

There one or two rituals which had to be observed. For instance, the guests had to march to their allocated tables and clap on the first beat of every bar of Handel's *Scipio*, which we were playing. (There was a Master of Ceremonies keeping an eye on everything and telling us when to start playing what he called the 'Sipio' march!) Having to provide a grace for the vocal quartet was a more difficult assignment. I could not find a four-part one anywhere (and indeed have never seen one since), so I decided to compose one myself. It is based on the Latin words 'Non nobis Domine' and was later used at the dinners during the Summer Schools at Charterhouse.

During the playing intervals at The Mansion House, I remember looking down at the splendid proceedings and the banquet being served below us and being taken behind the scenes for a plate of sandwiches and a glass of beer at the end of the evening! Not that we expected anything more of course!

One of my nicest memories concerns music and cricket. I knew the baritone Harvey Allan, and we were both cricket fans. He asked me one day if I happened to

207

have a violin that I would not mind lending to the great cricketer, Colin Cowdrey, who was a friend of his and had a son who wanted to learn the violin. As it happened I had two that might be suitable and in due course arranged to take them down to Cowdrey's home leaving both for them to try out.

Sometime later it transpired that Cowdrey junior would prefer to learn the clarinet instead and his father arranged to come to my house to return the violins. He arrived early one morning and by way of thanks also brought a tea towel imprinted with scenes of Lord's cricket ground and a dozen bottles of Mouton Cadet, a wine which has remained a favourite of mine ever since. With renewed thanks as he gave them to me, he said he hoped I would drink to the future of music and cricket. As he left, the postman passed him on the drive and asked me if I had been giving an early morning violin lesson!

In one of the early years of the Edinburgh Festival I was on my way to a holiday in Pitlochry, Perthshire, when I took it upon myself to call on the Professor of Music at Edinburgh University, Sidney Newman. He was previously head of Armstrong College in Newcastle-on-Tyne and we had first met at the Royal College of Music. My self-imposed brief was to seek publicity for the London Symphony Orchestra as I felt it was about time we were invited to play at an Edinburgh Festival. Newman said he would do his best but his plea on our behalf was turned down. It would be another few years before the L.S.O was considered worthy enough for an invitation to appear as part of the Festival north of the border!

I would like to mention three more light-hearted memories. Two occurred in the town of Reading. In my day, the College was asked from time to time to send a few reinforcements of string players to various venues not far from London, to bolster up an orchestra for a concert. Possibly this practise still obtains. The first time this happened to me, I was somewhat surprised that an orchestra of well over 100 in number would require any further addition. But I was also pleased as it was one of the few times I was paid additionally for a concert appearance. The conductor of the Reading University Orchestra, Dr Dawtry, appeared very easy going and I recall him asking his horn players if they were sure he was not making them play too fast!

The second trip to Reading was to play with the local symphony orchestra. The final item was Tchaikovsky's *1812 Overture*. At the climax of the work a kind of enactment of the famous battle takes place with the sound of cannons being fired, with appropriate "noises off" behind the scenes. Due to the comparatively small concert hall and platform, there was not enough space for this, so the cannon "blanks" had to be let off beneath the wooden floor of the stage. There were gaps between the floorboards. At the appropriate moment, the "firing" started and in no time the stage was so full of smoke that we could hardly see the music and breathing became somewhat of a hazard! It was a new experience which thankfully I experienced only once!

The third of this sequence of memories occurred more recently. A young flautist, Anthony Walker, sent me a number of old undated cuttings concerning the L.S.O. of which his grandfather Gordon Walker, had been chairman and principal flautist. His father, Eddie, had also been a leading L.S.O flute player. One of the pieces concerned myself and I have no recollection of how it came to be written or by whom. Under the heading 'B. flat please', it reads:

> "Mr Ralph Nicholson, a violinist of the London Symphony Orchestra tells of the day in the Albert Hall when an American wearing a hat and brown overcoat, strode up as a rehearsal began and demanded a 'B. flat'. After a large number of 'B. flats' from the orchestra, he seemed satisfied and walked off. When Sir Malcolm Sargent had finished conducting, the mystery man was identified as Danny Kaye".

James Blades was a delightful man, and was without peer in his skill and knowledge as a percussionist, and world-renowned.. He also had a tremendous sense of humour which is illustrated by this story he once told me of a visit he made with an orchestra to play for King George VIth at Windsor Castle many years ago. The King met some of the players after the concert and had been particularly intrigued with Jimmy's side-drum part which has the well known, 'tum, tiddly tum, tiddly tum, tum' beat which goes on continuously throughout the whole of Ravel's *Bolero* which had been part of the programme. He asked Jimmy how he knew where he had got to in the work. "Well, Your Majesty, one doesn't bother to count each repeated section as it is played, because you know that four bars before the end, the three trombones and tuba come in and then you know exactly where you are!" answered Jimmy. The King then asked what would happen if they did not come in and Jimmy replied that in that case there would be four new faces in the orchestra the next day! Humour has been very important in my life. Among my musical colleagues it is rare to find someone without a sense of humour. I have described some of the gems of wit and these have helped to enliven many of my working days.

In the early part of the century, George Bernard Shaw was the music critic of the Evening Standard. He did not sign the notices with his own name but used the pseudonym 'Corno di Basseto', the name of a very old woodwind instrument. He became bored with this and thought it would be amusing to change it to 'Bono di Corsetto' and nobody noticed! But humour apart, what critics write, is of great importance, especially to those about to set out on a career in music. A really enthusiastic notice can start a budding artist on the road to success.

But what to make of completely opposite views being expressed of the same event by two critics in September 1954 following a performance of Princess Ida. The Times critic wrote, " . . . the singing as a whole is indifferent- even the chorus shout with a very shrill tone . . . Sullivan's scores have been so battered by overwork that Mr Isadore Godfrey pushes them through without obtaining real precision of ensemble and not much lyricism anywhere. Some day the copyright will run out and then fresh minds can be brought to bear on them." The critic of the Daily Mail on the same performance: "The singing of the chorus could not have been bettered under Isadore Godfrey. This opera sparkled!" Take your pick!

I hope I have shown in the foregoing pages that variety really has been the spice of life for me. I have had a life of wonderful music-making with a great deal of humour and fun, together with moments of sadness and others of moving experiences like a great concert, a magnificent view, or an exciting cricket match! I think some of the most necessary ingredients for a happy life are satisfaction in work, friendships, the ability to laugh and a loyal family, with a good dollop of sunshine thrown in for good measure!